CRISIS IN CONSCIOUSNESS

CRISIS IN CONSCIOUSNESS
The Thought of Ernst Troeltsch

ROBERT J. RUBANOWICE

with a foreword by
JAMES LUTHER ADAMS

A Florida State University Book
UNIVERSITY PRESSES OF FLORIDA
Tallahassee

University Presses of Florida is the central agency for scholarly publishing of the State of Florida's university system. Its offices are located at 15 NW 15th Street, Gainesville, FL 32603. Works published by University Presses of Florida are evaluated and selected for publication by a faculty editorial committee of any one of Florida's nine public universities: Florida A&M University (Tallahassee), Florida Atlantic University (Boca Raton), Florida International University (Miami), Florida State University (Tallahassee), University of Central Florida (Orlando), University of Florida (Gainesville), University of North Florida (Jacksonville), University of South Florida (Tampa), University of West Florida (Pensacola).

BX
4827
,T7
R8

Library of Congress Cataloging in Publication Data
Rubanowice, Robert J.
  Crisis in consciousness.
  "A Florida State University book."
  Bibliography: p.
  Includes index.
  1. Troeltsch, Ernst, 1865–1923. I. Title.
BX4827.T7R8   230'.044'0924   81-16085
ISBN 0-8130-0721-6   AACR2

Typography by G & S Typesetters, Austin, Texas

Printed in U.S.A.

To Harry J. Marks, teacher and friend,
I dedicate this book.

Contents

Foreword

James Luther Adams

Ernst Troeltsch's reputation has ebbed and flowed in this century. Sixty years ago his name was almost universally known and respected among scholars in the fields of theology, theological ethics, philosophy of religion, history of philosophy, philosophy of history, social ethics, and sociology of religion. A wide swath indeed. By 1910, he and Max Weber, colleagues at the University of Heidelberg, had given to the sociology of religion a major thrust for the twentieth century. Troeltsch's comprehensive *Social Teachings of the Christian Churches* of 1911 appeared in English translation two decades later, to be republished in paperback in 1960 with an introduction by H. Richard Niebuhr (who in 1925 had written a doctoral dissertation at Yale University on Troeltsch's philosophy of religion). *Social Teachings* has remained unsurpassed for half a century, and no rival to it is on the horizon even now. In 1922, the first volume of Troeltsch's equally massive work *Historicism and Its Problems* appeared in Germany, the second volume remaining unfinished because of Troeltsch's death the following year. Various chapters of this work had been published previously in learned journals, together with several hundred other articles on a wide variety of subjects.

In the 1930s Troeltsch's reputation suffered a decline. Theological students from Germany in my classes in the 1940s and the 1950s, for example, repeatedly expressed surprise that *Social Teachings* was still the major text in the history of Christian ethics. When I asked them what work had replaced Troeltsch in this field, they would shrug their shoulders. When I asked why they did not read Troeltsch, they responded, "His work is *vorbei* [passé]"—the quickest way to dispose of any scholar or movement, especially in the decades of the dominance of Barthian theology. Indeed, anything by Troeltsch (and also the writings of Friedrich Schleiermacher, one of his major mentors) was practically *verboten*.

Since 1960, however, the writings of Troeltsch have been enjoying a significant recovery of reputation. Particularly important in this connection is the recognition that neo-orthodox theologies and idealistic philosophies have not properly confronted the crisis in consciousness of which Troeltsch was acutely aware. In the present volume, Professor Rubanowice centers his attention upon this crisis and upon directly related matters, presenting his findings and reflections on the basis of an impressive range of the literature both primary and secondary. He rightly sees Troeltsch as a pivotal representative of the early twentieth-century "crisis in consciousness," an analyst possessing unique qualifications by reason of the scope and depth of his concern with economic, political, sociological, theological, philosophical, and ethical changes and issues in past and present. As the present volume properly indicates, the "crisis in consciousness" was more than psychological in the ordinary sense. For Troeltsch, this crisis signified the emergence of a new period of history in the West.

We need not repeat here the vivid description of the dissolution of the dominant certainties of the nineteenth century, which is Professor Rubanowice's point of departure—a new malaise that questioned even the vaunted merits of "civilization" itself. We should stress, however, that this new outlook on the world which had been aborning for well over a century cannot be ignored or bypassed, as if the modern mentality could overcome the malaise simply by returning to good old ways. The new outlook, the new consciousness is here to stay. We now realize that consciousness itself does not rest on an immaculate pedestal outside history but is embedded in a historical, sociopolitical process. We appreciate also that our values, likewise, do not escape this process. Therefore a new method of understanding is required, a method that Troeltsch described as historical-psychological. In short, one recognizes today that human beings and human society are historical phenomena conditioned by contingent factors of time and place—what is called "historicism."

The term "historicism" is generally unfamiliar in English-speaking countries, and when it is used, the definitions are unclear and confused. Although historicism was current among scholars in Germany by the middle of the nineteenth century, no general consensus regarding its meaning obtained, for already it had acquired a variety of connotations both positive and pejorative.* In the 1830s Ludwig Feuerbach, for example, interpreted the term to denote cultural relativism and "the uncritical acceptance of the world as it presents itself." In this view,

* See the extensive account of this variety of connotations in the substantial article by the American scholar Georg C. Iggers in the *Dictionary of the History of Ideas*, III, 1973.

historicism, in addition to promoting cultural relativism, represents a conservative preference for the status quo. This and other definitions themselves reveal differing reactions to the "crisis in consciousness."

In *Historicism and Its Problems* (1922), Troeltsch analyzes and assesses the variety of meanings appearing in the numerous philosophies of history in the nineteenth and twentieth centuries (the while also boldly identifying, in turn, the deficiencies of these philosophies). In doing this he posits what he considers to be a proper definition. Historicism sees everything in history as involved in a "web of mutually interacting activities of the human spirit which are never independent and absolute but always interrelated, and therefore understandable only within the context of the most comprehensive whole." Moreover, these interrelations are constantly subject to change, as in a flowing stream.

Of crucial significance here is the recognition that history and the historical process cannot be understood in terms of a naturalism that attempts to interpret them under the categories of nature—for example, in terms of a billiard-ball idea of causation. History properly understood is an arena of freedom and of conflicts of value and meaning not to be found in nature, an arena in which human culture and the creative human spirit develop. This "development," to use Troeltsch's term, is not to be understood in terms of naturistic perspectives. In nature one does not encounter crises of consciousness; it is a source of fundamental confusion to attempt to interpret crisis under the rubric of nature. In Troeltsch's extensive treatment of naturalism, however, we should observe that he is generous in his recognition of contributions that have been made to modern existence by naturalism, especially in the areas of daily life and technology.

For the interpretation of history, not only naturalism but also the older, "dogmatic" approach is rejected, for this approach regards particular conditions, isolated revelatory events, and ideas as simply "given," and therefore it absolutizes them into immutable norms. The historical-psychological view rejects supernaturalism, miracles, authoritarian sanctions, and, especially, fixated revelation. Troeltsch at times seems to assert that the historical-psychological method relativizes everything, but he means that it sees everything as interrelated, and that it rejects absolutes. He does not mean that this method eliminates every standard of judgment and ends in nihilistic skepticism. Such a dissolution of standards Troeltsch calls "base historicism." Professor Rubanowice clarifies this matter in the pages that follow.

Troeltsch's intention, then, in *Historicism and Its Problems* is to present the problems and also the dangers of historicism, at the same time avoiding its identification with an empty cultural relativism. In this connection Professor Rubanowice points out Paul Tillich's error in speaking of Troeltsch's historicism as cultural relativism. A major problem of historicism is to set forth a basis for values *in* history, in changing history. For Troeltsch, these values cannot find sanction in something above history. The search for sanctions above history can be found even among those who reject naturalism and who make a distinction between history and nature. Values are to be discerned, however, in the interplay out of which standards emerge, undergo analysis and criticism, and perhaps anticipate or create new consensus. In crises of consciousness, the question arises acutely as to how to ride out and overcome the crisis. Relevant values do not appear in splendid isolation, they are entangled in previous situations. These values may in turn find new relatedness and new formulation in the context of a new situation. In this connection, Troeltsch speaks of history overcoming history. We must return to this theme.

We have considered one important aspect of Troeltsch's conception of historicism, the emphasis on historical relatedness. Karl Mannheim has spoken of this as "relationism." We must now refer to another concept indispensable for Troeltsch's view: individuality. The river of history consists of once-happening events and situations. Here one may recall Xénopol's distinction between *les faits de répétition* and *les faits de succession*. The former occur in nature, the latter in culture—that is, in the individualities of history. This distinction, to be sure, has been challenged repeatedly, toward the end of stressing elements of succession rather than of repetition in nature, but not successfully with respect to culture and its posited values (nonexistent in nature).

In an essay entitled "The Ideas of Natural Law and Humanity," published one year before his death, Troeltsch sets forth again the view that wherever one looks in the history of culture one finds uniqueness of outlook, uniqueness in cultural styles and *Gestalten*, uniqueness also in the "individual totalities" manifest when a culture has achieved its characteristic qualities. This recognition of individuality he attributes to Romanticism. Moreover, the contribution of Romanticism, he avers, is a peculiarly German insight to be seen in contrast to a characteristic outlook of the West. In Western Europe and America he finds the culture oriented to "an eternal, rational and divinely ordained system of Order, embracing both morality and law and asserting the unity of Humanity." In Germany, "on the other side, we begin to see individual, living, and perpetually new incarnations of a historically creative Mind." Here particularity, individuality, is of the essence. History is seen as

> an ever-moving stream, which throws up unique individualities as it moves, and is always shaping individual structures on the basis of a law which is always new. . . . This view is bound to consider the west-European world of ideas as a world of cold rationalism and equalitarian atomism, a world of superficiality and Pharisaism.

Professor Rubanowice is charitable in not stressing this set of ideas in his presentation. Troeltsch for his part, we must emphasize, traces the course of Romanticism through its many vagaries down to the brutal realism appearing when it goes as an animal on all fours. All sorts of difficulties emerge in considering Troeltsch's view if one questions the adequacy of his characterization of the West (where, for example, the idea of Natural Law has virtually disappeared except in Roman Catholic circles). Moreover, Romanticism (which began in England) has assumed a great variety of forms in the West. In the philosophical field, one may recall that Whitehead saw in the sensitivity to feeling among the English Romantic poets an anticipation of his own concept of "prehension."

In identifying Romanticism's proclivity for individuality, Troeltsch could have found many an illustration in the Romantic painters, who gave birth to an abundance of styles. Potentially, they envisaged an unlimited number of styles. At the same time, these painters presented in their work an "interplay of mutually interacting activities," each artist striving for a unique style. Their several individualities were not isolated phenomena, of course. Moreover, each of them exhibited an attachment to some phase of the past, feeling linked to it by "elective affinity." Thus, they represent in part a revival of aspects of previous styles. Altogether, one can see here an illustration of Troeltsch's view of the interplay of past and present in a new creativity in a new cultural situation.

An even more precise illustration of Troeltsch's conception of mutual interplay, of his idea of the conflict and mutual enriching of meanings and perspectives, and of finding values *in* history and not above it is to be observed in the history of Anglo-American law. This sphere is of special interest because the decisions of courts take effect through the coercive power of the state, therefore achieving visibility sooner than do other phenomena of social conflict and social change.

The most familiar example of the interplay of perspectives is the development of the law of equity alongside the common law and also of separate courts for these respective spheres. Court decisions are of course recorded, setting precedents that are regarded as authoritative. Common law, we should recall, is unenacted law—distinct from statutes and ordinances—and it is common to the whole land. Historically, knowledge regarding it has become increasingly familiar to professional lawyers, schooled by the Inns of Court in the history of law in relation to the developing culture. By the fifteenth century it was recognized that, in certain types of cases, no relief could be secured from the common law, now become rigid, yet relief was deemed worthy according to the ideas of the time. Certain cases that could not secure relief from the common-law courts could be brought before a court of equity, which could supplement the strict law in the name of "grace" and of "conscience." The courts of equity became a source of remedies in accord with changing needs of society and with new conceptions of fairness.

Under the influence of equity, significant reforms have been effected in common-law procedure, relaxing its earlier rigidity. This process still obtains today. The two types of court also continued to exist in the United States at the time of the adoption of the federal constitution. Even after the merging of the two courts in the nineteenth century, a petition for equitable remedy was valid, and lawyers today continue to make a distinction between law and equity. For centuries, then, the two perspectives continued in interplay—interplay not only between them but also between present and past, especially through the authority of precedent, the "reservoir" of values in past history.

The rule of precedent also illustrates the means whereby both continuity and social change became legally possible. A precedent tended to be established only when the previous situation was deemed to be essentially analogous. It is possible to document ways in which precedent has been interpreted not only to resist but also to sanction change, as well as to reveal a situation demanding exception.

In all of these processes that which called itself logic was repeatedly relinquished. Flexibility was demanded. To be sure, procedures had to be contrived to deal with abuses. Moreover, changes in the law oc-

curred when rights were extended to groups. As a consequence, even
the conception of the sovereignty of the state in face of "subjects"
underwent change. Speaking of the role of law in civilization, Oliver
Wendell Holmes, Jr., a century ago could say, "The actual life of the
law has not been logic; it has been experience." In short, we have in
this whole sphere what Troeltsch had in mind when he defined sound
historicism; it does not eliminate standards but finds them *in* history.
Yet, viewing the whole development, Troeltsch would say that here too
individuality or particularity is of the essence. Moreover, he could support the view that an understanding of the whole development requires
a conception of periodization, a periodization that discerns, for example, the development of individualism and the subsequent transition to
a more holistic approach.

   With illustrations like these (in the history of art and in the history of
law), one can see the cogency of Troeltsch's adumbration of the aspects of history to be recognized by the historian in the *actualities* of
history and not to be sought in categories transcending history. Here
the search for the actuality is a search for originality and uniqueness,
also a search for complex totalities and for development. The work of
the historian cannot have the scientific precision possible in the natural
sciences; it requires intuition and risk. This requirement becomes obvious if the reader examines Professor Rubanowice's admirable exposition of the eleven basic categories that make historical knowledge
possible (chapter 4). A mere listing of these categories, or concepts,
reveals Troeltsch's originality: individual totality and development,
originality and uniqueness, narrow selection, representation, unity of
value or meaning, tension between general spirit and particular spirits,
the unconscious, the creative, freedom in the sense of choice, and
chance. One can see that by including "chance" among these concepts
Troeltsch does not overlook Pascal's dictum "If the nose of Cleopatra
had been shorter, the whole face of the earth would have been changed."
Troeltsch observes, by the way, that Vico had already detected historical elements in Pascal. One recalls Pascal's speaking of the contradiction: that which is just on the west side of the Pyrenees is unjust on the
east side.

   What we have been dealing with here is what Troeltsch called "the
formal logic of history"—the nature and ingredients of history. Historicism also raises the question of the status of values in a shifting, pluralistic world—and especially in a pluralism of religious persuasions.

If no absolute religion is available or possible, and if each religion now appears as a substantial individual in its own right and tradition, what is the adherent of any particular religion to claim?

Troeltsch's answer to this question is that the true believer (who does not view his own religion as absolute) must respect and take seriously the other religions and their convictions. Here, then, Troeltsch adopts the idea of "polymorphous truth," individuals mutually recognizing that which is truth for the other. It is a striking thing that, in adopting this idea, Troeltsch was providing in his own procedure an illustration of the historicist recognition of the functioning of the past in the present. The germ of the idea of polymorphous truth had been anticipated in the German historian Leopold von Ranke's view that "every age is immediate to God." Troeltsch undoubtedly accepted this view from von Ranke. In the fifteenth century, Nicholas of Cusa had suggested that the various religions severally stand independently and immediately before God. A number of figures in the next two centuries adopted a similar view. John Saltmarsh, approvingly read by Troeltsch, had written that "every beam of light is light; every truth is a sparkle of truth itself."

Here we may introduce a term not used by Troeltsch. If we apply the idea of polymorphous truth to the interrelations between the religions in their differing perspectives, we could call the Troeltschian view a form of henotheism. Henotheism is to be contrasted with the implication of the First Commandment that other gods are held to be false gods, a view that has been accepted historically by many Christian thinkers.

The henotheist view is readily evident in Troeltsch's assessment of "the experience of Christianity." This experience he sees to be unavoidably a part of the cultural community of the West. It is truth *for us*, but only for us. The experience, however, does not preclude the possibility that "other racial groups" in other places will experience their "contact with the Divine Life in quite a different way absolutely [!] valid for them." In Troeltsch's view, this idea of polymorphous truth is not properly called "cultural relativism," for each religion is acknowledged to stand in some sense "immediately to God."

The idea of polymorphous truth may relieve the hostilities engendered by the demon of the absolute, but it does not come fully to terms with "the crisis in consciousness," the malaise of our time, where the center no longer holds. Here intrinsic values are required. History must overcome history. To assist here is the creative task of a "material philosophy of history." The "formal logic of history" deals mainly with the past. The material philosophy of history must be concerned also with the present and the future, not only through contemplation but also through new creativity. It is teleological. Historicism properly understood means not only the consciousness of standing in history but also of being responsible for the coming history (a task that is a legacy of the Enlightenment?). This means that the material philosophy must be concerned with new "development." But the development must take its rise from the situation as a whole and not in piecemeal analysis.

To be sure, one may discern types of social complex in the historical situation or process, and Troeltsch, like Max Weber, has for example identified types of religious association such as church, sect, and mystical group. But such types are only elements within the larger complex.

At given times history manifests itself in a unique whole of meanings (though there are always tensions). Troeltsch speaks of this as an "individual totality." The unique whole of meanings in which we find ourselves he calls "Europeanism," which contains a number of major value traditions in development and in interplay, now one, now another in the ascendant in various kinds of synthesis.

Occasionally in the past, when a major crisis in consciousness has appeared, a new cultural synthesis has come to birth in the attempt to overcome the crisis—a great creative act giving new meaning and relevance to past values, resulting in the rise of a new "historical individual totality." The period of Catholicism preceding and following the fall of Rome is not to be understood merely as a period of syncretism; it was a period of synthesis. Another period of this kind was the Enlightenment, which represented a creative thrust throughout Europe— a thrust, to be sure, engendering heat as well as light and containing ambiguities and flaws. So decisive was this change that Troeltsch identified it rather than the Reformation as the beginning of the modern period. Indeed, the philosophy of history as a new discipline emerged in this period, the beginnings of a philosophy that aimed to read the contours of life out of actual history instead of imposing them from above. Indeed, in one passage Troeltsch defines philosophy of history "in its full meaning" as "the perception of the aims of life out of history."

The twentieth-century crisis in consciousness and the reactions to it are the seedbed out of which a new cultural synthesis may be worked for and constructed. Here, as Troeltsch said, is "the one possibility for a solution to our problem—the problem of damming and controlling the historical stream of life." The needed individual synthesis must draw upon values in the past, not upon merely abstract "formal values" but upon more complex "cultural values." Nor can it be the work of one philosopher; it requires the interplay of various contributors for a generation or more. Although Troeltsch did not live to set forth amply his own material philosophy of history, he recognized that the task would be an enormous one in a time of turmoil when the world, as he predicted, would be dominated more and more by massive military powers and technologies.

He therefore held that values, even rich cultural values, can scarcely be accepted as imperatively obligatory if they are sanctioned only by history. They require a religious or metaphysical grounding. Judging from hints he has given, Troeltsch would find this grounding in a Leibnizian view relating a pluralism of persuasions to a divine, individuating, creative power. He speaks of "the identity of finite minds with the infinite mind" as "the key to the solution of our problem." Here we see a recovery of the Romantic idea of Schleiermacher, the immanence of the infinite in the finite. Tillich in the same vein speaks of the paradoxical presence of the infinite in the finite. Troeltsch for his part relates this conception to a Christian doctrine of God. Indeed, he goes beyond this. In a significant number of essays he adumbrates a doctrine of revelation and of other doctrines in Christian theology—all compatible with his historicism. These writings represent Troeltsch the theologian going beyond the level of the philosophy of history.

This is not the place to attempt to detail the influence of Troeltsch in our time. Such an attempt would have to take into account the marked increase in the last few years of translations and of creative and critical essays about his writings in different fields of investigation (some of which have been assembled in England by John Powell Clayton and introduced by Robert Morgan and Michael Pye*). Work is proceeding on the translation of the enormous tome *Historicism and Its Problems*. Wilhelm Pauck's engaging book has abetted this revival of interest. Moreover, an Ernst-Troeltsch-Gesellschaft has been founded in Germany under the presidency of the distinguished scholar Trutz Rendtorff, with its first international congress scheduled for March 1983. Currently the complete writings (extensive indeed) are being republished in Germany.

Paul Tillich's appreciation (and critique) of Troeltsch's writings ap-

---

* See bibliography for these and other references to recent works on Troeltsch.

pears in several essays (in German) and in his substantial essay review-ing *Historicism*. Tillich dedicated his book *The System of the Sciences* to Troeltsch, and he has spoken of Troeltsch's work on the philosophy of history as the presupposition for any concern with that subject. I would venture the judgment that Tillich's writings on the nature of history and on the modern period—its character, its problems, and its possibilities—as well as his writings on religious socialism and his elaboration of his concept of theonomy (Troeltsch had used the concept of "autotheonomy") all taken together approach "the contemporary cultural synthesis" asked for by Troeltsch. Indeed, one can trace through his writings a persistent interest in synthesis past and present.

The gracious and judicious volume before us will be a boon to all who in this period of Troeltsch revival are concerned with his philoso-phy of history. It lucidly traces its theme through a plethora of writings by and about Troeltsch, indicating the changes and growth in his thought and his political activities, cogently presenting the proposals made and the haunting questions raised by this fascinating and devout scholar on the meaning and the responsibilities of living in history, especially in our own time of "crisis in consciousness."

Preface

In studying the work of Ernst Troeltsch over the past fifteen years I have been convinced that this exemplary thinker of the late nineteenth and early twentieth centuries has been buried prematurely. For forty years after his death in 1923 Troeltsch's thought was relatively neglected. Only in the 1960s and 1970s has this prolific writer begun to receive the belated recognition that is due him as one of the most significant and representative minds of the turn-of-the-century crisis in consciousness. James Luther Adams has cautiously hinted at a genuine "Troeltsch revival" in our own times.[1]

Troeltsch's more than five hundred publications—from the 1890s through the early 1920s—fall into the categories of theology, church history, sociology, ethics, historicism, philosophy of history, and political analysis, among others. This "towering figure in the world of German scholarship" has been called "the greatest theologian of German Protestantism" and "the greatest German philosopher of history since the days of Hegel."[2] In the arena of practical politics Troeltsch was even considered a possible candidate for the presidency of the newly formed Weimar Republic.

From my perspective as a historian of ideas I have lamented repeatedly that the indexes of most books dealing with late nineteenth- and early twentieth-century European thought—and even books on modern Germany—tend to skip from Toynbee to Trotsky with no mention at all of our subject.[3] Walther Köhler's advice of 1941—that "the time has not yet come" for Troeltsch's intellectual biography—appears to me to be now well out of date.[4]

The current renewed interest in Troeltsch began in religious circles and has reached such proportions that Robert Morgan could shortly ago observe that "no theologian from before the First World War has featured so prominently in the footnotes of learned journals in recent years as Ernst Troeltsch."[5] The grand neglect into which Troeltsch had fallen, spearheaded by dialectical theologians of neo-orthodox persuasion, is no longer permissible in the pluralistic context of contemporary theology. Today we have come to recognize, as Wolfhart Pannenberg has suggested, that Troeltsch articulately posed "the truly important questions and responsibilities of theology in the twentieth century." [6]

The Troeltsch revival has become international in scope and is concerned with the full spectrum of Troeltsch's thought. Representative book-length studies of Troeltsch from the 1970s include Klapwijk's examination in Dutch of Troeltsch's historicism, Rapp's Italian study of Troeltsch's political thinking, Apfelbacher's German monograph on Troeltsch's theological program, and the papers from the predominantly English-speaking colloquium on Troeltsch and the future of theology held at the University of Lancaster in 1974. [7] Given Troeltsch's own broad interdisciplinary concerns, it was inevitable that interest in his religious thought should spread to other areas as well. Indeed, as Hans-Georg Drescher pointed out at the Lancaster colloquium, "unlike the theology of Barth, Bultmann and Gogarten, Troeltsch had had an influence which went beyond theology as a single university discipline, out to philosophy, the history of ideas and sociology. . . . It is his permanent contribution to have demonstrated that theology is an open discipline which lives by cooperation with other sorts of intellectual endeavours." [8]

The present work is an introductory survey of the range of Troeltsch's writings. It is intended to be more extensive and more detailed than any substantial overview in English that has yet appeared. Ogletree's *Christian Faith and History* and Reist's *Toward a Theology of Involvement* tended to dwell primarily on the religious dimensions of Troeltsch's thought, as did Sleigh's much earlier *Sufficiency of Christianity*, which also omitted an examination of Troeltsch's mature writings. [9] I approach Troeltsch from a transdisciplinary perspective that seeks to characterize his thought within the field of modern Western intellectual history. [10] I include for the first time in English an extended treatment of Troeltsch's political writings.

While I have referenced the most important secondary literature on Troeltsch where appropriate, I have generally not conducted a running dialogue with Troeltsch's interpreters. I have not, for example, become excessively involved in such issues as whether Troeltsch's "first phase" ended in 1902 (as Drescher maintains) or in 1909 (Bodenstein's view). [11] Instead, I have sought to engage the mind of Troeltsch himself. As the documentation indicates, this essay in intellectual history rests principally upon Troeltsch's own works—many of which are as yet untranslated into English. I am often haunted by Nietzsche's excoriation of pallid scholars, sitting aside, "waiting and staring at thoughts that others have thought." [12] Troeltsch's own characterization of certain scholarly tempests-in-teapots in the theological disputes of his time is still appropriate. He called these "harmless conventicle diversions, children quarreling while the house is on fire." [13]

I wish to thank James Luther Adams and Max L. Stackhouse for valuable critical readings of the manuscript in its first draft.

Robert J. Rubanowice

1

Representative of an Age of Crisis

Noch herrscht in unserem geistigen Leben die Mattigkeit
und die Verwirrung.

Troeltsch (1903)

Heute ist wieder eine Zeit schwerster kritischer Tage im
kulturellen und religiösen Leben Europas.

Troeltsch (1921)

The period during which Ernst Troeltsch flourished experienced a cultural crisis of enormous proportions. During the third of a century in which he wrote, from the 1890s until his death in 1923, European values were profoundly transformed. As his contemporary Charles Péguy expressed it, "the world changed less since Jesus Christ than in the last thirty years." [1] Troeltsch absorbed the dominant changing currents in European thought so thoroughly that his writings as a whole are a veritable microcosm of this turn-of-the-century intellectual turmoil.

A Paradoxical Age

With the hindsight of intellectual historians, we can now view the period from around 1880 or 1890 through World War I and the 1920s as the seedbed of much of the discontent with traditional values that erupted more visibly in subsequent decades. Standard interpretations of this pivotal period have tended to agree on the fundamentals. Roland N. Stromberg, for example, in his treatment of "The Crisis of European Thought: 1880–1914," referred to these troubled years as "the critical ones for the future destiny of Western man." [2] Gerhard Masur was "deeply perplexed by the profound transition which took place between 1890 and 1919"; Egon Friedell saw the dominant theme of the era as the "collapse of reality"; and H. Stuart Hughes detected

1

in the several decades after 1890 "an intellectual revolution . . . from which there emerged the new assumptions characteristic of our own time."[3]

Disciplines of thought and modes of expression as diverse and apparently independent of one another as psychology, art, theoretical physics, political thought, philosophy, literature, and religion, for example, all unmistakably share certain common characteristics during this pivotal period. It is hazardous to apply a blanket label to the numerous and complex varieties of European thought of the late nineteenth and early twentieth centuries. But if the attempt be made, the rubric "From Progress and Optimism to Crisis and Disillusionment" seems suitable, not because it captures all that can be said about the period but because of its fruitful suggestiveness. The age was a paradoxical one, and such a label—by contending that the dominant leitmotif of these three or four decades embodied a shift of emphasis from an optimistic faith to a pessimistic disillusionment—immediately grasps the contradictory nature of this age of "blooming, buzzing confusion."

On the one hand this pivotal period was *la belle époque*, a great time to be alive, an era in which European thought approached the zenith of its confidence. On the other hand this was also an era of dissolving certainties in which traditional, durable absolute values were being covertly undermined and—gradually—overtly rejected. It will be useful to examine both the positive and the negative aspects of this complex situation as a prelude to our focus upon Troeltsch's own thoughts on the subject.

Certainly, in Troeltsch's time European man enjoyed unprecedented material benefits. Troeltsch and his contemporaries had access to greater material prosperity and creature comfort than had yet been achieved in the history of the human race.[4] The industrialization of the European economy during the nineteenth century had been primarily responsible for ushering in Europe's Age of Materialism. Granted, there were defects and unfortunate abuses in this modernization of European society, but generally speaking the cumulative benefits of industrial capitalism had a profoundly beneficial effect upon the material welfare of Europeans. The living standards of the masses had never been so high. The longevity curve took a rapid upswing; breakthroughs in medical fields for the treatment and prevention of disease proceeded apace; sanitation, health practices, and dietary habits vastly improved; and inexpensive cotton clothing became readily available, allowing the average person to change his underwear more than twice a month.[5] It was all for the better.

The technological advances of this period are astonishing when measured against the relative absence of widespread technological achievement in preceding ages.[6] Kenneth E. Boulding persuasively argues that the technological revolution of the past century is comparable in scope only to the transformation from precivilized culture to civilization in the Neolithic period. Boulding maintains that "if anyone in an advanced society today were to be suddenly thrust back into the world of only a hundred years ago, he would feel utterly alien and strange."[7] It was in the midst of this century of progress and technological advancement that Ernst Troeltsch came to maturity.[8]

This was an Age of Materialism not simply on the level of its unprecedented accumulation of comfort, wealth, and power, but in a more profound sense. Its material prosperity buttressed a mood of confidence and optimism, a *Weltanschauung* proclaiming that the Enlightenment had not died with Voltaire but that perdurable enlightened ideas promised to make the future better than the past had ever been. Two hundred years earlier Alexander Pope had written:

> Nature and Nature's Laws lay hid in night;
> God said: Let Newton be! and all was light.

As the impact of the Newtonian scientific synthesis peaked, the late nineteenth century now willingly endorsed that refrain.

The basic controlling assumptions of the late nineteenth-century enlightened world view posited man as a gifted, rational animal. Not only was man rational but reality was ultimately fully intelligible as well. Mystery and doubt had been banished from the universe, a process that one of Troeltsch's Heidelberg colleagues, Max Weber, was to characterize as "the disenchantment of the world." Reason, science, and positivism either provided the necessary answers to man's basic questions or eventually would do so, given more time to work out some of the problems. The world was pushing onwards and upwards. God was in his heaven, all was right with the world.

Progress, endorsed as an idea by eighteenth-century *philosophes*, now appeared to be securely vindicated by actual events during the nineteenth century. The Law of Progress became enshrined as an inexorable Law of Nature, for Europeans in the late nineteenth century could see visible signs of improvement on every side—in the comparative freedom from sustained warfare since the time of Napoleon, in unprecedented material gains growing out of a rapidly industrializing economy, and judging by the astounding success of late nineteenth-century New Imperialism, in the evident superiority of European values vis-à-vis those of the rest of the world. (Indeed, by 1914 the white race emanating from Europe could claim control over 85 percent of the land surface of the globe.) The spirit of European man grew buoyant with confidence.

Crisis and Disillusionment

And yet, during Troeltsch's mature lifetime, European civilization underwent a profound cultural crisis. The period was also one of dissolving certainties. Perhaps it was inevitable, as Page Smith judges, "that the darkest pessimism should follow the exaggerated optimism that characterized the Enlightenment and its long twilight."[9] But some historians see the turn-of-the-century crisis as far more severe than the other fluctuations in values that characterize European culture every several generations. Georg G. Iggers, for example, has underscored its magnitude, writing that

> in the course of the nineteenth century a profound crisis in Western consciousness occurred, perhaps the deepest since the emergence of the great traditional value systems in Greece and Palestine two and a half millenniums ago. The fundamental metaphysical assumption of the Western intellectual tradition, the certainty of the ethical meaningfulness of the universe, collapsed. . . . Modern man confronted . . . the recognition that he lived in a world without objective value and hence without objective meaning.[10]

Traditional Western values were now seriously challenged in the most fundamental ways. Man's intrinsic rationality came into question, as did the notion that reality itself was ultimately fully knowable. The challenges were issued not only by *fin de siècle* neo-romantics but also by those operating from within positivistic and scientific premises. Truth became relative, uncertain. As William Butler Yeats put it, man might be able to embody truth, but he could not know it. Or, to paraphrase Dostoevsky, if everything was right, then nothing was right, and who could tell the difference?

The very concept of causality was questioned, and the apparently ascendant belief in progress and optimism yielded ground to encroaching disillusionment, pessimism, even despair. To quote Yeats again: "Things fall apart; the centre cannot hold; / Mere anarchy is loosed upon the world."[11] The feeling of dismay grew alarmingly, resulting in what George L. Mosse and others have called a "change in the public spirit of Europe."[12] In that age of splendid, unprecedented creature comforts, meaning drained away from bourgeois, materially based life-styles. Naive exhortations to virtue, like the stirring clichés of Samuel Smiles enjoining that "resolute determination in the pursuit of worthy efforts" would carry one energetically "onward and upward in every station in life," now became passé.[13] The bourgeois emphasis on religion, marriage, the family, and the great hunger for respectability seemed so much sham effort.[14] In a Pirandellian world, Europe became a vast stage on which people from all ranks of life sought vainly for a meaningful existence which was proving more and more to be an impossibility. With fundamental Christian and Enlightenment values no longer regarded as absolute, the very foundation of modern culture was disintegrating. Pitirim A. Sorokin has summed it up by referring to this extraordinary upheaval in values, whose momentum continued into the middle of the twentieth century, as "not one of the ordinary crises which happen almost every decade, but one of the greatest transitions in human history."[15]

This profound turn-of-the-century crisis was anticipated by sensitive thinkers during the nineteenth century proper, with the ranks of contributors to *Kulturkritik* swelling as the twentieth century approached.[16] The litany of writers included, for example, Arthur Schopenhauer, Thomas Carlyle, Karl Vollgraff, Jakob Burckhardt, Fyodor Dostoevsky, and Søren Kierkegaard. The tone of these nineteenth-century writers—all of whom more or less predated Troeltsch's own first appearance in print in 1890—is appropriately summarized by the British Victorian poet, Matthew Arnold, whose "Dover Beach" draws the following dismal conclusion:

> . . . the world, which seems
> To lie before us like a land of dreams,
> So various, so beautiful, so new,
> Hath really neither joy, nor love, nor light,
> Nor certitude, nor peace, nor help for pain;
> And we are here as on a darkling plain

Swept with confused alarms of struggle and flight,
Where ignorant armies clash by night.[17]

Among the more memorable classic statements of the cultural critics are the trenchant ambiguities of Friedrich Nietzsche.[18] Nietzsche's excoriations as "the leading spirit of this cultural criticism"[19] are well enough known, but it should be emphasized that subsequent writers have pushed his critiques even further. If Nietzsche saw men warped by the undesirable slave morality of a sterile, late-nineteenth-century materialistic civilization, Sigmund Freud saw them warped by civilization as such. Freud spoke about "certain difficulties inherent in the very nature of culture," questioning whether "human civilization . . . be the most precious thing we possess or could acquire" and frankly suggesting "that the whole thing is not worth the effort."[20] Carl Jung felt that "modern man has lost all the metaphysical certainties of his medieval brother. . . . Everything becomes relative and therefore doubtful."[21] The same situation prompted Georges Sorel to speak of the "charlatan dogma" of the idea of progress.[22] Not long after Troeltsch's death, Karl Jaspers wrote about man in the modern age that "there were periods in which man felt his world to be durable. . . . [But] man to-day has been uprooted, having become aware that he exists in what is but a historically determined and changing situation. It is as if the foundations of being had been shattered. . . . The foundations of life quake beneath our feet."[23]

One of the best ways to appreciate these judgments of "the awful sickness and disease of modern culture"[24] is to glance briefly at the radical transformations of values in some of the major areas of European intellectual life. In the area of natural science, for example, theoretical physicists were undermining the Newtonian scientific synthesis. Albert Einstein suggested that truth was not absolute but relative to the system in which it occurred. Werner Heisenberg insisted that "existing scientific concepts cover always only a very limited part of reality, and the other part that has not yet been understood is infinite."[25] And Max Planck averred that "if we take a closer look and scrutinize the edifice of exact science more intently, we must very soon become aware of the fact that it has a dangerous weak point—namely, its very foundation."[26] Laymen in the first part of the twentieth century might have continued to be impressed with the accomplishments of applied science, but theoretical physicists themselves were conducting a genuine upheaval within their own discipline.

Accompanying this theoretical revolution regarding nature and reality was a corresponding revolution in thinking about man. Pavlov suggested that the alleged rationality of man resembled the motivation of a salivating dog, and Freud's probing of the depths of the unconscious made the classic definition of man as a rational animal seem increasingly untenable. A recent bestselling book, deliberately iconoclastic, refers to man bluntly as "the naked ape." [27] Man the *irrational* animal became in the twentieth century a common leitmotif in politics, literature, philosophy, art, and other areas of endeavor. Political manipulators such as Adolf Hitler utilized the psychological insights of writers like Gustav Le Bon and William McDougall, and political theorists including Vilfredo Pareto, Graham Wallas, and Georges Sorel spoke fervently of man's radical irrationality.

Images of man in literature and art reflected the same themes. The Postimpressionists rejected the five-hundred-year Renaissance tradition that art should reproduce the surface of sensible nature. Beginning at least with the symbolists, creative writers spearheaded a breakup of literary traditions remarkably similar to the breakaway from Newton in physics. New emphases included the antinovel and antitheater, stream-of-consciousness techniques, the death of plot, the rise of the anti-hero, and—throughout it all—the message that man was not merely lonely but radically alone. Thomas Wolfe wrote:

> Naked and alone we came into exile. In her dark womb we did not know our mother's face; from the prison of her flesh we have come into the unspeakable and incommunicable prison of this earth.
> Which of us has known his brother? Which of us has looked into his father's heart? Which of us has not remained forever prison-pent? Which of us is not forever a stranger and alone? [28]

Problems of human communication were seen as rooted, not in individual personality deficiencies alone, but, more deeply, in human nature itself. To be alive, to be part of the human condition, was a claustrophobic experience with no exit; or, as one of Sartre's characters expressed it: "Hell is—other people!" [29] One contingent of the existentialist movement saw human life as merely an exercise in futility. Further examples of this disillusioned view could be multiplied virtually endlessly.

By the early twentieth century, a series of actual political and economic events began to occur that seemed to justify the pessimism of cultural critics and the apparently rudderless uncertainty of intellectuals and scholars. One catastrophic event after another suggested that these men of ideas were prophetic and indeed correct in their discontent and disillusionment. Common "little men," who might never have heard of Dostoevsky or Nietzsche or Burckhardt—nor have understood them if they had encountered their ideas—could understand full well the cumulative horrors of World War I. The war to end all wars shocked European consciousness to its foundations and "fortified and spread an intellectual revolt already under way against the standards of the nineteenth century."[30] Ernst Troeltsch's German compatriots, seeking meaning in troubled times, made Spengler's diagnosis of the decline of the West a best-seller in the immediate postwar years.

After the illusory "return to normalcy" of the Golden Twenties— more an American myth than a European reality—Europe was jolted by the shock waves of the Great Depression. Economic distress seemed to many to provide the *coup de grâce* to classical economic liberalism, and, more deeply, to liberalism itself as a world view.[31] Economic disruption and myriad political and social problems stemming from the Great War provided fertile soil for the emergence and growth of totalitarian dictatorship and autocracy. Although scholars are not in agreement about the precise causes and genesis of twentieth-century totalitarianism,[32] the point here is that the practices and abuses of the inter-war European totalitarian regimes aggravated on a widespread scale the existing disillusionment and pessimism regarding traditional Western values initiated by the intellectuals.

In light of such realities as the death camps, two "total wars" in one generation with loss of human life on an unprecedented scale, the bombing of Hiroshima and Nagasaki, and the sudden frightful awareness that atomic and hydrogen bombs could annihilate all forms of life on this planet, by the middle of the twentieth century the common man could feel justified in a pessimism and uncertainty that turn-of-the-century intellectuals had foretold. It had become commonplace to be assailed by political, economic, social, and intellectual crises, to be besieged by conflicting diagnoses, pseudo-remedies, and alternative solutions. As J. Robert Oppenheimer suggested at about mid-century, the "one thing that is new is the prevalence of newness, the changing scale and scope of change itself, so that the world alters as we walk in it."[33] This theme, the "death of permanence," has become common parlance through widely read books like *Future Shock*.[34] "It's a funny age, isn't it?" remarks one of the characters in Malcolm Bradbury's novel, *Eating People Is Wrong*; "there are so many literatures, so many religions, so many cultures, so many philosophies, one doesn't know where to turn." [35] To increasing numbers of people, Western civilization appears to have entered a new phase, the "accidental century." [36]

Troeltsch's Preoccupation: "Everything Is Tottering!"

That this profound cultural crisis was real, and that he felt himself personally involved in it, Ernst Troeltsch leaves us no doubt. "So-called modern thought," he wrote, "cannot produce a homogenous weltanschauung." [37] He detected in the modern period that "the general mind of our times . . . finds itself shaken to its depths and is in a state of change in almost every direction." [38] All around he saw what he called "the present anarchy of values and of mind" whereby traditional truths, hitherto seemingly permanent and everlasting, were apparently losing their durability. [39]

This crisis of consciousness preoccupied Troeltsch throughout his career. Shortly before he died, he declared that the contemporary relativization of values was "the very center of all my thought at the present time." [40] But more than twenty-five years earlier, near the beginning of his academic career, Troeltsch had literally disrupted a scholarly meeting with the same preoccupation. At a conference in 1896, after an eminent academician had just delivered a learned paper on the meaning of the doctrine of the Logos, Ernst Troeltsch sprang to the rostrum in the ensuing discussion, opened dramatically with the words "Gentlemen, everything is tottering!" and proceeded to corroborate his views. Finding his listeners unresponsive, Troeltsch stormed out of the gathering and slammed the door behind him. As Walther Köhler remarks in relating this anecdote, the older scholars were horrified at the incident, "but we younger ones pricked up our ears." [41]

Köhler rightly suggests that the phrase "Everything is tottering!" could be taken as the leitmotif of most of Troeltsch's work. The theme of "the fundamental transformation of human knowledge" certainly is rife throughout Troeltsch's writings on religion and church history, politics, philosophy, and the nature of history. [42] To combat the growing feeling of uncertainty in the air, Troeltsch urged the pursuit of "a new spiritual freshness, power, concentration, and discipline, which must everywhere be formed against the crudity, shallowness, and vulgarity of a trivialized or caricatured, increasingly disintegrated and desolate civilization." [43]

Troeltsch was convinced that his own anguish over the contemporary crisis in consciousness was not an idiosyncratic feature of his life alone but somehow part of a more widespread cultural ailment. As he put it, his own inner conflict was "no mere accident of my personal experience. It was rather the personal form in which a vital problem characteristic of the present stage of human development presented itself to me."[44] In fact, Troeltsch's personal intellectual development over three decades is a microcosm of general intellectual tendencies extending over several centuries in European culture as a whole. Adapting to our study of Troeltsch's thought a premise suggested by William Barrett, that "the philosopher cannot seriously put to himself questions that his civilization has not lived,"[45] it is clear, half a century and more after Troeltsch's death, that he did indeed deeply share in and admirably diagnose the serious transformation of values that his generation experienced.

Even in Troeltsch's own lifetime his immediate contemporaries sensed that an important part of his significance lay in his response to the *fin de siècle* malaise in a world jarred to its very foundations. R. S. Sleigh, who had met Troeltsch in Heidelberg before World War I, and who in 1923 was to publish the first major work on Troeltsch in English, described the age in which they both lived as pierced with a "modern iconoclastic mood" in which "no traditional insight or institution appears to be of any use."[46] Sleigh, who in terrifying imagery claimed that "men to-day are like miners trapped in a shaft with the awful sense that it is closing in upon them," also thought that "in Troeltsch the modern spirit [had] found not only a voice, but also its most comprehensive and penetrating expression. . . . The protests, the misgivings, and the forces of the age surged and struggled within his mind and his intuitions [seemed] to indicate the direction at least in which our generation [might] find rest for its tired and tried and deeply entangled spirit."[47]

Another contemporary, Leicester Lewis, writing several years earlier, spoke eloquently of the

> wide chasm [that] was steadily obvious in the last few years before the war, and [that] seems unpleasantly clear at present. . . .
> We are living in a new epoch. . . . In the last twenty-five years of the nineteenth century, a silent though mighty change was taking place at the outposts of intellectual activity. I say outposts because although the change promises to be the mightiest that West-

ern culture has felt for nearly a thousand years, the push of the movement has not yet percolated through to the masses. . . . It does involve a new world outlook and philosophy, and . . . a new theological temper. . . . We are experiencing the birth-pangs of a new epoch. . . . The world of today differs in practically every form of intellectual activity from the world prior to the eighties. . . . Troeltsch . . . is the prophet of a new era.[48]

Who was this man whom contemporaries and subsequent generations alike have found so representative of the turn-of-the-century Age of Dissolving Certainties?

Ernst Troeltsch was principally an intellectual. A university teacher and scholar for his entire adult life, the chief highlights in his career were the academic posts he held, the principal milestones his many publications. And he was a prolific writer. In addition to the 3,500 pages of his *Gesammelte Schriften*—consisting of his lengthy *Social Teachings* as well as 82 journal articles, reviews, and addresses— Troeltsch wrote more than 350 additional published books, monographs, essays, articles, and reviews.[49] Troeltsch has earned his reputation in the areas of theology, church history, ethics, and the sociology of religion, but his writings are hardly restricted to these fields alone. Americans in particular have tended to be oblivious to his contributions to the philosophy of history, historicism, and political analysis. Hugh T. Kerr, for example, typifies this narrowness of appreciation when he considers Troeltsch's "most important books" to be principally those in fields of religion written before 1914.[50]

Born in Augsburg in 1865, Troeltsch soon evidenced two tendencies, supported by both his family life and early schooling, which he was to retain throughout his life and which as an adult clashed within him. One tendency was a deep religious temperament, molded in the form of Lutheran evangelism; the other was a sensitivity to the historical and natural world. Shortly before his death in 1923 Troeltsch observed that "the historical studies which had so largely formed me, and the theology and philosophy in which I was now immersed, stood in sharp opposition, indeed, even in conflict, with one another."[51] The theme of "two souls struggling within one breast" in Troeltsch's case had deep roots in the past.

Looking back on his life, Troeltsch remarked that "my intellectual tendency was oriented from my youth to the historical world, just as Dilthey's was."[52] The Bavarian secondary school he attended "provided substance and nourishment for this tendency of mind," and Troeltsch referred approvingly during the last year of his life to this earlier "predominantly humanistic and historical education . . . using the terms 'history' and 'humanity' in the sense . . . of a contemplation of objects which covers as far as possible the whole extent of human existence, and which finds delight in all the abundant diversity and ceaseless movement characteristic of human experience."[53] The atmosphere of his home life supplemented these early classroom experiences. His father, a Bavarian physician, inculcated in the growing boy an appreciation for scientific reality which Troeltsch never lost. He wrote that his father "very early encouraged me in natural science observation and collection. He had [at home] skeletons, atlases, electric machines, plant books, mineral books, and so forth. So it happened that from the beginning I learned to regard all historical, cultural, and philosophical problems in the framework of a worldview of natural science, and at the same time to experience the relationship of both worlds to each other as a burning theoretical and practical problem."[54]

But when it came time to enter university life, Troeltsch did not follow these earlier naturalistic and historical interests in any narrow sense. After vacillating among history, jurisprudence, classical philology, medicine, and philosophy, he finally decided to become a theologian. With his broad interests he felt that "in theology one had . . . the only suitable admittance to both metaphysics and extremely exciting historical problems. And metaphysics and history . . . were the two most exciting problems which had stimulated me at home."[55]

It is somewhat difficult to enumerate precisely the influences upon Troeltsch's thinking in his theological studies at Erlangen, Berlin, and Göttingen. He tended to be a voracious reader, eager and willing to absorb diverse ideas. Adolf von Harnack has commented on "his extraordinary capacity to learn from others. . . . The flow of his thoughts surged through the life-works of great philosophers and thinkers, tore from their banks enormous pieces and dissolved them in his own waves."[56] Two of the significant early influences upon Troeltsch's thought were Albrecht Ritschl, one of the dominant figures in the late nineteenth-century German theological world, and Paul de Lagarde, a biblical scholar and classical philologist to whom Troeltsch dedicated the second volume of his collected works. Other important early influences included Hermann Lotze and Wilhelm Dilthey.

Troeltsch's scholarly and personal concerns with religion were inseparable throughout his life. His deep personal religious temperament—the underpinning of his professional theological orientation as well as a source of genuine anguish as he grappled with the contemporary crisis in values—is clearly revealed in several letters he wrote to his friend and admirer, Baron Friedrich von Hügel. Troeltsch married in May, 1901, at the age of thirty-six, and after almost five years of childlessness and his wife's chronic illnesses, he wrote: "I am clearly conscious of the schooling by pain and trials throughout my entire being, and have found opportunity not only to utter my faith but to live it. . . . People [ought not to] fight shy of serious demands made upon them and of definite acceptance of God in the full sense."[57] In July, 1913, after his wife's health had been fully restored and their only child had been born, Troeltsch wrote von Hügel: "It is impossible to express how deep are the thanks I owe to God for this happiness. We have indeed to take all things from His hand, even the heaviest, and can demand nothing, not even what may be most essential to our life. But when, after trouble, the free gift of God reaches the soul and tarries within it, it is easier to resign oneself thus fully into His hand."[58]

Yet Troeltsch's deep religious temperament did not interfere with his rigorous standards of scholarship. In a book on the influence of Protestantism on the origins of the modern world, he insisted that the historical phenomenon of Christianity "must be treated with complete objectivity and impartiality. . . . The investigation must be strictly historical, and in no way biased by theological prepossessions." He added that "if any reader finds [this book's] spirit too purely objective or skeptical, I will only ask him to remember that this is not due to any lack of religious convictions on my part, but to the fact that I have thought it right to reserve their expression for another place."[59] Had Troeltsch not maintained his personal religious values while simultaneously investigating, as a scholar, the decline of religion in the modern world, he would undoubtedly not have felt such deep spiritual anguish in his own life.

Troeltsch's choice of a dissertation topic at Göttingen affords an early insight into his concern with the problems of the historical appreciation of religion, a theme upon which he continued to work for the next three decades. Initially, in typical youthful and inexperienced scholarly zeal, he set for himself a formidable task, ponderously expressed: to comprehend "the universal history of the development of the religious spirit, in terms of the basis of its ultimate contact with a universal life, and the special place and contribution of Christianity within this universal development."[60] Persuaded of the vastness of this problem, Troeltsch narrowed its focus to the development of the spirit of Christianity within the context of the history of European culture. It was still unmanageable, as he soon came to realize, but the very posing of these historically grounded theological questions illustrates his intellectual concerns while still a university student. Further—as one of his own students later remarked—in this early work Troeltsch "realized fully how radically such a program differed from the traditional theological studies, including ecclesiastical history and the history of doctrine."[61] The actual topic upon which Troeltsch finally wrote, for which he was awarded the Licentiate in Theology, was limited to certain aspects of sixteenth-century Protestant thought. It was soon expanded to become his first publication, *Reason and Revelation According to Johann Gerhard and Melanchthon: A Study in the History of Early Protestant Theology*, and suggested a general conclusion similar to one which Wilhelm Dilthey had reached—although Troeltsch was careful to point out that he had reached his interpretation independently—namely, that the Protestant Reformation was more medieval than modern in character.[62]

After brief periods as a Lutheran minister in Munich and as a Privatdozent (unsalaried academic instructor) in Göttingen, Troeltsch's first academic appointment was at the University of Bonn, in 1892, as Extraordinarius Professor on the Theological Faculty. Then in 1894 Troeltsch accepted what was to become the longest academic post of his career, an appointment as Ordinarius Professor on the Theological Faculty at the University of Heidelberg, where he remained for two decades.

It was at Heidelberg, where he principally taught systematic theology and the philosophy of religion, that Troeltsch wrote most of his finest works on questions of religion. (His significant writings in this area are examined in Chapter 2 and the first part of Chapter 3.) He reacted decisively against his earlier Ritschlian influence, establishing himself as one of the founders of the sociology of religion and becoming the principal spokesman for the new "history-of-religions school" (*Religionsgeschichtliche Schule*). He further became a philosophic convert to neo-Kantianism's attempt to update Kant's original three

Kritiken by constructing a new "Critique of Historical Reason." At Heidelberg Troeltsch realized the insight he had had at the beginning of the 1890s, namely, "that he would revolutionize theology through historical studies."[63]

Near the start of the world war, Troeltsch moved to the University of Berlin, where he remained until his death in 1923. In a sense this was a double move, not only from one academic center to another but also from a teaching position on the Theological Faculty to one on the Philosophical Faculty. The chair of systematic theology had become for Troeltsch increasingly narrow and confining. H. Stuart Hughes has remarked that by the outbreak of the Great War Troeltsch as a theologian had become somewhat of an oddity, for "his thought was to take the most extraordinary and unorthodox course—until in the end he remained a theologian in little more than name."[64]

During the Berlin years Troeltsch turned explicitly to the themes of historicism and the philosophy of history. Indeed, the philosophy of history became for him the "essential problem."[65] He had lectured on questions of philosophy during his last five years at Heidelberg, but his full attention to philosophical matters awaited the move to Berlin, where in addition to his research, publications, and heightened political activities, Troeltsch taught courses in the philosophy of history, philosophy of religion, philosophy of culture, introduction to philosophy, ethics, and the history of philosophy. His most important single work in Berlin, written during his most mature period of scholarship, was the still untranslated *Der Historismus und seine Probleme*, a significant statement on the philosophy of history (see especially Chapters 3 and 4). It was in the creation of a viable philosophy of history that Troeltsch sought a solution for the contemporary European crisis in consciousness.

But Troeltsch's scholarly philosophical interests did not signal a removal from the so-called real world. In Berlin his political activities intensified. He was not a stranger to politics, having been the elected representative of the University of Heidelberg to the Badenese Parliament for eight years, but in Berlin his political experience enlarged considerably. Living in the capital city of Germany during the Great War and observing the turmoil of postwar Weimar politics gave him valuable experience and perspective. He defended the war effort in a series of addresses and essays from 1914 to 1918, and after the Armistice contributed to the prestigious journal *Der Kunstwart* a series of monthly political analyses that H. Stuart Hughes has called "the most judicious and at the same time the most moving commentary on the new Republic's struggle for existence."[66]

This brief summary of Troeltsch's career demonstrates the wide range of his personal and professional concerns. In all his writings the underlying leitmotif is the turn-of-the-century crisis in consciousness. Within the four principal areas of his work—religion, historicism, the philosophy of history, and politics—the expressions of this pervasive crisis may vary, but Troeltsch's belief that "Everything is tottering!" is evident throughout.

2

Ferment in Religion:
The Demise of Absoluteness

Die moderne Welt ist eine schwere Religionskrisis.
Troeltsch (1907)

Kirche und Religion ist Privatsache geworden.
Troeltsch (1909)

In the turn-of-the-century crisis in consciousness, traditional Christianity suffered a severe loss of status in European culture. Ernst Troeltsch was not only an exceptionally articulate and lucid analyst of this crisis in religion but also one of the principal intellectuals who helped undermine Christianity's privileged position.

Troeltsch wrote voluminously on religious topics, from his dissertation on sixteenth-century Protestant theology, published in 1891, to his collected lectures, entitled *Christian Thought* and published posthumously in 1923. In this third of a century, his views on religion in general and Christianity in particular underwent several decisive transformations. Troeltsch began his career as a traditional nineteenth-century theologian, influenced by the school of the eminent Albrecht Ritschl. As the decades passed, however, his theological thinking became unorthodox and controversial, so that he came to anticipate—and even, to a certain degree, to effect—many of the breakthroughs in religion that have concerned theologians in the later twentieth century. Benjamin Reist has recommended that "indeed, one of the most illuminating ways to deal with the issues that now confront Protestant theology in these middle decades of our century is to ponder them in the light of the unanswered problems that Troeltsch has left us."[1] As an "important link between nineteenth- and twentieth-century religious thought," some scholars now regard Troeltsch as "perhaps the most sophisticated theorist among the liberal protestants who dominated

German theology between 1870 and 1920."[2] Wolfhart Pannenberg has even suggested that Troeltsch might be considered "the most significant theologian of the twentieth century."[3]

Troeltsch's writings on religion, of course, sometimes incorporate his other intellectual concerns, and thus his contributions to the "history of religions school" are treated in the following chapter on historicism. Here I concentrate on Troeltsch's writings in the three basic areas of the crisis in religion, the decline of the churches, and the absoluteness of Christianity.

Crisis in Religion

The writers' ink expended on the modern world's religious crisis is staggering. I see no need to reproduce here this flood of words, sometimes an impassioned protest against "Western civilization . . . lurching to its death" without religion,[4] sometimes a cool description of traditional Christianity as "a posture, a matter of convention, a religious commodity like the factory-made bric-a-brac that adorned the typical Victorian home."[5] The crisis is great and is not restricted solely to theologians. It is the common experience of a wide public, as various popular catchwords today bear witness—death of God, religionless Christianity, secular city, world come of age, and so forth.[6] Nor has the crisis always been lucidly confronted. The ideological battles of the closing decades of the nineteenth century, what Carlton J. Hayes has called that "queer sort of fight between 'science' and 'theology,'" were marked by the widespread "intransigence or muddleheadedness of Christians who utilized what was imagined to be theology in order to combat what they regarded as the errors of science."[7]

Whether or not the twentieth century is fulfilling Kierkegaard's dire prophecy—made the decade before Troeltsch was born—that "men will fall away from Christianity by the millions,"[8] one finds evidence almost everywhere that "the central fact of modern history in the West," as William Barrett has written, "is unquestionably the decline of religion."[9] Many now find themselves suspended between two impossible worlds: one in which they can no longer believe, a world directed by religious directives and considerations; and one which they cannot bear, a world without these directives and premises. In our time many thinkers virtually take for granted that "contemporary religion is marked by relativism, the increasingly pervasive feeling among many educated church members that their church's beliefs, values, and organizational structure are patently the work of culturally conditioned men rather than the direct embodiments of a divine will."[10]

In numerous books and articles, with an ambivalent mingling of orthodoxy and heterodoxy, Troeltsch diagnosed the causes and content of the religous turmoil in modern times. Some of his works were of extraordinarily large scope—such as *Social Teachings*, which treated almost the entire history of Christianity—but most were more circumscribed, model essays or vignettes of European intellectual history. Indeed, Troeltsch was a pioneer in the writing of intellectual history long before this discipline achieved the fashionable status that it now enjoys.[11] One is able to piece together a compelling picture of Troeltsch's diagnosis of the complex career of religion in Western civilization from historically oriented works such as "The Ancient Church" (1913), "Augustine, Christian Antiquity, and the Middle Ages" (1915), "Renaissance and Reformation" (1913), "The Significance of Protestantism for the Formation of the Modern World" (1906), "The Enlightenment" (1897), "Deism" (1898), "Schleiermacher and the Church" (1910), "The Nineteenth Century" (1913), "Modernism" (1909), "The Essence of the Modern Spirit" (1907), and "The Church in Contemporary Life" (1911), to name only a small selection of the available sources.

The central premise running through all these works is a simple one: "It is undeniable that there is a severe crisis of religion in the modern world."[12] Not simple, however, was Troeltsch's diagnosis of this "certainly extremely intricate" problem. He presented a complex picture of an emerging modern mentality and spirit increasingly indifferent to religion.[13]

Troeltsch maintained that some tension always existed between religion and culture, regardless of the historical period.[14] In the modern period, however, the tensions had become exceptionally exacerbated. The growing spirit of the times was unprecedented hostility or indifference to traditional Christian values. They had been attacked, rejected, or ignored as simply irrelevant to the modern mentality. Organized religion—Judaism as well as Christianity—had become "extraordinarily weak and lifeless. . . . no longer capable of producing or sustaining a Church-directed civilization."[15] Troeltsch did not believe that the church-dominated medieval period of Western civilization ever perfectly overcame all discord between religious values and those of political, social, and economic spheres of life, but he held that a model for accord had been created.[16] In modernity, however, "the ecclesiastical world of the medieval period has come to an end, with its authority, its supernatural interpretation of nature and history, anthropology and psychology, and its inspired books and sacred traditions."[17] He saw that churches as viable institutions were defunct, noninstitutionalized religious groupings were confused, indifference and enthusiastic atheism were prominent, and surrogate religions everywhere abounded.[18] While individuals might still possess some religious beliefs, "religious uniformity in the modern world is simply inconceivable."[19]

To understand fully Troeltsch's analysis of this crisis, we must understand his historical perspective, his interpretations of the nineteenth century, the Enlightenment, the Renaissance and Reformation, and the Middle Ages. In Troeltsch's view, not only did the present religious crisis have deep roots in past history, but European civilization in general, in its "depth, exuberance, complexity, and dynamics," could not be appreciated fully without an awareness of its medieval (and even its ancient) cultural sources.[20] Troeltsch was a thorough historicist. In the following brief chronological appraisal of the successive phases of Christianity's influence in European civilization, I have endeavored to keep prominently in mind Troeltsch's own injunction that "the understanding of the present is always the final goal of all history."[21]

Troeltsch tended to endorse the familiar tripartite division of Western civilization into ancient, medieval, and modern.[22] His foil for the secular, individualistic, relativistic modern period was clearly the European Middle Ages.[23] In disagreement with the usual analysis, however, Troeltsch thought that modernity—neutral if not hostile to traditional religion—began much later than commonly believed; in his view the influence of the ecclesiastically based medieval period lasted until at least the eighteenth-century Enlightenment. In his time Troeltsch was a foremost revisionist writer on this subject, consciously rejecting the general assumption (which many still maintain) that the "Renaissance and Reformation are the starting-points of so-called modernity."[24] Indeed, not until his own age did Troeltsch see a genuine swing away from religion on other than an elitist basis, a "pendulum oscillation" away from "an epoch distinguished essentially by its religious ideas" towards an emerging epoch "basically worldly-minded and religiously feeble."[25]

Despite the implications of the title *Protestantism and Progress* (one of Troeltsch's few works which have been translated into English with the choice of title not his own), Troeltsch unmistakably regarded the Protestant Reformation as medieval and not modern. "The significance of Protestantism must not be exaggerated," Troeltsch cautioned; "a large part of the basis of the modern world . . . arose quite independently of Protestantism." [26] On this highly complex and polemical topic Troeltsch unequivocally said that

> the genuine early Protestantism of Lutheranism and Calvinism is . . . entirely a Church civilization like that of the Middle Ages. . . . Protestantism—especially at the outset in Luther's reform of the Church—was, in the first place, simply a modification of Catholicism, in which the Catholic formulation of the problems was retained, while a different answer was given to them. . . . Protestantism cannot be supposed to have directly paved the way for the modern world. [27]

Only in post-Reformation Protestantism—when "old" and "modern" Protestantisms separated, sometime in the later seventeenth century— did a "single-moulded Church civilization" end. [28] With this seventeenth-century split, a genuine crisis in confidence in traditional Christian values began to emerge quite openly.

In the meantime, however, Protestantism was effectively stifling the breakthrough towards modernity initiated by the fourteenth- and fifteenth-century Italian Renaissance. "The peculiarity of the Renaissance," Troeltsch wrote, "lay in its modification of the direction of interests, whereby for the first time there really showed up an increasing estrangement from the world beyond, from preparations for the grace of the Church, and from the monastic idea." [29] The Renaissance accelerated what Troeltsch detected as an incipient secular attitude already existing in the later medieval period, and although it did not produce fully drawn modern secular thinkers the Renaissance did exhibit "significant anticipations of the modern mentality." [30] (Apropos to the term "secularization," Ronald Gregor Smith has pointed out that "it was apparently Troeltsch who first used the word in its full modern connotation.") [31]

With the intemperate ideological struggles of the sixteenth-century Confessional Age, however, "such beginnings of a free and secular civilization as had already been toilsomely established" were swept away, and because of the Reformation era, "in spite of the contemporary diffusion of the ideas and manners of the Renaissance, Europe had to experience two centuries more of the medieval spirit. . . . It was only the great struggle for freedom at the end of the seventeenth and in the eighteenth century which really brought the Middle Ages to an end."[32] The confessional struggles of the Reformation and Catholic Counter-Reformation also enhanced "the unification of political and ecclesiastical powers," with church-state separation, espoused during the Renaissance, delayed for another several hundred years.[33]

Yet despite the Reformation's dulling of the Renaissance spirit, Troeltsch recognized that at least indirectly and unconsciously Protestantism contributed to the distinctively modern trends of secularism, individualism, and the eventual separation of church and state.[34] To Troeltsch secularism, "the limitation of the interests of life to the present world," was a prominent characteristic of modern European civilization.[35] "Religious asceticism in the form of negation of the world and self-disciplining with a view to a super-earthly life-aim has disappeared from the modern world," he noted.[36] But how had Protestantism—with its medieval heritage and its primary focus on the world beyond—contributed to this? Troeltsch's answer was that although Protestantism certainly did not foster secularism as an end in itself, it nevertheless inadvertently "promoted secular work and secular interests" because of its special meaning of the concept of vocation.[37] According to Troeltsch, life "in the world" rather than a monastic or other-worldly ascetic existence had been generally demeaned by the medieval religious temperament—aside from the somewhat secular element in the late Middle Ages, as previously mentioned. Protestantism succeeded in changing this basic other-worldly orientation by affirming and sanctifying the world (the term Troeltsch used, *Weltbejahung*, literally means a "saying yes to the world").

Although paradoxically the early Protestant reformers remained medieval in many ways, they emphasized that the world was "the natural and divinely ordained arena for the activity of the Christian." Consequently they asserted that "there is no doubt that the world and secular life do have a place of honor as the substance and form of faith's activity."[38] With his twentieth-century vantage, Troeltsch was able to appreciate that "the sanctification of the world was a dangerous and double-edged matter more easily favorable to the world than to sanctification."[39] He had as evidence the modern temper that endorsed secular values and activities as ends in themselves and no longer regarded "world affirmation" as a step in the pursuit of other-worldly goals. "A very thin boundary-line indeed stretches between the Protestant Christian animation of this secular labor and the secularization of state, economy, and society which is no longer Protestant."[40]

Not until the eighteenth-century Enlightenment, however, did the first concerted attack on traditional religious values take place. Of all the intellectual movements in the past five to eight hundred years, the Enlightenment, according to Troeltsch, provided the most direct challenge to the privileged status of religion in European culture. "The Enlightenment is the beginning and foundation of the intrinsically modern period of European culture and history, in contrast to the hitherto regnant ecclesiastically and theologically determined culture."[41] The Enlightenment was the great watershed in European history. Before it was medievalism, but after it, a "thorough fight against ecclesiastical supernaturalism."[42]

Although the essence of the Enlightenment was its "opposition to the hitherto existing schism between Reason and Revelation and to the practical imposition of supernatural Revelation on the happenings of life," initially this intellectual movement was not hostile to religion so much as it was seeking to emancipate various areas of thought and action from the influence of religious and theological tenets.[43] In the process of this self-styled emancipation, however, the enlightened criticisms of the *philosophes* and their admirers effectively "demolished the fundamental bases of the theological culture" which had prevailed till then.[44]

Isolated elements of modernity contained in the Renaissance, the Reformation, the scientific revolution, the rise of *raison d'ètat* in politics, a burgeoning economy, and the growth of a large middle class seemed to coalesce in the eighteenth century, the first modern century in European history. In all areas of European life, Troeltsch detected radical changes in the position and influence of religion. In politics, religion completely lost its long-held esteem, and "the state no longer appeared as an establishment of God, but as the work of an agreement resulting from human reason."[45] Concomitant with this political secularization, the prominent socio-economic development was the emergence of the *Bürgertum* or middle class, avidly desirous of achieving status and freedom not available in a theocratic, feudal, and agrarian world.[46] This rising middle class demanded a culture and literature consonant with its own tastes and independent of religion. The new political, economic, and social theories not only minimized religious explanations but also frequently displayed antitheological and antisupernatural turns of mind. In the writings of the great national econo-

mists like Quesnay and Adam Smith, Troeltsch located the most influential and characteristic Enlightenment values, such as the optimistic
belief in universal law and in humanity.

In surveying the higher thought of the Enlightenment—the new mechanical and mathematical sciences, historiography, philosophy and
the philosophy of history, the national literatures, educational reform,
ethics, and theology—Troeltsch found everywhere a declining belief
in the exclusive priority of religious values.[47] The cumulative picture
he drew of these intellectual disciplines prefigured what others after
him have called a come-of-age world which no longer needed religion
as an integral part of its life.

In the religious sphere proper, perhaps the most important development among thinkers was Deism, often said to be the foundation of the
modern philosophy of religion.[48] Deism—"more a symptom than a
source of the internal religious metamorphoses of the era"—was a
rational, critical, "freethinking" attitude towards religion, in contrast
to the earlier attitude based upon faith, divine revelation, and theology.[49] Whereas during the Confessional Age Protestants and Catholics
alike tended to share many values and beliefs despite often vehement
Reformation and Counter-Reformation disputes, during the Enlightenment proponents of the "natural religion" of Deism were decidedly
antagonistic to Europe's traditional, supernaturally based, institutionalized religion.

Widespread satiation with the religious fanaticism and excesses of
the Confessional Age, together with emerging approval of tolerance,
also made fighting and persecution for the sake of religion seem anachronistic. An additional undermining of traditional Christianity as absolute religion was the comparative study of Christianity and non-Christian religions, occasioned by the expanded global knowledge gained
through recent extensive colonizing and missionary work outside of
Europe.[50]

Traditional ecclesiastical Christianity recovered partially during the
first part of the nineteenth century, but then a reversal set in once more.
For the hundreds of years of Christianity's career, Troeltsch in fact saw
a recurrent ebb and flow of religious values: a very high tide in the
medieval and early modern periods, a low during the Enlightenment
era represented by Voltaire's "crush the infamous thing!," an incoming
tide once more during the early nineteenth-century Restoration, then
the lowest ebb in his own period when hostility and indifference to
organized religion reached unprecedented proportions. As we shall see

later in examining Troeltsch's philosophy of history, he did not attempt to superimpose any a priori pattern—such as a progressively or retrogressively linear pattern—on the variety of existential history, but rather tended to endorse what has been called a "philosophy of the jagged line."

Troeltsch had accurately recognized the complexity of the Age of Enlightenment—and with this acumen he stood in the forefront of historians of his era who sensed the danger in viewing the eighteenth century monolithically as a pure Age of Reason—but he was even more insistent on the complexity of the nineteenth century proper.[51] Similar to Matthew Arnold, a near-contemporary who viewed the nineteenth century as an "Age of Multitudinousness," Troeltsch regarded nineteenth-century intellectual history as "remarkably many-sided and full of contrasts."[52] The course of religion was turbulent indeed, beginning with an initial "profound religious reaction against the Enlightenment" and ending in disorder with a counterreaction.[53] The early nineteenth-century Restoration, crystallized at least by 1815 with the final fall of Napoleon Bonaparte and the settlement of the Congress of Vienna, "destroyed the meaning of the eighteenth century."[54]

Closely related to the "flowering of theology during the first part of the nineteenth century"—which Troeltsch identified in part as a "neo-orthodox reaction"—was the restoration of the established churches, with attendant close ties between church and state.[55] A central paradox of nineteenth-century religious development arose from this so-called "throne-altar alliance" whereby the revived churches enjoyed the important support of the political establishment. Although politically the Restoration was ended by a series of English electoral reforms beginning in 1829, by the continental revolutions of 1830 and 1848, and by the unification of Germany and Italy "on the basis of politically liberal institutions," the benefits of the throne-altar alliance to the restored churches were significant.[56] In sum, as the nineteenth century progressed, "restored ecclesiastical Christianity was too strong to be able to be ignored, but too weak to be able to control the common life."[57]

Decline of the Churches

Troeltsch's own generation inherited the early nineteenth-century inconsistency: as organizations and institutions the churches were viable, but they had only feeble influence over the minds and hearts of men.[58] Troeltsch noted that "the future of the churches, whose place in politi-

cal and social life, morality and literature, has been completely transformed, constitutes a serious problem for anyone who ponders it."[59]
By the early twentieth century, the churches—by which Troeltsch
meant traditionally oriented, institutionalized religious organizations
—had become increasingly irrelevant to the deeper spiritual needs of
the populace. Writing in 1913, Troeltsch felt that it was "an extremely
difficult and perilous cultural problem, whose possible solution still lay
in complete darkness."[60] He found a major clue to the dilemma of the
twentieth-century churches, however, in the modern situation of
church-state separation.

The appropriate relations between church and state is a venerable
theme in European history, dating at least from the early medieval
period and highlighted by problems such as Byzantine Caesaropapism,
the Gelasian "two swords" theory, the significance of Charlemagne's
crowning in 800, the subsequent Investiture Controversy, and so forth.
Troeltsch's own interpretation of the theme was straightforward. In his
view, "the relation of state and church is essentially irrational. . . . [It
is] the relationship of two sovereign powers which can neither get
along without one another nor yet endure one another."[61] In other
words, Troeltsch tended to define man both as a political and a religious animal whose two sides supplemented each other in one fashion
or another—with some notable exceptions, such as the Enlightenment
and the post-Restoration period. For most of European history, close
church-state relations had been the norm, with what Troeltsch called
the *"System der Einheitskirche"* far more prevalent than the modern trend of the *"freikirchlichen System."*[62] Unmistakably Troeltsch
thought it proper to designate this *"separation of state and church* as
an essential characteristic of the modern religious situation."[63] He did
not, however, see the coexistence of independent churches and religiously neutral political states as the conclusion to a centuries-old is-
sue: "the separation of state and church will only shove the problems
in different directions, not solve them."[64]

The new religious crisis affected the churches in a threefold way:
first, established churches tended to be separated from political support; second, they were experiencing increasingly diminished control
over their surrounding milieux; and third, the most viable forms of
contemporary religous expression were occurring outside the churches.
As Troeltsch wrote in an article observing the Reformation Jubilee in
1917, "the religion of the churches is no longer the religion of spiritual
Germany: this fact is indisputable."[65]

Indeed, Troeltsch took careful note of the increasingly strong appeal in his own era of what he called "churchless Christianity" (*das kirchfreien Christentum*).[66] The center of contemporary religious activity was, in fact, the "disintegration of ecclesiastical [*kirchlichen*] religion."[67] Churches—Protestant, Catholic, and Jewish—represented the "organization of religious life of times gone by."[68] In modern times, he observed, "the churches are working with the ideals of past ages," whereas what appealed more and more to the modern mentality was "*religion outside the churches*" (*ausserkirchliche Religion*).[69]

Troeltsch even saw in his own time "scorn for the churches" as typified in a comment made by a Black Forest farmer: "Ministers should call upon the sick, should pray for the dead, but should leave the healthy ones in peace."[70] On this same theme, Troeltsch took note of the disturbance of a young theologian who had sought his advice on whether or not to become a minister. "All the great men, such as the prophets and Jesus, had known nothing about a church, had wanted no church," the theological student exclaimed; "they were not pastors or ministers and had no need to be."[71] Troeltsch expressed sympathy with this disenchantment, remarking simply that truly "Jesus himself certainly founded no church. He had only scattered the seeds."[72] Troeltsch consistently endorsed the difference "between the religion of Jesus and the religion of churches and priests"[73] and thus came remarkably close to anticipating mid-twentieth-century phenomena such as "religionless Christianity" or the "underground church." As early as 1895, in one of his first published essays, he wrote that "the present has an exceptionally vigorous religious life but it has practically no connection with the churches, or only a loose connection."[74]

The increasing neglect of ecclesiastical Christianity did not unduly upset Troeltsch, for he personally did not equate or identify "religion" with "church." "Antichurchly religious individualism" meant, he stressed, "not unreligiosity but unchurchliness."[75] It was a spurious war-cry, he felt, to look at the decline of the churches in the modern era and thereupon to shout: "Religion is in danger!"[76] The churches might be dying, but not religion itself, which was but assuming other forms.

Troeltsch found in recent history ample harbingers of the contemporary spiritual upheaval in which he had become embroiled. New religious groupings of the sixteenth century and afterwards—including the Baptists, Quakers, Jansenists, and Conventicles—signified to him that in Western civilization "a new conception of religion was being formed everywhere."[77] Viable new religious tendencies during the Enlightenment era, such as Pietism in Germany and Methodism in England, further suggested a "series of religious movements which then proliferated throughout the European world in reaction to ecclesiastical-theological torpidity and as a presentiment of a vast impending spiritual upheaval."[78] Among his own generation Troeltsch observed that "the great modern religious movement, the reawakening of the need for religion, is arising outside the churches and in most cases even outside of theology."[79]

But what a bewildering diversity of eclectic religious tendencies Troeltsch noted in his own times! In a typically convoluted sentence, with a complexity that he relished, Troeltsch described these motley, extra-ecclesiastical phenomena:

> Sometimes it is simply an intensified Christianity which is amalgamated somehow with the modern world of ideas but which no longer has or seeks links with historical churches; at other times it is an after-effect of Kantian-Fichtean ethical idealism tempered with concepts of Goethe and Hegel as well as with religious ideas essentially originating in Christianity; now it is a frankly completely imaginative syncretism of all sorts of religious elements from the entire world derived from the scholarship of the history of religions; or it is a spiritualistic and occult community in which the most ancient early religions of the cult of soul and spirit are again resurrected; now it is a free-floating artistic religion which blends the aesthetic unity of form with the natural law unity of the world; or again it is a reawakening of pessimism and of the desire for salvation, but one which prefers the Buddhist form of renunciation rather than endorsing the Christian idea of personality; and sometimes it is a totally amorphous longing for religion, but one which shrinks back from every concrete religious plan.[80]

Despite his apparent playfulness in describing the extreme variegation, Troeltsch personally did lean favorably towards religious individualism.[81] In his fundamental distinction between religion and church he even opposed the two, describing religion as "the direct opposite of the rigid form of the church."[82] Religion was something fluid and throbbing, something "inward, personal, individualistic and spontaneous," whereas the church was static, generally monolithic, and inclined to neutralize the immediateness and directness of the religious experience in favor of some form or another of prescribed outward conformity.[83] Troeltsch did not regret the passing away of a bygone era in which church and religion had been identified, in which one could not be religious except in and through a church.

The Absoluteness of Christianity

Troeltsch's thinking contributed to the twentieth-century ferment in religion in yet another way. Even more radical than his rejection of churches as an absolute part of Christianity was his challenge of Christianity itself as absolute religion. Here Troeltsch struck at the very heart of the modern European crisis in religious values, and in so doing paradoxically challenged the very values to which he tenaciously held. Carlo Antoni has concluded in assessing Troeltsch's work that Troeltsch "was destined to witness (and even to aid) the precipitous decline of those faiths and ideas into which he had been born and within which he had grown to maturity."[84] Troeltsch not only recorded and described the turn-of-the-century crisis in religious consciousness, he personally contributed to it.

It is important to note, however, that although Troeltsch helped to challenge traditional religious values he did not attack faith itself. He was no enemy to religion and thereby is remarkably distinguished from what Warren Wagar describes as "the majority of avant-garde twentieth-century thinkers and artists [who] have been, for all practical purposes, unbelievers."[85] Troeltsch remained a believer throughout his life. But his endemic revisionist attitudes in theology, church history, and the sociology of religion had the cumulative effect of seriously transforming the system he was wont to defend. Indirectly and gradually, Troeltsch did help alter the very religious values which lay at the center of his own temperament as well as at the center of European civilization itself. A parallel contemporary revolution occurred in the physical sciences, when scientists such as Planck, Einstein, and Heisenberg did much to undermine the prevailing traditional Newtonian view of a positivistic-materialistic reality. One of Troeltsch's contemporaries actually referred to him as "a kind of Einstein of the religious world," and James Luther Adams has more recently described him as "the Heraclitus of historiography."[86]

The Absoluteness of Christianity and the History of Religions, initially made public in 1901, is one of Troeltsch's most important books.[87] It is entirely proper to consider this essay "as a pioneer work in the field of thinking theologically about the relationship between

Christianity and other religions . . . [and] as a minor classic of German theology."[88] It is further proper to regard *The Absoluteness of Christianity* as "the embryo for all that followed" in Troeltsch's writing career, but it is misleading—Troeltsch's own description notwithstanding—to designate this work "the starting point of his thought."[89] This classic essay appeared fully ten years after Troeltsch's first publication, a decade in which he clarified his thinking in several dozen writings published while he was on the faculties of Bonn and Heidelberg. My point is simply that during this ten-year period, through his teaching and writing, Troeltsch's mind was developing in such a way that *The Absoluteness of Christianity* may rightly be regarded as the *conclusion* of a decade of work—none of which had been published in English translation through the 1970s. I believe an examination of the most important trends of these writings of the 1890s will illuminate Troeltsch's mature outlook on the absolute and relational aspects of Christianity.

Over the course of the years, Troeltsch changed his basic theological views several times. The key to understanding this development lies in his response to the first decisive theological influence he felt, that of Albrecht Ritschl. "In the last quarter of the nineteenth century," writes H. R. Mackintosh, "no influence in the field of theology could compare, for breadth and vigour, with that of Albrecht Ritschl of Göttingen. . . . Harnack was not far out in calling him the latest of the Church fathers."[90] Gustav Krüger has suggested that "what Bismarck did for the German nation Ritschl achieved for German theology."[91] As Troeltsch himself said, it was "in the impressive teaching of this energetic and great scholar" that he was nurtured as a student.[92] Ritschl was at Göttingen for a full quarter-century, beginning his teaching career there the year before Troeltsch was born.

The program of Ritschl and his school was oriented towards a systematic theological superstructure erected upon a systematic theological foundation. Theology, in short, was to be based upon theology and not upon any extraneous (that is, nontheological) principles, be they philosophical, scientific, historical, or otherwise. Ritschl's was a *Heilsgeschichte* in which the supernatural far outweighed the natural, in which the mysterious and miraculous clearly outdistanced history and reason. Against this approach Troeltsch reacted. "Within the group of Ritschl's own disciples divergent tendencies early began to appear," comments John R. Van Pelt, who locates Troeltsch "at the extreme left" among "a group of men who, after having stood for a time under the influence of Ritschl, early struck out for themselves a new path."[93]

Troeltsch's divergence from Ritschl actually began as early as his first publication, his expanded doctoral dissertation appearing in 1891 as *Vernunft und Offenbarung (Reason and Revelation)*. Seven years later Troeltsch was to comment that little by little he had developed an opposition to the Ritschlian system, but this initial publication showed he had already begun to part ways with his Göttingen master.[94] The very title itself posited a relationship that Ritschl had sublated. As Troeltsch concluded in this study: "the old [sixteenth-century] theologians had possessed and worked out with great vigour and clarity a trustworthy, intelligible relation between reason and revelation that the new ones do not possess. . . . [These latter] have terminated the most manifold alliances and conciliations with philosophy."[95]

Despite the apparent narrowness of this case study, the issues at stake for Troeltsch were broad and far reaching. Contrary to Ritschl's basic view, Troeltsch asserted that dogmatic religious values did depend at least in part upon their nontheological milieu. In particular, Troeltsch maintained that sixteenth-century (*altprotestantischen*) Lutheran theology was rooted not merely in biblical revelation but also in both the contemporary cultural milieu and specific events, such as the proceedings at the Imperial Diet at Spires in 1526.[96] In this regard Troeltsch clearly pioneered in what Horst Stephan was later to call "extensive theology" (that is, a theology open to the world and to natural knowledge) rather than a more traditional "intensive theology" which looked inward upon an inherited scriptural core.[97] In making this emphasis Troeltsch helped immeasurably to develop the methodology of the *Religionsgeschichtliche Schule* as well as the emerging scholarly discipline of the sociology of religion.

One detects in virtually all Troeltsch's writings of the 1890s the conclusion—or, perhaps more properly described, the controlling assumption—that Christianity is absolute and clearly superior to the world's other religions. But his treatment of this theme contained subtle changes of emphases, uneasy compromises among divergent views, and a curious admixture of both religious orthodoxy and heterodoxy. As the decade unfolded the gradual rejection of Ritschlian *Heilsgeschichte* was increasingly evident in favor of a view regarding Christianity as a historical phenomenon accessible to the standard tools of historical research (*Geschichtsforschung*). Several examples will clarify this trend.

In a lengthy early essay, "The Christian World View and Its Counter Tendencies," Troeltsch accepted the Ritschlian premise that Christianity was uniquely different from all other religions, remarking "that Christianity stands in acute contrast to all other religious development. . . . [It is] a new principle in relation to the entirety of non-Christian religions"; and further, "that any investigation of the genesis of Christianity leads deep into the mystery of the supernatural world."[98] He kept this belief in Christianity's superiority, but in his writings several years later based his approach not upon an alleged unique miraculous origin of Christianity but upon a somewhat empirical comparison of Christianity with other religions. He wrote that "it is clear today that Christianity is the profoundest, mightiest, and most fertile deployment of the religious idea," but his proofs were of a different nature.[99] Conceding that the Christian world view might not be definitively proven correct, he still judged it to be superior to alternative and competing world views, which also lacked ultimately demonstrable proofs.[100] At the core of his argument was a growing ecumenical attitude basically contrary to the Ritschlian school's religious exclusiveness, which tended to judge that "other religions, afflicted with so many errors, enigmas, and uncertainties, without Jesus eventually lead only to atheism."[101]

Not long after, in an essay on "History and Metaphysics," Troeltsch unequivocally rejected this narrow Christian exclusiveness, insisting that Christianity was not aloof from history but a part of it. Focusing upon the approach of the eminent Ritschlian Theodor Kaftan, Troeltsch wrote that "since Kaftan maintains a specific Christian-theological method and . . . I, on the other hand, contest the possibility of such a salutary method and entrust myself solely to that universal method practiced in the profane scholarly disciplines, this is the antithesis of two modes of viewing, of which the former is accustomed to be prevalent more among theologians, the second more among non-theologians, so far as these latter own up to a personal religious faith."[102] For Troeltsch, proofs for the claims of Christianity were subject to verification by the same methodology as other historical assertions. Any form of "miraculous" proof he rejected as untenable, ridiculing Kaftan for maintaining that Christianity alone had a historically inaccessible supernaturalism.[103] "Only one who roams through the history of religions simply as an apologetic hunter and is merely on the lookout for illustrations of arguments for the inferiority of non-Christian religions, but not one who goes through this sublime world of marvels as a hushed and reverential wanderer, is able to bring home his supernaturalism intact from such disputatious expeditions."[104] It was impossible, Troeltsch maintained, to isolate the origins and development of Christianity from history, or to separate within Christianity the natural from the supernatural, or to claim a supernatural genesis for one religion while denying it to others.[105]

And yet, despite these patently clear rebuffs of Kaftan and orthodox Ritschlian theology, Troeltsch was not willing to have theological truths totally dependent upon the ebb and flow of history. Despite the appeal of the comparative historical method, in this early work Troeltsch still tended to regard history somewhat suspiciously as a weak foundation. As he wrote in 1898, a dependence on history might lead to historicism (*Historismus*), and historicism in turn to pernicious dangers:

> Playful relativism, for which everything is growth and decay, conditional and approximate, the . . . renunciation of every personal conviction, the asphyxiation of all productiveness and . . . simple confidence in generally valid standards, the disintegration of scholarship in the creation of endless duplications of what has already formerly passed, the habituation to the destitute routine of historical specialization, these are the oppressive defects of historicism, which are now and then so strident that they can make one apprehensive about the continuation of our civilization."[106]

Later in his career, most notably during his Berlin years after 1914, Troeltsch was not so apprehensive about the phenomenon of historicism, as we shall see. Nevertheless, even though the youthful Troeltsch—still in his predominantly theological, pre-philosophy-of-history phase—regarded historicism as bristling with dangerous portents, he tended to endorse the historical viewpoint over the dogmatic religious viewpoint as the better of two available alternatives. "Historicism will not let itself be shaken off again," he felt, "and supernaturalism will not be called back again."[107] In ending his first decade of scholarship in 1900, Troeltsch concluded that the method required at the present time was the "idea of a religio-historical [*religionsgeschichtliche*] theology," which he also referred to as a "theology of historicism."[108]

The ambivalence towards Christianity evident in his writings of the 1890s is still present in *The Absoluteness of Christianity*, but Troeltsch has clarified the issues. At the start of his second decade of scholarship, Troeltsch was still unmistakably biased towards Christianity, stating that

> among the great religions, Christianity is in actuality the strongest and most concentrated revelation of personalistic religious apprehension. It is even more than that. It occupies a unique position in that it alone has worked out in a radical way the distinction between the higher and lower worlds. . . . It alone . . . takes empirical reality as actually given and experienced, builds upon it, transforms it, and at length raises it up to a new level. . . . Christianity represents the only complete break with the limits and conditions of nature religion.[109]

Troeltsch did not deny that religions other than Christianity might also be revelations of God, but he insisted that "Christianity remains *the* great revelation of God to men."[110] Further, "Christianity is the pinnacle of all religious development thus far and the basis and presupposition for every distinct and meaningful development in man's religious life in the future. There is no probability that it will ever be surpassed."[111]

But Troeltsch's description of the absoluteness of Christianity was not without qualification. He was bothered by what he regarded as a weakness of *Heilsgeschichte* or of any nonhistorical method concerned with a supernatural entity "that stands within history but does not derive from history."[112] He felt obliged to admit that "the Christian religion is in every moment of its history a purely historical phenomenon, subject to all the limitations to which any individual historical phenomenon is exposed, just like the other great religions. It is to be investigated, in every moment of its history, by the universal, verified methods of historical research."[113] Troeltsch had concluded—and continued to insist for the rest of his career—that Christianity was phenomenological ("the sphere of the individual and nonrecurrent") and consequently could be comprehended by the standard historical methods; "it is evident, therefore, that the attempt to present Christianity as the absolute religion is untenable."[114] As a historical phenomenon, Christianity could not be both historical and absolute. If something is absolute, it is not historical; and if it is historical, then it is not absolute. Simply put, "the absolute lies beyond history."[115]

Then Troeltsch's argument took another turn, as he tried to blend the best of two worlds. Although one could not unqualifiedly possess the absolute within history, nevertheless he maintained that historically conditioned truths leaned towards, or participated in, the absolute. Since God was "the source of all historical life," this meant that within history and through historical phenomena like Christianity one did have access to a world of permanency.[116] It was largely a "problem of how to discern, in the relative, tendencies toward the absolute."[117] This problem preoccupied Troeltsch for the rest of his life, as he wrestled with the premise that man "has access to this absolute . . . only in a historical way, a way conditioned by the context of which he is a part. It is available to him only in historically individualized revelations of the absolute. To wish to possess the absolute in an absolute way at a particular point in history is a delusion."[118]

The implications of Troeltsch's perspective on the absoluteness of Christianity are extensive. An examination of two specific examples— Christian missionary activity and the person of Jesus Christ—can serve to illustrate the shock waves of his historically oriented approach upon the hegemony of the orthodox, dogmatic method in theology.

Five years after publication of *The Absoluteness of Christianity*, consistent with his rejecting the idea that Christianity had been static and monolithic for two thousand years, Troeltsch redefined the meaning of Christian missionary activity. "The mission of the present is something other than the ancient Christian mission," he asserted. "It is something other than the mission of the Middle Ages. . . . Finally, it is also something other than the pietistic evangelical mission. . . . Today's mission is the promulgation of the world of religious ideas of Europe and America in intimate association with the extension of the European sphere of influence."[119] Troeltsch had come to believe so firmly that Christianity and European history were intimately wedded that, aside from the question whether Christians indeed had the right to promulgate their religious beliefs in alien religious circles, he raised doubts "whether Christianity really is transferable to all the stages of the development of civilization, and whether there possibly might not be peoples who after all are not fit and destined by fate for it."[120] Conversely, he questioned the introduction of Oriental religions into European culture.[121] These doubts contain the germs of two ideas which Troeltsch later developed in his mature philosophy of history: the idea of "individual historical totality" featured in his formal logic of history and the idea of "Europeanism" prominent in his material philosophy of history (both are discussed in detail in Chapter 4).

Despite these revisionist views of the role of Christian missionary activity, however, Troeltsch still was sufficiently orthodox to declare that Christianity, if not the perfect religion, at least neared perfection. In the same essay Troeltsch persisted "in the assurance that the Christian religion, in its blending with the heritage of ancient European civilization, is the most sublime form and power of the spiritual life, in spite of all the infirmities, contradictions, and foulness of our civilization." [122] At times, in his yearning to reconcile his own apparently contradictory thoughts, Troeltsch is like the proverbial person who wants to have his cake and eat it too. [123]

Five years after this essay on missions Troeltsch entered squarely into a turn-of-the-century controversy that was still being debated in scholarly religious circles: whether or not Jesus Christ was a genuine historical figure. The controversy had reached a peak just before World War I with the appearance of Arthur Drew's *Die Christus Mythos*, which ventured to prove that Jesus Christ had never lived. [124] Troeltsch's own position was that "the contention of the non-existence of Jesus is unquestionably a monstrosity, and likewise, the contention of the unintelligibility of the main features of his preaching is a severe overstatement." [125] Because the cult and symbol of Jesus Christ was so central to the worship of the Christian community, Troeltsch insisted that "thereupon under these circumstances a neglect of historical-critical research is by no means possible. . . . Faith can interpret, but not determine, the data." [126] Troeltsch rejected out of hand what he regarded as the Ritschlian view, which put "the personality of Jesus, by a value-judgment of religious faith, outside the residual history, characterizing him as a miracle of revelation standing opposite this remaining history." [127] Troeltsch urged that facts about the person and teachings of Jesus Christ "must be able to be established as historical actualities by means of historical-critical means, if the 'Christ symbol' is to have a firm and strong spiritual foundation in the 'factual' Jesus." [128] Despite the unmistakable uncertainty and relationism entailed in this insistence on proofs for the historicity of Jesus Christ, Troeltsch still recommended the historically oriented approach over that of a dogmatic religious exclusiveness, concluding that "people who are able to be happy in their own beliefs only if these are thereby binding upon millions of years to come, know nothing of the real freedom and greatness of religious faith." [129]

This conclusion is reminiscent of the chiding contained in *The Absoluteness of Christianity* that "absoluteness is a universal characteristic of the naive way of thinking. . . . Comparison between religions and the realization that one has to make adjustments in his initial, naive outlook has a shattering effect on absoluteness and paves the way for *thinking*."[130] Troeltsch preferred not to be a member of "the superficial crowd that strives self-confidently for perfect solutions."[131] His emphasis on historicity and relationism was a central aspect of the heritage which he bequeathed to twentieth-century theology. Half a century after Troeltsch's remarks, the theologian Heinz Zahrnt has reiterated that "the fundamental problem of all theological work is still *history*. . . . The attempt to use dogma as it were to overrun history has proved a failure."[132]

On the other hand, Troeltsch's heritage has not been without difficulties. Hubert Cunliffe-Jones, for example, judged that Troeltsch "provided no firm basis for the Christian faith he held" because the constantly shifting ground of a historically rooted religion lacks any absolutely valid permanency.[133] Cunliffe-Jones raised a further, more serious point, that Troeltsch had no "firm basis . . . for his continuing to be Christian."[134] For if Troeltsch's prolific thought on religious matters ultimately failed to yield a convincing rationale for his own continuing acceptance of Christianity, might not others find themselves in the same predicament? This question reflects the position of Herrmann, Barth, Bultmann, and others not deeply sympathetic to liberal Christian theology. Thus, the dialectical theologian Emil Brunner complained in the late 1920s that Troeltsch had mutilated theology to the point that "a specifically christian consciousness of revelation can no longer be maintained here."[135]

But the problem is not a simple either-or dichotomy. Christian theologians have dual responsibilities both to an orthodox theological tradition and to the intellectual climate of their own day. If, as Morgan has said, "Troeltsch may be judged to have discharged the latter more successfully than the former," he erred as a daring pioneer.[136] Troeltsch formulated his concerns, in A. O. Dyson's words, "amid the general uncertainty and confusion of intellectual life in the late nineteenth century."[137] He contributed appreciably to a revolution which "shook the theological world like an earthquake" in the early twentieth century.[138]

Troeltsch has been aptly described as a "complexifier."[139] For him, theology and history were not mutually exclusive, watertight compartments of the human experience. He would have thoroughly repudiated Zahrnt's recent remark that with an immersal in history "from henceforth man no longer exists on two levels, a [secular] lower and an upper [divine] one. . . . Instead, he exists on one level alone."[140] For Troeltsch, passage between these two worlds was still affirmed. "The melancholy image of Troeltsch as a theologian who lost his faith" is unacceptable.[141]

One of the more balanced recent appraisals of Ernst Troeltsch's religious heritage was expressed by Robert Morgan at the Lancaster conference in 1974: "no responsible theologian now doubts the necessity of a critical and historical approach to bible and doctrine. . . . [Troeltsch's] openness to the real, social and economic, historical, world, makes him a more helpful guide to christian thinking at the end of the twentieth century than are either the followers of Herrmann who privatise religion and morality, or those who seek to evade the radical consequences of historical thinking and preserve a massive biblicist fortress in the midst of a secular world."[142] At the beginning of our century, in a time of crisis, Troeltsch was the most important spokesman forcing Christian theologians to take seriously the real world. There is no doubt that he "will continue to live in theology by the questions he raised."[143] Interest in Troeltsch is not an antiquarian curiosity. He is relevant today, and—it is humbling to reflect—we "have still not fully mastered his problems."[144]

3

Historicism: The Modern World View

*Die historische Methode, einmal auf die biblische
Wissenschaft und auf die Kirchengeschichte angewandt,
ist ein Sauerteig, der alles verwandelt und der
schliesslich die ganze bisherige Form theologischer
Methoden zersprengt.*

Troeltsch (1898)

*Um uns von der Historie zu befreien und souveräne
Herrschaft über sie zu bekommen, stürzen wir uns in
einen Ozean historischer Kritik und Rekonstruktion.*

Troeltsch (1922)

The ultimate rationale for Troeltsch's rejection of Christianity's absoluteness, as well as for his radically revisionist views on other
religious themes, lies in his endorsement and personal spiritual inte-
riorization of historicism (*Historismus*) as a world view. The theme of
historicism became the very center of his lifework. To trace Troeltsch's
development chronologically, one may say that during the two pre-war
decades at Heidelberg he elaborated his innovative historical method
—for the most part on religious topics—and then during the war and
immediate post-war period generalized from these essays to the development of human thought in general. It was as a persistent participant
in this turn-of-the-century European "revolution in consciousness,"
Van Austin Harvey reminds us, that "Troeltsch's problems still haunt
us."[1]

The emergence and flourishing of historicism as a world view has
been an integral part of this revolution, but cultural critics have been at
extreme odds in assessing its effects. For each critic who maintains
that the result has been turmoil and chaos—for example, that "the
death of God is caused in part by the historicizing of all our thinking"[2]—one can easily find another who maintains that the historical
outlook has been fruitful.[3] Nor were Troeltsch's views on this question

39

simple. He did advise that in the twentieth century "all thinking is obliged to become in some measure historical,"[4] but he wavered in his acceptance of the total implications of this premise. Although Troeltsch was remarkably close to Nietzsche's view that "everything has developed . . . there are no eternal facts, just as there are no eternal truths," the ramifications of this situation made him uneasy.[5]

Troeltsch in fact considered that the historical outlook posed a greater threat to traditional religious values than did the natural sciences. Both the emergence of mathematical-mechanical natural science and the comparable critical discipline of history had been products of the Age of Enlightenment. Contrary to prevailing popular opinion, however, Troeltsch thought it wrong to regard natural science as the principal threat to revealed religion. Since the eighteenth century the real foe lay, he thought, in a radical historicist attitude, supplemented by the shocks to traditional Christianity produced by the spate of new travel books, deism, the importation of Indian religious and philosophical views, philology, ethnology, and also "a great new discipline, *die Religionsgeschichte.*"[6]

"Religionsgeschichtliche Schule" and the Sociology of Religion

The phrase *"Religionsgeschichtliche Schule"* is virtually untranslatable. In keeping with Troeltsch's own remark that "the expression does not exist in English," the original German term is retained here rather than one of its inadequate English equivalents.[7] The year before hostilities erupted into World War I, Troeltsch composed a scholarly summary of the main features of the *religionsgeschichtliche* movement, which had first burgeoned in the 1890s and for which he is commonly regarded as the principal theoretical spokesman. This 1913 article not only characterized the movement as a whole but conveniently summarized as well Troeltsch's own outlook on his two decades of work at Heidelberg.

Although in this essay Troeltsch never mentioned Ritschl by name and made only a passing reference to "the school of Ritschl," his antipathy to Ritschlian orthodox *Heilsgeschichte* is obvious.[8] For example, the *religionsgeschichtliche* movement denied the miraculous supernatural origin of Christianity, located Christian values in their cultural milieux, rejected the claim that Christianity was absolute and unique, and encouraged the empirical historical study of comparative religions. As Troeltsch himself expressed it, the phrase *religionsgeschichtliche Schule* means in general nothing other than the recognition spread throughout the entire scholarly world that the religion of mankind exists only in a great number of particular religious formations, which evolve in multifarious reciprocal contacts and influences, and among which the judgment cannot be made with the old dogmatic means of the distinction between a natural and a supernatural revelation. . . . [Such dogmatism] suffices only so long as one lives essentially within the horizons of one's inherently customary religion and therefore obviously can impute to it alone a value supernaturally established without being contradicted by foreign claims. . . . The relationship [of one's own religion] to the religious life of humanity is from the scholarly viewpoint no longer that of the supernatural or philosophical apologetic of that special religion, but rather that of a comparison of the universal history of religions. . . . Indeed, the whole notion of the construction of a historical religion as definitive, perfect, and prevailing over all others is evidently doubtful and questionable.[9]

Although this approach to religion is not shocking to us today, in Troeltsch's time these views "not only [ran] counter to both orthodox and liberal theology but also [stood] in opposition to the ecclesiastical self-understanding of Christianity."[10] As far as Troeltsch was concerned, anyone pursuing religious questions qualified as a member of this protean *religionsgeschichtliche* movement so long as he sought "to answer questions purely on the basis of historical development with every renunciation of a supernatural information and foundation."[11]

Troeltsch's reappraisal of Christianity in this article is definitive and contrasts with his frequent earlier statements that Christianity held a privileged status as an absolute and unique form of religious expression. Troeltsch now unequivocally stated that "one can certainly not envisage [Christianity] as the idea of religion perfectly and eternally realized, or, in the words of Hegel, as absolute religion."[12] Since Christianity was a historical religion, Troeltsch insisted that "only an investigation of the history of biblical religion in a *religionsgeschichtliche* interpretation is possible. . . . Any simple biblicism is impossible."[13]

Confronted with the question "What is Christianity?" Troeltsch now felt constrained to avoid any answer that might suggest permanency; instead, historical-critical and historical-developmental thinking leads one to the point of regarding the entire extent of the world of Christian life as the gradual unfolding of a germinating power or rudimentary purpose manifesting itself therein. . . . Thus the 'essence' [of Christianity] can be understood only as the appropriately productive reapplication and readaptation of the historical Christian forces of each total situation at any given time. *For each era the essence is somewhat different.* . . . An unchangeable Christianity would mean the end of Christianity. It has never happened, and it will not be able to happen, provided that it once genuinely belongs to history.[14]

This statement about the essence of Christianity could hardly be farther from dogmatic absolutism. "At that time when critical historical research and, I hope, a *religionsgeschichtliche* way of thinking prevail," Troeltsch concluded, "then by all means it is entirely impossible to treat the Bible as the sole means of the generation of ideas, and to forget about the history lying between it and the present. . . . The Bible cannot be the sole instrument of the religious community, but to it must also be added the entire wealth of Christian history."[15]

As for the dogmatics of the *religionsgeschichtliche Schule*, Troeltsch not only suggested that the *Schule* was not a school—rather only "a more or less radically administered *religionsgeschichtliche* method" —but that its *Dogmatik* was not dogmatic.[16] He saw an intimate connection between a changeable Christianity and a changeable "dogmatics" intended to explain that shifting historical phenomenon. Calling attention to "the ambiguity of the word 'Christianity' and to the impossibility of hardening it into immutable first principles," Troeltsch was in effect offering what might be called an "undogmatic dogmatics."[17] The expression is an oxymoron, and illustrates well the paradoxical twist of Troeltsch's mind on this question. He fully expected the objection that "this is no 'dogmatics,' no unfolding of constant and invariable truths," but such an attack did not seriously trouble him.[18] His underlying rationale was simply

that as a matter of fact there is by no means any permanently unchangeable truth. Such truth is not merely imperceptible to man, but also out of the question altogether, because of the lively, changing character of the world, where there is no program readymade simply to be put into practice, but only the perpetually new and active comprehension of the nature of a reality itself profoundly in evolution. Such a dogmatics, however, is not on this account unalloyed subjectivism, because it takes shape out of the vast disclosures of history and is conscious of working its way in the direction of the absolute goal.[19]

Troeltsch's earlier, more tentative theological iconoclasm had now reached maturation.

In 1912 Troeltsch published the full text of what most English-language readers know as his most outstanding work, *The Social Teachings of the Christian Churches*. The complete German title is *Die Soziallehren der christlichen Kirchen und Gruppen*. In light of Troeltsch's view of the exceeding importance of nonchurch forms of Christianity, it is unfortunate that in the English translation of this title the last two words, "*und Gruppen*," were deleted. Nevertheless, this work (generally called "monumental" even by its most harsh critics) furnishes the best available illustration—though certainly not the most concise one—of the application of the dogmatics of the *religionsgeschichtliche Schule*. Though specialized scholarship in the decades since its publication have invalidated isolated parts of the work, in its general impact it is still regarded as a classic in its field, establishing Troeltsch as a pioneer in the sociology of religion.[20]

In the *Social Teachings* Troeltsch staked out as his domain of investigation no less than the entire two-thousand-year span of Christian history—"a direct survey of the Ancient World, of the Middle Ages, of the Reformation, and finally of the Modern World."[21] Confronted with his subject's vast time span and recalcitrant data, he could not possibly explore and master it singlehandedly. Consequently, he depended greatly upon others' efforts. As Roland H. Bainton has remarked: "Troeltsch, to be sure, was not absolutely original—who ever is?"[22] Bainton thereby underscored one of the weaknesses of the *Social Teachings*, but he also suggested its strength:

> The procedure of Troeltsch consisted in an effort to reconstruct the characteristic marks of Christianity in particular epochs and cultures, and then to compare the one manifestation with the other. He made no pretense of an extensive acquantance with the sources. His procedure was rather to take the best dozen or so books for each period and out of these to construct a picture of the dominant characteristics. The method has its obvious limita-

tions. Any work so executed is bound to be subject to the fire of the specialists. Yet there is scarcely any other way in which a sweeping synthesis can be achieved. This only must be borne in mind that conclusions reached in such a fashion must ever be regarded as tentative, and a work like that of Troeltsch should be canonized rather for its methodology than for its positive conclusions. At the same time a reviewer must not carp at details but should center attention rather upon the main thesis and only thereafter indicate less significant defects of fact or interpretation.[23]

Bainton's distinction—that Troeltsch excelled in methodology, not in conclusions—is valuable in any balanced assessment of the *Social Teachings*. What was this methodology? In a word, it was that of the *religionsgeschichtliche Schule*, which in turn ultimately reflected Troeltsch's emerging historicist attitude.

Focusing upon the social message of Christianity in its various phases of development, Troeltsch brilliantly constructed a massive case study revealing that this message could be understood only in changing historical contexts. A commonplace assumption today, in Troeltsch's own time his "sociological formulation of the problem" and his insistence that "my work recognizes no special theological or Christian methods of research" amounted to a controversial challenge to traditional standards for the treatment of Church doctrine.[24] He was, in effect, writing about theological issues not as a theologian but as a Church historian and sociologist. Ten years after the *Social Teachings*, in his impressive *Historicism and Its Problems*, Troeltsch referred in an aside to the *Social Teachings* of 1912 as an effort "which places side by side with the eminent, essentially ideological-dogmatic presentation of Christianity which Harnack has produced an essentially sociological-realistic-ethical one."[25] This was a remarkable understatement. As one commentator has phrased it, in offering the *Social Teachings* with its controversial new methodology, "Troeltsch was willing to counter the most celebrated student of the history of doctrine of his generation"; and further, "the real point to *The Social Teachings* will never be grasped until one is aware of the broad assault on all customary church history and all the accepted history of doctrine that generated it."[26]

The greatest influence upon the methodology Troeltsch used in the *Social Teachings* was Max Weber. Troeltsch remarked in an obituary tribute to the great German sociologist, who from 1897 had been his friend and colleague at Heidelberg, that "for years I came to know the immensely stimulating vigor of this man in daily communication, and I am conscious of being indebted to him for a great part of my knowledge and ability."[27] In the autobiographical sketch of his own intellectual development, Troeltsch recalled those Heidelberg years in greater detail:

> I was drawn anew into historical investigations concerning the nature and history of Christianity, in fact, with almost impetuous agitation. . . . I plunged myself into sociological studies which of course intimate less a ready knowledge than a new mode of observing. . . . At the same time I came into the sphere of influence of such an overwhelming personality as Max Weber, to whom these surprises dawning upon me had long since been foregone conclusions. . . . The formulation of the question, consequently, was this: to what extent is the origin, development, modification, and modern damming up of Christianity sociologically conditioned, and [to what extent is] this itself perhaps an actively forming sociological principle. Exceptionally difficult questions concerning which there were hardly any useful preliminary studies! And yet one could no longer speak about a history of the pure dogma and ideas of Christianity, if one had comprehended this problem.[28]

Troeltsch pursued these questions of the sociology of religion in intimate association with Weber. Indeed, the writing of the *Social Teachings* took place during a time that Weber and Troeltsch actually lived in the same household.[29] In discussing this "fruitful intellectual intercourse during those happy years when they were living together under the same roof," J. P. Mayer remarked that "it would be difficult to say whether Weber's sociology of religion is more influenced by Troeltsch's studies in this field or *vice versa*."[30] As in Troeltsch's intellectual relationship with another colleague, Friedrich Meinecke, there was a genuine cross-fertilization of ideas and not merely a one-way influence.

A prominent borrowing from Weber was the "ideal-type." Weber wrote that

> an ideal type is formed by the one-sided *accentuation* of one or more points of view and by the synthesis of a great many diffuse,

discrete, more or less present and occasionally absent *concrete* individual phenomena, which are arranged according to those one-sidedly emphasized viewpoints into a unified *analytical* construct (*Gedankenbild*). In its conceptual purity, this mental construct (*Gedankenbild*) cannot be found empirically anywhere in reality. It is a utopia. . . . It is a conceptual construct (*Gedankenbild*) which is neither historical reality nor even the 'true' reality. . . . It has the significance of a purely ideal limiting concept with which the real situation or action is compared and surveyed for the explication of certain of its significant components. . . . The ideal-type is an attempt to analyze historically unique configurations or their individual components by means of genetic concepts.[31]

The ideal-type, in short, is a heuristic device useful in social science research. "It is not a *description* of reality but it aims to give unambiguous means of expression to such a description."[32] Weber recognized that "whoever accepts the proposition that the knowledge of historical reality can or should be a 'presuppositionless' copy of 'objective' facts, will deny the value of the ideal-type."[33] However, Weber pointedly warned that "if the historian (in the widest sense of the word) rejects an attempt to construct such ideal types as a 'theoretical construction', i.e., as useless or dispensable for his concrete heuristic purposes, the inevitable consequence is either that he consciously or unconsciously uses other similar concepts without formulating them verbally and elaborating them logically or that he remains stuck in the realm of the vaguely 'felt'."[34] In the main Troeltsch endorsed these views, using them extensively in his own conceptual frame of reference for the *Social Teachings*. (Interestingly, when eventually Troeltsch turned against the viewpoint Weber represented, he veered towards the unknown biases and suspicious impressionistic accounts about which Weber had warned.)

In his intellectual portrait of Weber, Reinhard Bendix remarked, "Weber explicitly states that he abandoned the topic of Protestantism because his friend Ernst Troeltsch, who was a professional theologian, had initiated his work on *The Social Teaching of the Christian Churches and Sects*."[35] The evidence suggests that Troeltsch moved even beyond the scope of Weber's work into a broader area of concern, the most visibly prominent sign being Troeltsch's expansion of Weber's church-sect ideal-type construction into the scheme of church-sect-mysticism. This analytical, tripartite device was defined by Troeltsch in the conclusion of his *Social Teachings*:

> The Church is an institution which has been endowed with grace and salvation as the result of the work of Redemption; it is able to receive the masses, and to adjust itself to the world, because, to a certain extent, it can afford to ignore the need for subjective holiness for the sake of objective treasures of grace and redemption.
>
> The sect is a voluntary society, composed of strict and definite Christian believers bound to each other by the fact that all have experienced 'the new birth.' These 'believers' live apart from the world, are limited to small groups, emphasize the law instead of grace, and in varying degrees within their own circle set up the Christian order, based on love; all this is done in preparation for and expectation of the coming Kingdom of God.
>
> Mysticism means that the world of ideas which had hardened into formal worship and doctrine is transformed into a purely personal and inward experience; this leads to the formation of groups on a purely personal basis, with no permanent form, which also tend to weaken the significance of forms of worship, doctrine, and the historical element.[36]

These sociologically informed conceptual aids, which J. Milton Yinger has described as "the starting point for most current typologies of religious groups. . . . [and] of enormous significance in the development of the sociology of religion," Troeltsch used as his primary tools in organizing his survey of the various historical phases of Christianity's social teachings.[37] Aside from the brief statement on "Introduction and Preliminary Questions of Method" and the almost equally brief "Conclusion," the *Social Teachings* is divided into only three chapters: "The Foundations in the Early Church" (pp. 39–200); "Medieval Catholicism" (pp. 201–445); and the longest chapter, simply entitled "Protestantism" (pp. 461–990). Troeltsch treated his topic "exhaustively as far as the eighteenth century," remarking of subsequent history that "even if the undertaking were restricted to a mere description of the different Christian endeavours, schemes, and associations of the present day, the whole situation is so complicated that the subject would have to be treated in a separate work."[38]

Troeltsch's observations and conclusions in the *Social Teachings* are too sprawling and prolix to summarize economically at this point, where it seems more germane to our theme to focus upon Troeltsch's later attitude towards sociology as a whole, in an important corrective to the widely held assumption that he remained sympathetic to sociology to the end of his career.[39] The *Social Teachings* was an exemplary piece of scholarship in the young field of the sociology of religion, but in his later writings it is evident that Troeltsch felt he had moved beyond this sociological approach. Troeltsch might be "perhaps the most eminent sociologically oriented historian of Western Christianity," as Talcott Parsons claims, but he himself had a decided change of mind about sociology.[40] In *Historicism and Its Problems*, for example, he spoke clearly about its limitations. His main concern was that the generalizing social sciences should not be mistaken as acceptable surrogates for history as a discipline. Although he did have an occasionally favorable, positive comment about these disciplines as he knew them—for example, in his aside that "the modern history of economics, and sociology, teach us to perceive our own existence freshly and more accurately"—his more prevalent attitude is represented by the following remark: "All these abstract-historical sciences of laws and of types are for true, representative history [*Historie*] indeed only auxiliary disciplines, formulations of questions, categories, models, ways to observe and to classify, but furnishing in themselves no likeness and appreciation of the historical world at all."[41]

Although Weber's sociological influence had been valuable in the underlying conceptions of the *Social Teachings*, Troeltsch now reversed his judgment, referring to sociology as "certainly still an extremely immature discipline, which up to now has discovered not at all unambiguously either its central problem or the systematic arrangement of its subject-matter."[42] Troeltsch at Berlin unmistakably thought sociology to be inferior to history, a point generally overlooked by those commentators onesidedly preoccupied with Troeltsch's pioneering efforts in the sociology of religion during his Heidelberg years. Later Troeltsch shared the antipathy towards sociology that generally characterized members of the historical profession in Germany during the 1920s.[43] To those familiar with the pattern of Troeltsch's intellectual development this change in attitude comes as no surprise. Throughout his thirty-year academic career, he was influenced by, and later deviated significantly from, the ideas of thinkers such as Ritschl, Windelband, Rickert, and Dilthey, as well as Max Weber. Troeltsch had a constantly growing, developing mind, eclectic to an extreme. That he at one point sympathetically adapted Weber's ideas and at a later date criticized Weber's sociological approach is but one of several major intellectual shifts.

Fundamental to this breach with Weber was Troeltsch's view that the formalized rules and models with which the generalizing social sciences were concerned had little or no direct bearing upon individualized phenomena and were foreign to historical life—which, for Troeltsch, was equivalent to being divorced from reality. This rejection of sociology was similar in motivation to his earlier rejection of Ritschlian *Heilsgeschichte*; neither the Ritschlian nor the sociological approaches were sufficiently historically or phenomenologically grounded. "It is the historian," Troeltsch maintained, "who shows the basic phenomena [*Urphänomene*] of history to the psychologist and sociologist, and not vice versa."[44] The generalizing social sciences displayed for Troeltsch a too-close affinity with certain features of the natural sciences. The crucial underlying distinction was the dichotomy he endorsed between the *Geisteswissenschaften* and the *Naturwissenschaften*, terms explored in the next section of this chapter. In short, Troeltsch came to view the generalizing social sciences as defectors from the ranks of the *Geisteswissenschaften*, as prodigals aping the ways of the *Naturwissenschaften* and consequently potentially inimical to the discipline of history and the philosophy of history.

Despite the influence of a sociological approach on Troeltsch's religious writings during his later Heidelberg years, and despite his furthering of the young discipline of the sociology of religion, at Berlin he came to insist adamantly that sociology and the generalizing social sciences could be at best only auxiliary, supplementary disciplines [*Hilfswissenschaften*] and in themselves were only poor substitutes for history and the philosophy of history. Troeltsch's change of mind leads us to the important movement of *Historismus*.

Meaning of "*Historismus*"

A brief look at the context of the historicist movement, which Troeltsch came to personify, is helpful in appreciating Troeltsch's own interpretation of historicism as a modern world view.[45] Calvin Rand has remarked that "the German '*Historismus*'. . . . only became widely known in the 1920s through Troeltsch's writings."[46] The peak of discussion in German academic circles occurred between the publications

of Troeltsch's *Der Historismus und seine Probleme* in 1922 and
Friedrich Meinecke's *Die Entstehung des Historismus* in 1936, although the origins of historicism go back much further.[47] The term
itself is slippery and difficult to pin down. Walther Hofer correctly
claims that the interpretations of historicism have been "inconsistent;
it is a controversial notion [*Kampfbegriff*] generated, accepted, repudiated, and given new meanings in the turmoil of countless discus-
sions and polemics."[48] I would not go so far as John Lukacs, who
states that historicism is a "term so broad as to be useless."[49] However,
I do suggest that after sampling the literature on historicism virtually
all would agree with Rand's remark that "the arguments, pro and con,
in the last seventy-five years have distorted whatever clear meaning the
term might have developed."[50]

According to Meinecke, in his much cited classic description, "the
emergence of historicism was . . . one of the grandest spiritual revolutions that Western thought has experienced. . . . We see in it the high-
est stage attained up to now in the understanding of human things."[51]
Meinecke located the roots of historicism in the eighteenth century in
England, France, Italy, and especially Germany, where it reached its
fullest expression. "The core of historicism," Meinecke has written,
"consists in the substitution of a generalized way of thinking about
historical, human realities by an individualized way of thinking. This
does not mean that henceforth historicism excludes altogether the
search for general laws and types of human life. It must practice this
[search] itself, and blend it with its feeling for the individual. It was a
new consciousness for the individual which [historicism] awakened,
[for previously] precisely the innermost moving forces of history, the
mind and spirit of man, had remained under the constraint of a generalizing judgment."[52] With the genesis of historicism as a world view in
the second half of the eighteenth century, the German spirit, according
to both Meinecke and Troeltsch, deviated on an independent development away from the mainstream of Western Europe."[53]

Troeltsch's own brief characterization of historicism follows:

> The word 'historicism' . . . signifies the historicization [*Histor-
> isierung*] of our entire understanding and experience of the spir-
> itual [*geistigen*] world, as this came into existence in the course
> of the nineteenth century. Here we see everything in the river of
> becoming, in endless and always new individualization, in deter-
> mination by the past towards an unrecognizable future. The state,

law, morality, religion, and art are dissolved in the flow of historical becoming and are comprehensible only as ingredients of historical development.[54]

Historicism as a world view rejects any static view of eternal ideas, regardless of their source. It regards truth, values, and institutions as related to specific historical times and places.

Most decidedly, however, historicism did not mean in Troeltsch's mind the same thing as relativism. He would certainly have disagreed with the simplistic definition of historicism given by his Berlin colleague, Paul Tillich, as "an attitude of relativism towards history."[55] To be sure, as early as 1901 in the midst of his writings on theology and church history, Troeltsch had declared that "the historical and the relative are identical," and he died with the opinion that there are no absolutes within history.[56] But because of his important distinction that "the relativity of values is not relativism," he was able to defend the position that historicism itself was not relativism.[57]

This dubious association could not apply, in Troeltsch's opinion, to genuine historicism but to "the much censured, base historicism which appears to many today to be identical with historical thought as such, to the extent, to wit, that it is unbounded relativism, a playful preoccupation with things and a crippling of purpose and its own life."[58] Remarking the year before his death that "in linguistic usage at the present time the word 'historicism' is above all an invective [*ein Scheltwort*], a discharge of all sorts of complaints against historical burdens, complicated historical thought, and the validity of decisions of a debilitating historical fashion," Troeltsch set himself the task of rectifying its poor image.[59] Troeltsch's position was that although historicism did involve relationism (relating values and institutions to their historical and cultural contexts), which might lead to an unfortunate relapse into relativism, this potential was a difficulty, not a definition, of historicism. He believed that "scepticism and relativism are only an apparently necessary consequence of modern intellectual conditions and of historicism."[60]

Concern over the proper meaning of historicism was eloquently expressed throughout *Historicism and Its Problems*, where Troeltsch repeatedly said that he wanted to see "this word completely disconnected from its bad secondary meaning [*schlechten Nebensinn*] and to be understood in the sense of the fundamental historicizing of all our thinking about man, his culture, and his values."[61] Troeltsch believed that historicism as a world view was a healthy phenomenon, a significant advance in the development of the human spirit. Thus he stood in marked contrast to those who posited historicism as essentially defective, faulty, undesirable, a corruption of correct thinking, or a retrogressive slide from cherished values of Western civilization.

In a work suggestively labelled *The Poverty of Historicism*, for example, Karl Popper described historicism as "a method which does not bear any fruit" but which unfortunately has had a "persistent and pernicious influence upon the philosophy of society and of politics. . . . Its logic—often so subtle, so compelling and so deceptive . . . suffers from an inherent and irreparable weakness."[62] Granted that Popper's definition of historicism was peculiarly idiosyncratic and his argument somewhat misinformed, his invectives at least illustrate the strength of the opposition to Troeltsch's own attitude.[63] Troeltsch did not write a book on *The Problem of Historicism*—to paraphrase Popper's title—but on *Historicism and Its Problems*. That is to say, because Troeltsch regarded historicism as basically valuable and beneficial, his approach was that *historicism has problems but is not itself a problem.* He did admit that when the discipline of history (*Historie*) misunderstandingly adapted the methods of the natural sciences it led to a "wretched historicism" (*schlechten Historismus*).[64] But despite having certain unfortunate chronic illnesses, historicism itself, in Troeltsch's opinion, was not itself an ill.[65]

Troeltsch's meaning of historicism becomes clearer when contrasted with his concept of naturalism. In a sense, the contrast is analogous to Troeltsch's endorsement of the *religionsgeschichtliche* method over that of a more static *Heilsgeschichte*. Historicism and naturalism were "the two great creations of scholarship [*Wissenschaftsschöpfungen*] of the modern world, unknown in both antiquity and the Middle Ages."[66] "Naturalism has to do with ultimately purely given, inexplicable bodies in space, whereas historicism is the self-understanding of the spirit, inasmuch as it deals with its own procreations in history."[67] The common source of these conflicting world views was Cartesian dualism where the "double tendency" of both naturalism and historicism "was already given: the direction towards natural bodies and universal laws, and the direction towards the ego-based and historical-genetic contents of consciousness."[68] Although Troeltsch thought that Descartes and his followers had emphasized the former, naturalistic tendency, he considered the Cartesians to have inadvertently laid the foundations for historicism as well, despite their apparently overly rationalistic neglect of history. These initial gestures of Descartes were further advanced by Locke, Hume, Hamann, Herder, Schelling, Goethe, and Hegel, among others, so that since at least the early nineteenth century, despite their common taproot, Troeltsch perceived "a rivalry of naturalism and historicism which changes with the issues and atmosphere of the times."[69]

In this rivalry of world views Troeltsch obviously favored historicism, resenting what he regarded as the imperialistic invasion of naturalism into the domain of historicism—although he did grant that naturalism was a giant step forward over what it, and historicism, had replaced. "As a general principle of comprehension and interpretation of the world," a mathematicized naturalism, in Troeltsch's opinion, was "the most magnificent deliverance from chance and appearance, the most enormous widening and clarity, the most-far-reaching spiritual mastery of the changing and the individual, the most marvelous support of all technology, which the human spirit has at any time reached."[70] It should be noted, however, that despite this apparently glowing tribute to naturalism, Troeltsch's praise was not totally unequivocal. Preoccupied with the existentially historical, Troeltsch believed in the reality and importance of chance and appearance, change and the individual—as will become more evident from an examination of his formal logic of history in the next chapter.

Nature is not history. This fundamental distinction was the ultimate rationale for Troeltsch's objection to the infringement of naturalism upon historicism; he believed the two were radically different. This simple dichotomy between nature and history was also the basis for separating the philosophy of nature and the philosophy of history. Thus there were three separate pairs of antinomies, with the first pair primary: nature and history, naturalism and historicism, and the philosophy of nature and the philosophy of history.

Troeltsch was insistent that history—in the existential sense of history-as-event rather than history-as-record ("Geschichte" rather than "Historie")—was not a part of nature and could not be reduced to nature. Nor were the reality of history and the reality of nature reducible to a common denominator. The stuff of which history was made and the stuff of which nature was made were simply not the same. This difference was objective, real, and independent of the historian or the natural scientist. It followed, consequently, because of this existential incompatibility between history and nature, that world views and philosophies based upon their separate spheres must also be incompatible.

Because of this radical separation of history and nature, Troeltsch tended to endorse the neo-Kantian distinction between the *Geisteswissenschaften*, to which history belonged, and the *Naturwissenschaften*. Although the preceding discussion suggests that Troeltsch made this distinction on the basis of the subject matter of these disciplines—as Wilhelm Dilthey had urged—he was not consistent in this emphasis. Elsewhere he tended to make the same distinction on the basis of methodological differences—as Heinrich Rickert thought proper. Troeltsch believed that history has not only a peculiar subject matter but also a peculiar methodology, or logic, with which to approach that subject matter. It was the nature of his mind forever to try to reconcile and synthesize diverse elements of thought, whether these elements were ultimately amenable to reconciliation or not.

Despite his open favoritism towards history rather than nature, in *Historicism and Its Problems* Troeltsch drew an exceptionally humble picture of history (that is, history-as-event), which still retains its vivid accuracy after decades of research and scholarship. Compared with the vastness in space and time of nature, the world of history—including even the period of unrecorded human prehistory—was portrayed as minute and paltry, "as fleeting as a puff of breath upon a frozen pane of glass."[71] In discussing Troeltsch's thoughts on the subject one is tempted to capitalize the term "nature," for it becomes almost like nature in the works of Thomas Hardy: the chief protagonist in life's drama, the primary antagonist against man. Troeltsch, for example, cited the reaction of Goethe's Wilhelm just after looking through a telescope for the first time: "What am I, then, compared with the universe. . . . How can I stand against it, how can I stand in its center? . . . How can man take his stand against the infinite?"[72]

Troeltsch regarded the scope of human history as infinitesimal in the light of the hundreds of thousands of years of vegetative and animal evolution and the four glacial periods that preceded the appearance of man. As he wrote in *Historicism and Its Problems*, only at the end of the fourth glacial period in Paleolithic Europe did the Neanderthal hunter emerge, and only within the Neolithic period about 25,000 years ago, when bronze and iron replaced stone tools, did *Homo sapiens* arise, and not until approximately 8,000 B.C. did the first "historical peoples" appear along the great rivers of Asia, Egypt, and China.[73] This long-range perspective certainly dwarfed history; Troeltsch mused,

If one puts the question where and when man really originated in the development of living beings, and what proportion of time belongs to history proper [*eigentlichen Geschichte*], i.e., documented, spiritually filled cultural history, and what proportion of time belongs to nonliterate history, or prehistory. . . . How minute and brief is history proper in contrast with prehistory. . . . It is a proportion like that of the layer of humus in the earth's crust. . . . One does not know exactly where man begins, and undoubtedly he has been for an immeasurable period of time a creature of sheer nature and not a creature of culture.[74]

"We see all too clearly that all great systems of culture have a circumscribed duration and then decompose," he remarked, tentatively endorsing the prospect suggested by Dubois-Reymond "of the last man who roasts the last potato over the last piece of coal. . . . One must not conceal the possibility that this history is perhaps only a short-lived and imperfect blossom on the gigantic tree of terrestrial living organisms."[75] The vast disproportion between history proper, on the one hand, and prehistory and the extent of humanless nature, on the other hand, so impressed Troeltsch that he was led to entertain the doctrine of the plurality of worlds: "Indeed, without the thought of a great number of spiritual realms, a *pluralité des mondes* as Leibniz said, human history, and the human spirit, is a startling anomaly in the world."[76] His acknowledgment of the humble brevity of human history and his assessment of its implications are in themselves fine illustrations of the application of historicism as a world view—and also excellent examples of the attitude that opponents of historicism criticized as the excessive relativization of values.

Summary and Recapitulation: Polymorphous Truth

In summary, as a principal representative of the *religionsgeschichtliche Schule*, Troeltsch was concerned with the general phenomenon of historicism, a concern that grew from his particular interest in the historicizing (*Historisierung*) of Christianity. It is incorrect to assume that Troeltsch's crisis in consciousness was rooted no further back in time than the disturbances wrought by the Great War. Although the crisis of the war undoubtedly stimulated his concern with historicism, nevertheless, as the review of the Heidelberg writings has shown, a major source of his concern lay in his pre-war preoccupation with the apparent relativization of absolute religious values.[77] Aware that formerly durable theological truths had become deabsolutized, Troeltsch widened his vision: "all rationally necessary ideals of government and society are carried away into the whirlpool, and there is no longer any immutable codex of knowledge. . . . The ready-made, supernatural absolutes of the old dogmatics belong to the spiritual atmosphere of ready-made metaphysical truths and eternal ideas of government and society. In the atmosphere of the modern historical relativization of all things, they no longer breathe healthily and ingenuously."[78]

Increasingly, Troeltsch remarked, in studies of "the development of political, social, ethical, aesthetic, and scientific ideas . . . I encountered the same difficulties in each of these provinces—they were not confined to religion."[79] Problems in the relativization of a Christianity hitherto pictured as absolute emerged as equivalent problems in studying culture as a whole. As Troeltsch described his efforts in the short autobiographical essay written the year before his death, "It is the old problem of absoluteness in a much broader sphere of activity, considered in terms of the entirety of cultural values and not merely in terms of the religious situation alone."[80]

Troeltsch's "latent theology of historicism"—a phrase he had first used in 1898—had mushroomed wildly.[81] His tendency to look at theology historically, rather than to look at history theologically, had led him right into the heart of historicism as a modern world view.[82] In short, Troeltsch shifted over his scholarly career from asserting the absolute validity of Christian values, through sensing the contingency and *zeitgebunden* character of Christianity, to, finally, regarding all the values of Western civilization—not just its religious ones—as in a state of historical flux. He tended to gravitate more and more to the view that "outside history there can be no reality."[83]

Troeltsch had truly traveled a long way towards cultural relativism. In one of the last essays he wrote, looking back upon his work of two decades earlier, Troeltsch commented that "the individual character of European civilization, and of the Christian religion connected with it, receives now much greater emphasis, whilst the somewhat rationalistic concept of validity, and especially of *supreme validity*, falls considerably into the background."[84] On the same theme Troeltsch remarked in *Historicism and Its Problems* that "the singularity of Christian social teachings and of the problems of European religion and culture had not yet been sufficiently recognized" in the *Social Teachings* of just over a decade earlier.[85]

How was Troeltsch able to accomplish this reversal? His underlying intellectual framework was the concept of "polymorphous truth," which provided him a place of compromise between a dogmatic view positing absolute truths and a sceptical view endorsing historical relativity. The concept of polymorphous truth was venerable, rooted at least in the sixteenth- and seventeenth-century views of Karlstadt, Schwenkfeld, Sebastian Franck, and Castellio. For example, John Saltmarsh, the seventeenth-century English divine whose works Troeltsch read approvingly, had written that

> every beam of light is light; every truth is a sparkle of truth itself. . . . They who break a Chrystall, may see their face in every peece and parcell; so in everything of Christ there is an image of Christ. . . . Our severall and distinct goings are but like so many Travellers to the City of London; some travell from the north, some from the south, and from the west, some from the east, yet all thither.[86]

Although Troeltsch ultimately did accept the existence of absolute truths, he believed they belonged to the domain of faith and ethics, not history. In history there could be only relative truths, truths conditioned by time and circumstances.[87] Nevertheless, these relative truths did have overtones of absoluteness. They were, though relative, not absolutely relative but rather relatively absolute. As Troeltsch said in one of his last papers, in rejecting what he called a "spirit of scepticism or uncertainty": "A truth which, in the first instance, is a *truth for us* does not cease, because of this to be very Truth and Life. What we learn daily through our love for our fellow-men, viz. that they are independent beings with standards of their own, we ought also to be able to learn through our love for mankind as a whole—that here too there exist autonomous civilizations with standards of their own."[88]

This idea of polymorphous truth—of truth valid and binding in certain historical circumstances but not in others—came to the fore in Troeltsch's discussion of the nineteenth-century philosopher Rudolf Eucken. Though Troeltsch elsewhere was severely critical of Eucken's body of thought, he did agree with him "that we may admit our historical restrictedness without having to forego, on that account, truth and eternity, a proposition which matches the Rankean expression about the immediateness of every eopch."[89] Troeltsch unmistakably endorsed the romantic and historicist view, associated with the great German historian, Leopold von Ranke, that "every age is immediate to God."

As an example of a relatively absolute historical truth, Troeltsch cited the idea of "personality." In Oriental history, he pointed out, the idea of the dignity and even sacredness of the individual personality did not obtain as it did in European history. "The idea of Personality," he thought, "is, after all, a Western belief, unknown in our sense, to the Far East, and preeminently and peculiarly the destiny of Europeans. But in view of the whole of our history we cannot but believe that *it is for us the truth.*"[90] In other words, although the idea of human personality was not accepted by all peoples, although it did not have what Troeltsch called a "timeless and everlastingly immutable validity," nevertheless it was truth for typical Europeans.[91] It did not need the endorsement of the whole of humanity to be a truth. As Troeltsch expressed it, in typically convoluted fashion, "not every universality is valid for all mankind," because "universalities are founded upon individual specific constructs."[92] These words, and other similarly expressed sentiments, by their nature defy definitive clarification. However, he apparently desired to absolutize to the maximum extent possible what he had to admit were nonabsolute, relative truths. It was obvious to anyone familiar with the data of comparative history that all mankind did not believe in what he called "the truth of personality" as an absolute truth; but, since the mainstream of Western civilization tended unqualifiedly to endorse this truth, Troeltsch felt he had no other choice than to insist that for "Western man" the value of individual personality was an absolute. The term "absolute" here meant not a truth eternally binding upon all minds, but rather what might be called the best available truth for someone in a given time and place. One clearly detects in Troeltsch's sometimes ambiguous prose a yearning for the security of solid ground, the desire for absolute security in the face of relativity.[93] This personal ambivalence illustrates well Troeltsch's own diagnosis of the late nineteenth-century crisis in values, that "the longing for absoluteness is the consequence of an age of relativism."[94]

Another example of polymorphous truth—also a case of a truth absolute for a European but not for all mankind—was the phenomenon of Christianity. Troeltsch endorsed here the viewpoint of Gotthold Lessing, who in his eighteenth-century drama *Nathan the Wise* espoused the desirability of a harmonious coexistence among followers of the Jewish, Moslem, and Christian religions.[95] Lessing disagreed with the assumption that there could be one, and only one, true religion. Troeltsch, himself a devout Christian, would not have it otherwise. As he expressed it in his posthumously published essay on "The Place of Christianity Among the World Religions," "we cannot live without a religion, yet the only religion that [Europeans] can endure is Christianity, for Christianity has grown up with us and has become a part of our very being."[96] In Troeltsch's opinion, because the European cultural community had known in its development primarily only the experience of Christianity,

> this experience is undoubtedly the criterion of its validity, but, be it noted, only of its validity *for us* [*sic*]. It is God's countenance as revealed *to us*; it is the way in which, being what we are, we receive, and react to, the revelation of God. It is binding *upon us*, and brings *us* deliverance. It is *final and unconditional for us*, because we have nothing else, and because in what we have we can recognize the accents of the divine voice.
>
> But this does not preclude the possibility that other racial groups, living under entirely *different* cultural conditions, may experience their contact with the Divine Life in quite a *different* way, and may themselves also possess a religion which has grown up with them, and from which they cannot sever themselves so long as they remain what they are. And they may quite sincerely regard this as *absolutely valid for them*, and give expression to this *absolute validity* according to the demands of *their own* religious feelings.[97]

This notion of polymorphous truth was not restricted to the phenomenon of religion but was applicable to historical reality generally. For example, in endorsing this concept in his historical epistemology, Troeltsch in effect recognized that individual historians as well as individual groups or generations of historians would have conflicting claims to validity. Thus, he allowed that "a Christian or humanist or pessimist or hard-headed realist [*Machtrealist*] will construct [historical accounts] with the strictest devotion and critical assurance, but always in contrasting ways, because the operative and decisive factors must appear to be different to each one."[98] Yet, Troeltsch maintained, the Christian, humanist, pessimist, or hard-headed realist each had a genuine claim to truth. Similarly, Troeltsch cited approvingly a remark made by Radowitz in 1851 that "political truth is generally not absolute, but relative to time and place," and commented that relative truth, "mark my words, notwithstanding that, endures as truth."[99]

Further, no particular viewpoint could claim to have a sole monopoly on truth to the extent that conflicting points of view were automatically null and void. Though frequently particular, finite viewpoints masqueraded as absolute, objective sources of truth, nevertheless, Troeltsch urged, no particular historically conditioned viewpoint deserved this status of exclusiveness, for no particular historically bound point of view could effectively grasp reality as it was in itself (*das An-sich*); only the absolute spirit (*Geist*) could do this.[100] Consequently, Troeltsch laid an epistemological foundation for the historiographical position that, though actual historical events did not change in themselves, the accounts about them did change, and must change. Though past *Geschichte* remained the same, its corresponding *Historie* was never constant or absolutely definitive, with each particular *Historie* able to voice its claim to genuine validity—provided, of course, that it had been adequately constructed according to proper historical intuition and the categories of the formal logic of history.[101] With this provision, Troeltsch anticipated a pronounced tendency in twentieth-century academic historical circles, as expressed, for example, by Edward Hallett Carr: "It does not follow that, because a mountain appears to take on different shapes from different angles of vision, it has objectively either no shape at all or an infinity of shapes. It does not follow that, because interpretation plays a necessary part in establishing the facts of history, and because no existing interpretation is wholly objective, one interpretation is as good as another, and the facts of history are in principle not amenable to objective interpretation."[102]

Yet Troeltsch both praised the relative historicist view as a positive advance in man's interpretation of reality and regretted its effects. Although he loftily remarked on the question of absolutes that "what is primarily important is not an ahistorical, eternal, and ever unfolding principle but a living, individual complex of concrete reality, a whole that has become what it is under very specific conditions," nevertheless he lamented historicism as one of the crucial factors in the contemporary crisis in values.[103] He regarded the advent of historicism as, at least initially, a boon to the development of spiritual life and thought, but he also acknowledged that at first "what had been liberation and deliverance became a burden and a confusion."[104] The contemporary crisis in historical consciousness consistently gnawed at Troeltsch's mind. It was the same problem with which Meinecke had incessantly wrestled: "How can we preserve, in the face of the relativistic conclusions of historicism, the firm and secure faith in something Absolute and Eternal, which we need to meet both our theoretical and practical needs?"[105] Troeltsch described this profound crisis as having veritably shaken "the general philosophical foundations and principles of historical thinking."[106] Incidentally, he was scrupulously careful in the opening pages of *Historicism and Its Problems* in clarifying that the crisis lay in the philosophical underpinnings of historical thought and not in the realm of academically based historical research (*Geschichtswissenschaft*, or *technisch-historischen Forschung*).[107]

Wherein lay the solution to the present crisis in values brought about by historicism? Troeltsch answered: in the philosophy of history. The answer to the present revolution in historical consciousness could not be found in pat formulae or aphorisms, he maintained: "it can only be found in a fundamental philosophical mastery of the essence of history and of the question of its spiritual aims and contents."[108] The situation was paradoxical, indeed, for history was the source of the *problems* as well as the source of their *solutions*. Troeltsch would have totally disagreed with the view that "it is necessary to surpass history by an act of faith if one wants to accord it a meaning."[109] Historicism for Troeltsch was a given, a controlling premise lying at the heart of his thought. "In order to liberate ourselves from history and to obtain a superior control over it, we plunge ourselves into an ocean of historical criticism and reconstruction."[110] By urging an immersal in history, Troeltsch was in effect rejecting dogmatic, absolute, nonhistorical, extrahistorical, or transhistorical solutions to the contemporary crisis in consciousness. History was to be overcome through history—that was the motto and goal which informed Troeltsch's work during his mature, Berlin years. That was also the motivation behind his own efforts to construct a viable philosophy of history, which to him was certainly not an ivory tower game of words and concepts divorced from reality, but an attempt to provide solutions to the problems of historicism and the crisis of values in contemporary Occidental culture.

4

Philosophy of History: Solution to the Crisis

> *Das Bedürfnis nach Synthese, System, Weltanschauung,*
> *Gliederung und Stellungnahme ist ausserordentlich.*
>
> Troeltsch (1920)

> *Erkennt man die Normen der Lebensgestaltung nicht*
> *mehr in kirchlichen oder seinem Nachkömmling, dem*
> *rationalistischen Dogma, dann bleibt nur die Geschichte*
> *als Quelle und die Geschichtsphilosophie als Lösung.*
>
> Troeltsch (1922)

Although the concept of polymorphous truth was helpful to Troeltsch in confronting the modern "anarchy of values," his most ambitious attempt to cope with the modern crisis in consciousness was the construction of a model for a viable philosophy of history. As we have just seen, history—in the form of *Historismus*, or the method of the *religionsgeschichtliche Schule*, or some other variant of the historical attitude—Troeltsch perceived to be at the root of the crisis in values at the start of the twentieth century. In turning to the philosophy of history, Troeltsch was in effect clarifying for himself and his contemporaries what he considered to be the principal source of values for modern man, namely, existential history. As he put it, since his age no longer recognized either "Church dogma or its offspring, rationalistic dogma," as the fountainhead of life-shaping values, the best available alternative to faith or reason was history.[1] History was all that man had, and the supreme way to master the kaleidoscopic complexities of existential history was through the philosophy of history. In short, although history was responsible for the modern crisis in values, in the philosophy of history one would find the solution to that crisis.

Unfortunately for twentieth-century man, however, Troeltsch believed no one had yet created a philosophy of history sufficiently formidable to cope with this modern crisis in consciousness. All previous attempts to construct philosophies of history had been failures, from Antiquity to Troeltsch's own times. Not a single attempt to create a philosophy of history in the past twenty-five hundred years had been totally free from defects. From the ancient Greeks to his own contemporary Europe, Troeltsch saw a tradition of disappointing and only semisuccessful efforts at best. The history of the philosophy of history was filled with excesses of rationalism, empiricism, irrationalism, iconoclasm, and theologizing, to cite the most significant defects. It was a record of ambiguities, misunderstandings, omissions, and downright errors. Troeltsch recognized no single movement or philosopher as having constructed what he could accept as a thoroughly viable philosophy of history.

These sharply revisionist criticisms would be readily understandable in a budding young scholar eager to make a name for himself by impetuously taking to task the entire preceding efforts of his academic profession. But such was not the case. Troeltsch maintained his perfervidly critical judgments as an established university professor of thirty years standing with hundreds of publications to his name. He could not have been more serious. He felt that all previous philosophies of history had been faulty, without exception, and he explained why. One may not agree with his explanations, but at least one can appreciate his intent: only by clearly identifying and overcoming specific errors that had vitiated past philosophies of history could one construct the philosophy of history which modern European culture urgently needed for its guidance and direction.

Friedrich Meinecke called Troeltsch's reconstruction of the history of the philosophy of history "a scarcely surpassed, outstanding achievement of modern historicism."[2] One need not go as far as Kurt Kesseler's appraisal that "Troeltsch was the greatest German philosopher of history since the days of Hegel," but one certainly can appreciate that his stature in this field was impressive.[3] Indirectly, a glance at Troeltsch's history of the philosophy of history also affords insights into his own efforts to construct a proper model of the philosophy of history. With his own scholarly penchant towards the *Referieren*, Troeltsch found it most congenial to first examine previously significant thought on a topic before expressing his own viewpoints.[4] Before my review of Troeltsch's history, it should be noted that although he was critical of all previous efforts from the ancient Greeks through his own times, he did see some actual improvements during the eighteenth-century Age of Enlightenment, as well as some further promising developments during the nineteenth century. Even that generalization requires qualification, but it at least indicates that he detected occasional breakthroughs in the most recent past. In addition, Troeltsch believed that his work would help create the first totally genuine philosophy of history in Western civilization. He specified that "only joint labor can solve these problems" and that his own role lay in a clarification of the preliminary steps (*Vorstufen*), but he seemed convinced that if contemporary thinkers were only to follow his guidelines they would arrive at an acceptable program.[5]

History of the Philosophy of History

Troeltsch began his panoramic survey of the history of the philosophy of history with the Greeks.[6] He granted that the ancient Greeks' sense of history was somewhat philosophically based, and he further recognized their prodigious natural and historical mythology as well as their ingenious theories about the nature of political life. But he rejected the view that ancient Greek thinkers constructed the first philosophy of history in Western civilization, maintaining to the contrary that the Greeks "did not have a philosophy of history which took its decisive impulse for a view of life and the world from the observation of events and the principles discerned in them."[7] The fundamental flaw was a gross emphasis upon premises external to history. Predicated upon metaphysical views containing timeless, unalterable ingredients—be they Platonic Ideas, Aristotelian Forms, Stoical Natural Laws, or the like—Greek thought overexaggerated the nonhistorical. Proto-existentialist that he was, Troeltsch complained that the Greeks gave precedence to essence over existence. For them, "The means to understand essences did not arise *from history*, but, on the contrary, from a consideration of essences arose an understanding *of history*, insofar as human affairs and creations appear to be now a vague and uncertain, now an improved and progressing approximation of these ideals."[8] In this view human history had meaning only to the extent that it mirrored suprahuman essences or values; Troeltsch rejected this idea, in keeping with the early twentieth-century German historicist movement which he endorsed. As one commentator has pointed out, "no one among the thinkers of his generation perceived the problems of historicism so early, so clearly, but also so agonizingly as Ernst Troeltsch."[9] Invariably, rightly or wrongly, Troeltsch consistently incorporated historicist trends into his critical appraisal of the philosophy of history.

A related defect in Greek thought was the doctrine of eternal recurrences, a variation of the cyclical view of history that interpreted human affairs as repeatedly unsuccessful attempts to realize and embody the eternal essences. Though human affairs might approximate this world of absolutes better at some times than at others, history remained always inferior to the perfect, transhistorical realm of which it was at best merely a muddy likeness. In Troeltsch's view, a cyclical philosophy of history was a contradiction in terms because of its lack of appreciation for historical contingencies.[10] His final conclusion about the ancient Greeks was that with their assumptions "no philosophy of history was in fact needed; history sufficed solely as the elucidation of political events which one experienced and from which one could draw definite practical lessons, or as material for the delight in storytelling and the pleasure of discovery of a traveller who shrewdly compares his homeland with faraway places. We know from the examples of Thucydides and Herodotus that in both these respects one might accomplish grand results with these propositions."[11] Neither these "grand results," however, nor the accomplishments of any other Greek thinker or writer ever met Troeltsch's ideal for a philosophy of history.

In the post-Grecian world of late Antiquity, Troeltsch thought that an improvement took place in the attitude towards history, especially with the coming of the Christian era, reaching an apogee in the writings of St. Augustine.[12] Christianity endorsed the supremacy of a suprahistorical realm but also found value in the realm of history itself, which was regarded as the visible expression of an accessible monotheistic deity. The status of the historical individual totality (*Individuell-Einmaliges, Individuelle Totalität*) was enhanced, with a certain coherence in human history newly discovered in the sinfulness, redemption, and final consummation of individual persons in the kingdom of God. The earthly kingdom of human history, though perishable, was meaningful.

Christianity brought about, "without any doubt, an enormous transformation, and an immense significance of history for a worldview," Troeltsch remarked; then he immediately qualified his statement: "but basically this history was not [genuine] history, and this fundamental reflecting about history not philosophy of history."[13] Despite the acknowledgment that the temporal order had value, the central role of miracles in the Christian vision produced an overall vitiation because miracles "are not really history, consequently theorizing about them is not philosophy but faith in dogma, which is shored up by authority and revelation, and which for its part is concerned with the agitation and finiteness of human life only externally and formally." [14] Speculation about the conjoining of timeless and time-bound spheres of reality in the Incarnate God-Man was ultimately an unsuccessful, though praiseworthy, attempt to unite the historical and the unhistorical. Including the ancient Stoics in this scheme did not ameliorate matters. [15] The best that the early Christian synthesis could produce was church history and dogmatics, but certainly not a viable philosophy of history. Citing Julius Africanus, Eusebius, Jerome, and Augustine, Troeltsch concluded: "One is accustomed to call them philosophers of history, but they were, on the contrary, only compilers and dogmatists who fitted all events into a framework based upon miracles and upon the conventional historical approach of Antiquity." [16]

During the Middle Ages, this dogmatic, church-influenced vision of human history prevailed as the dominant frame of reference of historical thinkers. Medieval writers like Otto von Freising were as "far removed from genuine historical thinking" as the ancients before them. [17] It would be only with an entirely changed cultural situation at the beginning of modern times that this faulty view of history was displaced, with continuing esteem for this dogmatic theologizing about history seen as late as the seventeenth century, as Bossuet's *Discourse on Universal History* reveals.

Neither the Renaissance nor the Reformation produced any genuine philosophy of history, according to Troeltsch, although tentative steps were taken in this direction. "The peculiarity of the Renaissance lay . . . in its modification of the direction of interests, whereby for the first time there really showed up an increasing estrangement from the world beyond, from preparations for the grace of the church, and from the monastic idea." [18] The Renaissance did advance the cause of historiography (*Geschichtsschreibung*), but historiography and the philosophy of history (*Geschichtsphilosophie*) were not the same. Tending to regard the Renaissance in Italy as the sign of a rupture in the medieval cultural fabric, Troeltsch nevertheless rejected the more enthusiastic Michelet-Burckhardt version of the Renaissance as the first chapter of modernity, preferring to evaluate that movement more modestly as containing only "important anticipations of modern thought." [19]

For Troeltsch, the fundamental reason for Renaissance humanism's merely prefiguring but not achieving modernity was the debilitating effects upon it of the Protestant Reformation. The matter was somewhat complex. On the one hand, Troeltsch recognized certain aspects of Protestantism as leading towards a philosophy of history. For example, "Protestantism encouraged a certain spirit of historical criticism, which subjected the Catholic ecclesiastical tradition and the current conception of Church history to a severe and suspicious examination."[20] On the other hand, however, though the Protestant reformers seriously undermined Church-controlled thought (*Wissenschaft*), Troeltsch's controversial view was that early Protestantism remained basically a subspecies of the existing Christian attitude towards history, representing "the same traditional attitude towards life as was prescribed by Catholicism."[21] The Reformation could not possibly make a contribution to the philosophy of history, for "the scholarship of Protestantism was a Scholasticism furbished up by Humanism; its historical criticism was a polemic on behalf of absolute truth against devilish deceit; its general information consisted of a farrago of universal knowledge collected from the ancients and all kinds of curious sources; its theory of jurisprudence was a modification of the old Church doctrine."[22] Because of the inter-Confessional struggles generated by the appearance of Protestantism, and despite certain Renaissance breakthroughs towards modernity, "Europe had to experience two centuries more of the medieval spirit."[23]

The true dividing line between medieval, church-dominated thought and modern philosophizing was the system of Descartes.[24] "Modern philosophy, that is to say, as Descartes established it, is a philosophy of consciousness—an analysis of consciousness in terms of its contents and the laws setting these contents in order. That is its distinction from the philosophy of Antiquity and from that of the Middle Ages (which merely had given the ancient style a religious garb), both of which emanated from ontology."[25] Cartesianism gave rise to a twofold tendency: both towards a mathematical orderliness and modern naturalism and towards history and historicism. This latter tendency came to the fore "as soon as one saw this consciousness not only in light of its aprioric, mathematical and physical creations, but rather in an aposterioric fashion in terms of specific genetical transformations and accomplishments."[26] The English tradition especially, as seen notably in Locke and Hume, focused on this historical emphasis. Descartes, however, did not personally create a philosophy of history, and notwithstanding any innovations he might have encouraged, the seventeenth-century intellectual atmosphere generally prevented the development of any full-fledged philosophy of history, for "quite certainly, they had not yet arrived at a historical way of thinking."[27] Troeltsch suggested by this latter comment (which his *Referieren* substantiated) that the vital distinction between critical and speculative branches of the philosophy of history was not yet appreciated.

Nor did Troeltsch agree with the view that Giambattista Vico at the turn of the century produced the first philosophy of history in European thought.[28] He did favorably describe Vico's *Scienza Nuova* as "the most considerable breakthrough [thus far] towards a philosophy of history" and as "certainly the sharpest and most deliberate antithesis to Descartes' rationalism, his ahistoricalness, and subjectivism."[29] Vico, however, suffered from the drawbacks of an eclectic approach; his pioneering contributions to the philosophy of history were blunted by an unfortunate admixture of Catholic dogmatic teachings about Providence as well as by his acceptance of the operation of natural laws in history.

Not until the Enlightenment proper did a radical change take place. As Troeltsch clearly put it, "the philosophy of history is a modern creation, a child of the eighteenth century."[30] Helping to emancipate both history-as-record (*Historie*) and history-as-event (*Geschichte*) from the sway of religious values, the historical investigations of eighteenth-century Enlightenment thinkers

> destroyed the hitherto existing picture of the world, . . . revealed a formerly unknown and disregarded world, opened up unfathomable time-periods of history, banished the Fall of Man from its central point in history, and constructed an entirely different primitive condition as the point of departure. But above all it brought into play a pragmatic method, in which the political conception and practice of the time was reflected, and which was also the historical equivalent of the atomistic, mechanical method of the natural sciences. Individuals became the elementary units of history; from their unconscious, methodological, calculated reciprocal actions they built up the social structure.[31]

The net results of these innovations in method was that "a universal, secular, and philosophical historiography took the place of the hitherto prevalent theological, juridical, and philologically antiquarian polyhistory."[32]

Troeltsch's "Yes . . . but" mental disposition is by now familiar. His view of the Enlightenment was no exception. Regardless of the Enlightenment's accomplishments, Troeltsch's final judgment about this movement was that the "philosophy of history in the full sense, the perception of the goals of life out of history, had not yet developed. To that end it was still too rational."[33] Having banished God's Providence as the unifying interpretive principle of an entangled mass of historical occurrences, the thinkers of the Enlightenment unfortunately substituted the idea of natural law—a major defect in Troeltsch's view, for it was merely the replacement of one faulty approach by another inadequate one. With his rejection of *Methodenmonismus* in human thinking, Troeltsch located natural laws within the logic of the *Naturwissenschaften* and rejected their applicability to historical thinking; they were not sufficiently attentive to spontaneous, contingent human historicity.[34] Although eighteenth-century history became rid of supernatural forces and eighteenth-century philosophy became emancipated from its medieval status as a handmaiden of theology, the era of a genuine philosophy of history had only dawned but had not yet developed into full daylight. A view of history based upon an endorsement of secular natural law could be no better than a "preparatory surrogate of the philosophy of history."[35]

Troeltsch's reservations and apparent inconsistencies regarding the Enlightenment as the wellspring of a genuine philosophy of history are evident in his remarks about Voltaire and Rousseau. Initially he nominated Voltaire as the virtual creator of modern philosophy of history,[36] then appeared to reverse his judgment in favor of Rousseau, whom he also called the first Romantic. Rousseau, he wrote, "gave the strongest impetus to modern philosophy of history, specifically in its two main branches, the Anglo-French positivistic one and the German speculative one, an impulse which was further augmented by the French Revolution, which seemed to spring out of Rousseau's ideas, and by the opening of a new age, which doubly compelled a consideration of history. Out of opposition to it, with the retention of its impulse to teleological and universal thought, for the first time ever a peculiarly modern philosophy of history sprang up."[37]

Troeltsch's ambivalence in locating the emergence of the first genuine philosophy of history in Western civilization is not really surprising, remembering that he found delight in paradox, that complexity did not upset him, and that he always felt obliged to examine all aspects of a question regardless of whether this meant eventual difficulty in constructing any coherent synthesis. These traits of his thought are aptly illustrated by his treatment of nineteenth-century philosophy. Troeltsch's general conclusion regarding nineteenth-century thinkers was typical: they had gone far towards building viable philosophies of history—farther than in all previous centuries—but they had not accomplished the task.

In criticizing contributions to the nineteenth-century philosophy of history, Troeltsch was notably fair in his choice of subjects, directing his remarks not at weak straw men but at the most prominent and significant thinkers in the field, for example, Kant, Hegel, Schopenhauer, Marx, Comte, Nietzsche, Dilthey, Croce, Bergson, and Rickert. When one bears in mind that in Troeltsch's view these were defective thinkers whom he himself intended to surpass, his audacity appears great indeed. Since it would be prohibitive to explore in depth here each significant nineteenth-century thinker or movement, the following treatment will be restricted to selected representatives of the half-dozen or so philosophic movements which Troeltsch himself emphasized, beginning with idealism.

Troeltsch had a high regard for early nineteenth-century philosophic idealism, which took deep root and flourished in Europe, especially in Germany.[38] Simply put, German idealism "denotes the metaphysical theory which, as regards the primary and most certain datum of experience, takes its stand upon consciousness and its contents. . . . Idealism implies that the relation of subject and object is one of the essential starting points of philosophy, and in its view of that relation it lays down the decisive principle that objects can exist only for a subject, and that the subject which carries the objects within itself is the higher category, and as such must determine the process of philosophic thought."[39] German idealism was not monolithic, of course, which Troeltsch recognized in his treatment of individual thinkers, such as Kant, Hegel, Schelling, and Schopenhauer.[40]

In Troeltsch's view "Kantianism is the characteristically German philosophy, the nucleus of German philosophy, and even to the present day all the great systems either emanate directly from it or define their position by critical reference to it."[41] But despite Kantianism's importance, Troeltsch regarded it as too rationalistic a system ever to become the foundation of a genuine philosophy of history. The Kantian preoccupation with "generally valid, unchangeable, timeless ideals" did not give due respect to "the value and content of history, its concrete, individual liveliness and the tension-filled play of its tendencies."[42] An examination of the loyal Kantian school at Marburg led Troeltsch even more vehemently to "observe with horror the distance of their world of abstract aims from genuine history. . . . The dogmatic intolerance of such a rationalism is equivalent in its distance from real history to any ecclesiastical, dogmatic one."[43]

Nor did the Hegelian system fare much better before Troeltsch's barbs. Again, despite his glowing tribute that Hegel afforded "the most magnificent attempt to solve the problem" of the philosophy of history up to that point, Troeltsch judged Hegel's overall effort inadequate because it also was too rational and not sufficiently historical.[44] Troeltsch emphasized that Hegelian dialectics was not, like the Kantian formula, an aprioric deduction of historical data but rather a rearrangement of available data already presupposed to exist. Hegel "was really not the apriorizing fabricator that legend would have it."[45] Ultimately, however, because Hegelian dialectics rendered concrete phenomena intelligible only by arrangement into a rational pattern, and gave the pattern priority over historical events themselves, historical individual totalities became demeaned as only "marionettes and material for the artfulness of reason."[46] The end result of the tension between the real and the rational was that "a monstrous violation is done to actual history, despite the profound views which Hegel had about the nature of concrete, individual, historical formations."[47]

An additional fault in the Hegelian system was its defective sense of cultural synthesis. Hegel's vast synthesis—indeed, "a grander synthesis has never been seen"—was oriented in the wrong direction; that is, it pointed from the present towards the past instead of from the present towards the future.[48] In Troeltsch's opinion, a genuine philosophy of history must have what he called a "*gegenwärtige Kultursynthese*" whereby "the strictness, versatility, and devotion employed in investigating the past [*die Erforschung des Gewesens*] must be combined with handling a future-oriented inclination."[49] Only with such a contemporary cultural synthesis, in the attempt "to mold the future organically out of the past," could any speculative philosophy of history be complete.[50] Because Hegel regarded his own historical period as the apogee of the dialectical unfolding of history, as the point where the absolute was most fully revealed in time, he lacked incentive, Troeltsch felt, to speculate about any future-oriented cultural synthesis of values.[51]

Also within the boundaries of philosophic idealism was the German organological school. Organology was antirationalistic, emphasizing "the concept of Life in place of the Idea of Hegel; intuited, rather than constructed becoming; a vitalistic idea of development."[52] Although according to Troeltsch the early nineteenth-century organologists were "the true parents of the history of cultural and intellectual thought,"[53] organology had severe defects as far as the philosophy of history was concerned, as was evident in the work of its best example, Schelling.[54] Schelling may not have had the excessive logical rationalism of other idealist philosophers, but he, like Hegel, incorrectly understood the need for a contemporary cultural synthesis; and because of his romantic, intuitive proclivity his best efforts amounted to "a fantastic, rhetorical utopia, the rebirth of the world through Art and Religion."[55]

If Schelling was nonlogical, Schopenhauer outdid him by being antilogical; he viewed history as essentially a negative, blind process without rhyme or reason. "Under these circumstances," Troeltsch thought, "history and the philosophy of history lost all meaning."[56] One of Troeltsch's primary requisites for a genuine philosophy of history was that it should "overcome history," by which he meant overcome the problems, such as relativism and an apparent anarchy of values, attendant upon historicism as a world view. But if human history as such had no meaning—if "history was depreciated and nullified" to the extent that it was in Schopenhauer's view—then any attempt to overcome it was simply not worth the pyrrhic victory.[57] If "all culture was illusion and madness," as Schopenhauer suggested, any construction of a contemporary cultural synthesis would inevitably be hollow.[58] Schopenhauer did not lack an appreciation for all cultural values whatsoever, Troeltsch readily admitted, but those values towards which he was inclined were principally from Oriental thought, particularly Buddhism. In constructing a philosophy of history which early twentieth-century Europe required, Troeltsch was willing to allow "a few sideglances at the East," but he remained adamant that Europeans could really understand fully only their own culture, namely, Europeanism.[59]

Though Troeltsch judged all the idealists to be ultimately unsuccessful, he regarded their efforts as signs of a promising burgeoning in the philosophy of history. This early nineteenth-century philosophizing did not enjoy uninterrupted development, however. "The years after 1848 are the time of the collapse of all philosophy and the readvancement of the mathematical and mechanical natural sciences."[60] In this mid-century decline, according to Troeltsch, efforts in the area of philosophy of history degenerated into mere history of philosophy. Remarkable achievements were made in the second half of the nineteenth century in historical investigation (*Geschichtsforschung*), but empirical history "formed its standards independent of the comprehensiveness of any philosophical system, rather out of the narrower and more urgent practical interests of the day, above all out of the contemporaneous nationalistic movements."[61] The advancement of historiography was admirable, but the accumulation of data and the growing academic specialization generally lacked a philosophical basis, a phenomenon Troeltsch regarded as part of the disillusionment of confidence in spiritual forces after mid-century.[62] During this heyday of the empirical natural sciences—and the preference of historiography for a "scientific" rather than a "philosophic" foundation—two outstanding examples appeared of what are commonly regarded as philosophies of history, namely, Marxism and positivism, both of which Troeltsch considered extremely important.

Although Troeltsch thought Marxism one of the most creative philosophic systems of the nineteenth century, he disapproved, for a variety of reasons, of Marxian dialectics as the basis of a viable philosophy of history. His basic objection was that the Marxian "system of values did not emanate from history and development, but from biased belief and enthusiasm."[63] Marx claimed to have naturalized the Hegelian dialectics, to have bowdlerized the mystical and metaphysical from Hegel, and to have substituted the empirical and realistic in its place. But Troeltsch considered these claims illusory, suggesting that Marx had merely substituted a new mystique and a new metaphysics for the old.[64] Further, from Marx's "adulterated dialectics and natural law . . . a contemporary cultural synthesis could not be obtained at all."[65] Troeltsch also found unacceptable the substructure-superstructure dichotomy with its gross attention to economic factors as the "sole independent variables."[66] The centrality of social class conflict was also for him an unwarranted reductionism and an erroneous oversimplification. Overall, despite Troeltsch's indebtedness to the insights of Marx, he found in Marxian dialectics too many discrepancies, contradictions, and obscurities to recognize it as a fully respectable philosophy of history.[67]

Contemporaneous with Marxism was a philosophic movement Troeltsch thought equally significant, as well as equally defective, the largely Anglo-French school of positivism, which in contrast to the German idealist tradition "declared the problem of subject and object to be insoluble and of no consequence, and recognized the phenomenal order of nature as of no less decisive import for the mind than an order metaphysically declared."[68] The positivist Herbert Spencer, for example, "twice began to read Kant but immediately laid him aside on account of his apriorism of the mind."[69] Auguste Comte was perhaps the most famous early positivist. His Law of Three Stages identified an advance from previous theologically and metaphysically inclined ages, and in so doing sought to extirpate the residue of prepositivistic, non-scientific ways of thinking from the field of history, which to Comte had remained "the paradise or asylum for romantics, theologians, visionaries, constructors, aesthetes, and pathetics."[70] But Comte ultimately was caught up in a vicious circle from which he could not escape. Though he professed that his positivistic approach to history was a value-free observation of the particularity of historical facts, with no superimposed theoretical frame of reference, Troeltsch retorted that there was no such thing as a presuppositionless science. Comte did not appreciate "that the selection, interpretation, and meaning of facts themselves already presuppose certain assumptions, and to that extent 'facts' are surely initially created by reflection itself. . . . The Law of Three Stages, in particular, is for him an assumption which prevails everywhere and determines the grasp of facts."[71] To the positivists' claim that they simply discovered but did not create universal natural laws of history, Troeltsch countered "regularly the 'natural laws' are laden with the ideals of the French Revolution, or of the English gentleman, or of American democracy, or of socialistic brotherhood." He gave as an example H. G. Wells' *Outline of History*, whose so-called universal laws Troeltsch insisted were narrowly Anglo-Saxon.[72] Although positivism did give more consideration to historical phenomena than had the *vormärz* idealistic systems, it also ultimately failed to clarify satisfactorily the relationship between that which was rational and that which was historical, too important a defect to establish positivism as a viable philosophy of history—viable, that is, in the eyes of Troeltsch. For as John Higham points out, by the beginning of the twentieth century "philosophy of history in the Anglo-Saxon world had become positivistic."[73]

Towards the end of the nineteenth century Troeltsch detected a general reawakening of the philosophy of history; it had been "half dead or completely so since 1848."[74] Since the positivistic natural sciences had by now been firmly established, this reawakened philosophy of history did not try to replace or reject them, but rather "sought a position where it could simultaneously both acknowledge them and also claim recognition as their own prerequisite, whereby in a certain sense its priority of spirit was again secured in relation to them."[75] The common denominator of this philosophic revival Troeltsch called historical realism (*historischer Realismus*), a diversified movement combining elements of *vormärz* idealism and mid-century empirical positivism without the extremes of these two antithetical positions. Besides the metaphysicians who attempted to provide an ontological rationale for the loosely coherent camp of historical realism—such as Hermann Lotze, Eduard von Hartmann, and Rudolph Eucken—Troeltsch delineated three main groups of thinkers, which he labelled the psychologizing philosophers of life, the apriorizing philosophers of form (both of which were centered in Germany), and the positivistic neo-romantics of France and Italy. Our résumé of Troeltsch's history of the philosophy of history will conclude with a brief look at a representative thinker from each of these three groups.

Friedrich Nietzsche represented that branch of historical realism which Troeltsch called "*die psychologisierende Lebensphilosophie*," a cumbersome label intended to denote simultaneously that this current of thought was basically a philosophical attitude, that it was concerned with psychological reality, and that it was above all oriented to "life" itself. Psychologizing philosophers of life—including Dilthey, Spengler, and the George school—held that life is essentially movement and development which cannot be reduced to the static, abstract concepts and formulae of natural science. Troeltsch saw these thinkers in the vanguard of "the whole modern battle against mechanization and intellectualism."[76] Nietzsche, for example, "the master of this psychology," concerned himself with the total mind of man—not just the rational, logical side alone—and achieved results comparable to the probing depth psychology of a Stendhal or a Dostoevsky.[77] Troeltsch thought Nietzsche had an exceptional historical consciousness in pursuing his own brand of *Geistesgeschichte*, despite Nietzsche's academically iconoclastic attitude towards professional historical circles.[78] Nevertheless, Troeltsch was dissatisfied with Nietzsche's focus in *Geistesgeschichte* upon mind and spirit as an elite phenomenon, as the general exception to the humdrum existence which typified the masses. Specifically, the vision of a utopia of supermen Troeltsch unequivocally rejected as fantasy.[79] In the final analysis, Troeltsch rejected the entire corpus of Nietzsche's writings as simply not fulfilling satisfactorily the primary tasks of a genuine philosophy of history, such as delineating the nature of historical thinking by clarifying a formal logic of history, constructing a contemporary cultural synthesis as a guide for a troubled world, properly respecting traditional European values as a source for this new reconstruction, and so forth. On the other hand, Troeltsch did agree that despite these shortcomings Nietzsche, like his contemporary Karl Marx, had proposed "half-truths, but extremely fertile half-truths."[80] Nietzsche's contribution to the history of thought lay in the ferment of ideas which he let loose upon the European intellectual scene. As the nineteenth century turned into the twentieth, Troeltsch preferred to see Nietzsche not as a particularly successful philosopher of history but as a catalyst for a new age, "the leading spirit of the cultural criticism" which was to help precipitate the twentieth-century consciousness revolution.[81]

Georg Simmel typified the "apriorizing philosophers of form," an important group of thinkers with neo-Kantian overtones, which included Cassirer, Windelband, Rickert, Max Weber, Husserl, and Scheler. Simmel correctly recognized that historical accounts (*Historie*) never isomorphically reproduce the manifoldness of historical events (*Geschichte*) but unavoidably involve "selection, condensation, abridgment, restoration, and interpretation."[82] He also denied that history was the province of absolutely valid formal values, a departure from the neo-Kantian influence. Unfortunately, however, in Troeltsch's opinion Simmel never fully escaped from the dreary relativism of his early work, which degenerated into an unlimited scepticism and pessimism and contributed to his defective appreciation of historicism. Simmel said, for example, "the deliverance which Kant produced from naturalism, we also need from historicism."[83] Thus, in erroneously interpreting historicism as a burden upon thought and not as a magnificent accomplishment, Simmel was from the outset barred from success in constructing a genuine philosophy of history. Yet another basic flaw was what Troeltsch regarded as Simmel's vague and unconvincing grasp of the two central categories of Troeltsch's own formal logic of history, individuality and development.

Finally, we come to Henri Bergson, representative with Benedetto Croce of that branch of historical realism which Troeltsch called neo-romantic positivism, an equivocal label suggesting both the positivistic heritage upon which Bergson's generation had been nurtured as well as the growing neo-romantic endorsement of intuition, individualism, and the irrational. The spiritual paradox of the age—"the need to acknowledge and to surmount positivism at the same time"—found eminent expression in Bergson's philosophy with its respect for the "obviously irrational, supra-logical, metalogical, or supra-rational depths" of reality.[84] Troeltsch approved heartily, considering Bergson to occupy a central place in modern philosophy of history because of his resistance to stiff and rigid systematization, which Troeltsch felt "utterly destroys so far as it is possible traces of flowing and becoming, of continuity and incommensurable agitation."[85] Sounding suspiciously like an early nineteenth-century romantic himself, Troeltsch lauded the return which he saw in Bergson "to a sympathetic self-contemplation of life, to a participation in the living heartbeat of the Absolute."[86] Bergson's great contribution, he felt, was to "fall back upon an imaginative and poetic intuition of the feeling of life and reality—a feeling the object of which could neither be demonstrated in experience nor grounded in thought."[87] Bergson continued to publish after Troeltsch died (including his important *Two Sources of Morality and Religion*), and presumably Troeltsch would have been equally receptive to these later writings. He did think, however, that Bergson's writings were marred by gaps and incompleteness, and I suspect that the later work would still have disturbed Troeltsch by what he regarded as Bergson's occasional veerings towards dilettantism and a persistent vagueness on how the intuition of historical becoming was to take place.

Looking at the entire scope of Troeltsch's history of the philosophy of history, one's most overriding impression is his consistent critical severity in rejecting all previous efforts in the field. He provided his own summary of the bevy of errors detailed above:

> If one starts from ideas and standards, one falls into an unhistorical rationalism and loses the connection with empirical history [*Historie*] and its practice. If one starts from the historical-individual, and thereby remains in harmony with research, then a boundless relativism and scepticism threaten. If one seeks to approach both by ingenious conceptions of development, the two constituents consistently break apart. If you boldly base your stance on present day judgments, it is all too easy to lose both history and idea. When one becomes aware of the difficulties of the problem, then it becomes distressing, and one gladly reverts to the authorities and the revelations of the churches, as with very comprehensible motives both old and new romantics have done and will do again, or one turns away altogether from the historicizing Occident to the unhistorical Orient, to its mysticism and its Nirvana, as Schopenhauer attempted.[88]

Though recognizing his own personal limitations, Troeltsch was not intimidated by a proximity with great minds of the past who had also struggled with these issues. "The force of the problem is so vast and sweeping," he felt, "that the fear of competition with eminent authorities must not frighten one away."[89] A sense of urgency pervaded his own efforts, a yearning to create finally a philosophy of history that would offer "a realization of the aims of life out of history [*Geschichte*]."[90] Creating a viable contemporary philosophy of history by which European civilization might orient itself was, he knew, a gargantuan task, requiring the collaboration of many minds. Further, he believed that "an original system is possible only every several hundred years." But he nevertheless poured his energies into this task, regarding his own role more as offering incisive analyses of the problems rather than proposing definitive solutions.[91] His untimely death stopped him short even of this modest goal, with his legacy to us perhaps best appraised as a "prolegomenon to a philosophy of history."[92] Troeltsch had embarked on a heroic venture whose fulfillment taxed the abilities and resources of himself and his contemporaries.

Formal Logic of History

In the reawakening of the philosophy of history at the end of the nineteenth century Troeltsch detected approvingly a newly emphasized distinction between "the formal logic of history" (*die formale Geschichtslogik*) and "the material philosophy of history" (*die materiale Geschichtsphilosophie*). This distinction, which previous philosophers had generally lacked, was loosely equivalent to that between critical and speculative parts of a unified philosophy of history.[93] In effect, recognition of this distinction meant that the philosophy of history consisted of two separate parts or two related though separate groups of problems. For this reason Troeltsch intended to make *Der Historismus und seine Probleme* a two-volume work, "of which the first furnishes the abstract foundation and the second the material exposition of that which I can recognize as the philosophy of history."[94] He died while still in the process of writing the second volume.

The basic premise behind Troeltsch's justification of the formal logic of history was simple: there is not merely *one logic* of human thinking but *various logics*. Instead of a general, universal logic equally binding upon all the intellectual disciplines (*Wissenschaften*), Troeltsch saw instead "a plurality of fundamental methods."[95] He rejected the applicability to historical thinking of any elementary "metalogic," be it the Aristotelian-Scholastic version or otherwise, and was most intent on establishing the autonomy of the formal logic of history vis-à-vis that of the natural sciences. Here he basically accepted the neo-Kantian distinction between the *Naturwissenschaften* and the *Geistes-wissenschaften*. In this regard, his insistence that the formal logic of history was *sui generis* was part of a growing turn-of-the-century philosophical aversion to the alleged intellectual imperialism of natural science and natural science methodology. As Troeltsch wrote, "history once more stood up to naturalism and demanded from philosophy the proof of its claims."[96] Whether or not history actually made this demand is a moot point. I suggest as more accurate that while philosophers of history might have been railing against creeping naturalism, turn-of-the-century historians actually aspired that their adolescent discipline might achieve a status comparable to that of the positivistic natural sciences. At any rate, in Troeltsch's opinion, late nineteenth-century philosophers of history, rising to the challenge as they perceived it, had "constructed a historical logic which fundamentally tore to pieces monism of method [*Methodenmonismus*]."[97]

An important point about this antimonistical construction of a formal logic of history was that the venture was not a theoretical, academic exercise but rather was rooted in existential historical reality itself. Its formulation was based ultimately not upon any deductive analysis of the rules of logic but upon the data of empirical history. Troeltsch was saying that properly speaking logic is determined not by mind but by reality. In short, "the 'laws of being' of different regions must lead to very different logical orders."[98] For example, since actual causality in the existential historical realm was different from causality in the natural realm, it followed that the historian would use a different concept or category of causality from that of the natural scientist.[99] Another example Troeltsch cited was the process of abstraction (*Abstraktion*), again different for the historian and the natural scientist because the material (*Stoffe*) with which the historian dealt was essentially different from that which the natural scientist studied.[100]

For Troeltsch the formal logic of history was not a deductive, apriori schema of rules and concepts imposed upon empirical data; it emanated from those empirical data as from a source. Troeltsch would have unequivocally rejected the charge sometimes made against philosophers of history that they "construct models of historical knowledge which have little to do with the actual processes of history."[101] When Troeltsch described the formal logic of history, he maintained that he was doing neither more nor less than stating the actual thought processes of the practicing historian, that is, describing *how the historian actually knows*. "The logic of history," he wrote, "consists in certain logical presuppositions, principles of selection, of formation, and of combination, which, in comprehending the actuality of experience established through criticism or through spontaneous intuition we practice, to begin with, entirely unconsciously."[102] Troeltsch intended to make this logic conscious and explicit, recommending that since the historian unavoidably thinks about historical matters in a special way, it is preferable to become aware of these basic thought processes; practicing them unconsciously has an inherent proclivity to error.

Troeltsch's procedure was a discussion of the eleven basic categories, or concepts, which made historical knowledge possible. The two fundamental categories were individual totality and development. Secondary or corollary concepts were originality and uniqueness; narrow selection; representation; unity of value or meaning; tension between the general spirit and particular spirits; the unconscious; the creative; freedom; and chance. I turn now to a brief *ad seriatim* examination of these basic categories.

Individual Totality (Individuelle Totalität)

The most fundamental category of the formal logic of history—indeed, "the conception which dominates the whole sphere of history"—is that of the individual totality.[103] The flow of history, in Troeltsch's view, was incredibly complex, an "incomparable profusion of always new, unique, and hence individual tendencies, welling up from undisclosed depths, and coming to light in each case in unsuspected places and under different circumstances."[104] It was the job of the historian to put order into this kaleidoscope of images from the past. Consequently, "the method of historical science . . . is determined by the object of selecting from the flux of phenomena that which is qualitatively and uniquely *individual*, whether on a larger or on a smaller scale, and of making this intelligible in its concrete and specific relations."[105]

It should be noted that the individual totality (which Troeltsch at times synonymously called the historical individual totality, the historical individual, or simply the individual) more often than not referred to a collectivity or gestalt formation rather than literally to an individual person. In Troeltsch's usage, therefore, the category of the individual included "family, race, class, nation, circumstances of the time, total spiritual situation, and finally, the association of humanity; thus the real objects of scientific history have become less and less single biographical individuals, but, on the contrary, collective individualities, peoples, states, classes, social ranks, cultural eras, cultural tendencies, religious communities, complex occurrences of all kinds, like wars, revolutions, and so forth."[106] Consequently, although the phrase "historical individual" might occasionally pertain to a Napoleon or a Charlemagne, in Troeltsch's writings it more likely referred to a collective entity such as Antiquity, the Renaissance, or the German nation. Troeltsch detected among modern historians an especially favorable treatment given to the individual totality called "the state," a preferential interest dating back at least to the seventeenth century when "state and nation [Staat und Volk] appeared as the proper central subjects of history, in a way which was a reflection of the Age of Absolutism and of the accompanying transformation of Europe into a system of great powers."[107]

Consistent with his general characterization of the formal logic of history, Troeltsch insisted that the category of the individual totality was likewise existentially grounded in an extramental, extrapsychological way. The category of the individual totality, in other words, was not a formal mental construct imposed upon shapeless historical data to give them form and meaning. Rather, historical reality already contained an inherent form and meaning, which the historian grasped after the fact, sometimes instinctively and intuitively and sometimes more consciously with elaborate logical clarification. The important point, however, is that the historical individual was an objective reality, a thing in itself and for itself, with an existence independent of and antecedent to any mind which might know it.[108]

In making this insistent emphasis in his mature philosophy of history during the Berlin years, Troeltsch was in effect repudiating an important facet of the neo-Kantian tradition, as interpreted by Windelband and Rickert, which had very much influenced his thinking during his last decade at Heidelberg. On the one hand, Troeltsch did retain the nomothetic-ideographic distinction of Windelband and Rickert that the natural sciences tended towards a generalized knowledge of laws and types, whereas history tended towards a specific knowledge of concrete particularities. But on the other hand, Troeltsch rejected the Windelband-Rickert view that the historical individual totality was generated by the mind of a knowing subject and imposed upon reality. As a mature scholar Troeltsch thought this latter neo-Kantianism defective because it incorrectly made mind antecedent to reality, thereby making the historical object the "mere conception of the subject."[109] As we shall see repeatedly in each of Troeltsch's ten other categories of the formal logic of history, the categories used by the historian in properly thinking about the past arise not because the historian—as historian—has a distinctive type of mind, but because the data or material with which he deals—and ultimately the existential reality itself of which the data are traces—have themselves these distinctive qualities. The historian does not impose the categories of the formal logic of history upon existential reality, for they are already there.

Originality and Uniqueness (Ursprünglichkeit und Einmaligkeit)

The historical individual totality contains and implies the category of originality and uniqueness, which refers to the irreducible "onceness" of events in the historical realm. Every single concrete historical phenomenon is unique and "cannot be fully explained by universal laws, but always exhibits some special and distinct element not derivable therefrom."[110] There is "no single rudimentary analogue to the element of natural science" in the flux that is the ebb and flow of history, no repeatable modules or interchangeable units similar to the physical atom or the chemical element.[111]

Narrow Selection (enge Auslese)

In depicting accurately that which is unique and original about an individual totality, the historian should not crowd his account with an infinite plethora of details. It was a mistake, Troeltsch maintained, to think that a genuine description of a historical totality must include everything known about the totality. Certain features should be emphasized, others excluded. The operative principle here was "the necessity of *more narrow selection*, which not only cuts the subject out of the flow of things, but also emphasizes within the subject only the essential or characteristic features, as it were, the *vinculum substantiale*."[112] Achieving the best narrow selection possible was a skill. Simply put, some historians were better than others: Ranke's and Buckhardt's success in implementing this principle elevated them above those capable only of more prosaic results. Facets of successful selection are suggested in the next several categories.

Representation (Vertretung)

The historian must not only select a limited number of features when describing an individual totality but also must choose what is most essential, that is, what is representative. "This ability to represent countless details through the characteristic features contained in them is the indispensable prerequisite of any historical description."[113] Representation was not achieved through a cause-effect type of analysis, only sometimes through a conscious abstraction from empirical details, but most often through superior intuitive perception. Troeltsch again emphasized that success was directly related to the capabilities of the historical mind.

Unity of Value or Meaning (Wert- oder Sinneinheit)

The category of value or meaning further clarified the historian's task of making a limited and representative selection of what is original and unique about historical totalities. Here "the word 'meaning' is not intended as the conscious setting of design, but, on the contrary, as the perchance yet unconscious association of inclination and significance."[114] The meaning or value of past historical phenomena presumably might vary from age to age, necessitating the rewriting or updating of past history. But although historical accounts (*Historie*) must be continually rewritten, this did not necessarily establish the essential subjectivity of history. Rather, Troeltsch held, successive revisionist interpretations of the past illustrated deeper understanding of its hitherto unemphasized dimensions. The significance and meaning of a historical totality might change, but it always remained a thing for itself (*Ding für sich*), never losing its inner objectivity by becoming merely a thing for us (*Ding für uns*).[115]

*Tension between General Spirit and Particular Spirits
(Spannung zwischen dem Gemeingeiste und den Einzelgeistern)*

In Troeltsch's discussion of this category, which he called "the most complicated problem, without exception, in all history," it becomes evident that the historical individual totality has a composite nature.[116] That is to say, the individual totality is not one-dimensional but complex, involving "a considerable tension between the universal and the singular, between the general spirit and the particular spirits, society and individual persons, objective and subjective minds."[117] The unity of a historical totality is not to be denied, but this unity must be regarded as compound, a "unity of contradictions," and not as simplistic and uncomplicated. The historicist indebtedness to the romantic tradition, with its enshrinement of paradox and antinomy, is here evident.

The Unconscious (das Unbewusste)

The category involving general and particular spirits "is possible only with the help of a further fundamental concept of history, the concept of the unconscious."[118] Troeltsch used the term "unconscious" not with the usual psychological or psychoanalytic overtones, however, but to refer to "the fact established by history in a thousand ways, that our actions, emotions, instincts, struggles and decisions have many more assumptions conveyed in them than we are aware of and a much greater or completely different total and lasting meaning than we are conscious of."[119] Only occasional "rare geniuses" have maximum awareness of the historical totalities in which they participate. Most people are generally not conscious of the full meaning of the total configurations in which they are participants and contributors. For example, the total import of the Protestant Reformation involved meanings "beyond the actual consciousness of individual persons" contemporary to those sixteenth-century developments.[120] Thus Troeltsch concluded that the writing of "contemporary history" was a shallow pursuit because the historian in the midst of contemporary historical totalities could not know fully what had not yet been fully consummated.

The Creative (das Schöpferische)

The category of the creative helps account for the incalculable and unpredictable in the flow of history, "that which is not yet contained [*das Noch-night-Enthaltenen*] in the preceding elements" but which rises from their permutations.[121] The appearance of the "new" in the process of history "is no mere transformation of existing forces, but an element of essentially fresh content."[122] Such creation of new history out of old could not be explained, Troeltsch felt, by the ways of natural science. Just as he had rejected the notion of monolithic logic in favor of a multiplicity of logics, Troeltsch similarly held that there is *not one rationalism but various rationalisms*. If one accepted only the meaning of "rational" derived from natural science methodology, then history's creation of the "new" must indeed be considered irrational. But Troeltsch refused to accept the "normalcy" of the rationalism of natural science, though he appreciated the origins of this epistemological myopia as "the consequence of two hundred years of brilliant work in natural science and of the consequent domination of philosophy emanating from it."[123] Troeltsch was saying, in effect, that there is reason in history that the rationality of the natural scientist cannot perceive. Instead of a simplistic situation in which one type of rationalism assumed a monopoly on normalcy, Troeltsch favored a pluralistic coexistence of various forms of rationalism, each of which was normal for its own given discipline but none of which was absolutely obligatory for all situations. Troeltsch regarded Enlightenment reason not as the natural and normal form of human thought but rather as a *zeitgebunden* product of historical conditions.[124]

Freedom in the Sense of Choice (Freiheit im Willkürsinne)

The category of freedom supplemented that of the creative and was Troeltsch's answer to deterministic views of history. History was "fundamentally incalculable, and any notion of a uniform law embracing it completely" he ruled out, endorsing the view that the development both of individual persons as well as of individual totalities was a process of self-actualization, leading continually to unforeseen new and creative situations.[125] The free self-determination of individual persons and of individual totalities was not necessarily consciously or deliberately programmed but might operate partially or totally on an unconscious level. Indeed, Troeltsch thought that most self-directed choices of discretionary options occurred "with superficial, impetuous decisions, or entirely thoughtlessly."[126] History was the realm of the contingent, the unpredictable, the uncalculated, partially because of this element of freedom.

Chance (Zufall)

Closely connected with freedom was the category of chance or accident, the latter referring to the apparently haphazard fusion of heterogeneous factors. Troeltsch cited in illustration "the noted walker who is killed by a brick on the head," explaining that here the falling brick and the walking person belonged to different systems or spheres of activity whose intersection was totally unforeseen.[127] Examples of other chance occurrences included crop failures, famines, epidemics, severe climatological changes, the presence or absence of charismatic personalities in given situations, sharp changes in population, and discoveries of gold. Troeltsch insisted that the historian should look upon accident and chance not as an irrelevant or inconvenient factor but as part of the very warp and woof of history itself. Without the element of chance, history would not be history. Further, Troeltsch warned that although the phenomenon of accident and chance might be explained through some transcendent rationale—such as by the religious idea of providence—such a procedure was bad history. He did not deny that an extrahistorical realm existed—in fact, he claimed that "the transhistorical realm surrounds history"—but he urged the historian not to become involved with this transhistorical realm but to overcome history through itself.[128] The "leap beyond history" of Kierkegaard, for example, while it might be good faith, nevertheless was a violation of the formal logic of history.[129]

Development (Entwicklung)

Troeltsch's lengthy discussion of the category of development puts into proper perspective the preceding ten categories by emphasizing the dynamism of the historical process. The category of the historical individual totality, for example, might suggest a relatively frozen, static view of history, in the sense that a photograph might be said to freeze the movement of life into a static picture. Troeltsch wished to emphasize, however, that historical totalities "are a part of an uninterrupted flow of becoming and must be set into this flow."[130] The category of development remedied this need.

Devoting more space in *Historicism and Its Problems* to an explication of the meaning of historical development than to the other ten categories combined, Troeltsch furnished an exhaustively detailed treatment which he claimed was the first comprehensive publication on the subject. As usual, he had recourse to the *Referieren*, surveying especially the most significant interpretations of the concept in the previous century. Prior to the theory of Hegelian dialectics ("the first great theory of historical dynamics") Troeltsch thought that thinkers had not yet dealt with historical development in sufficient depth to warrant lengthy consideration of their work.[131] Rather than recapitulate here the entire scope of post-Hegelian, nineteenth-century theories, I focus instead on Troeltsch's own frame of reference, namely, his dialogue with Rickert's form of neo-Kantianism. Rickert was the primary influence on Troeltsch's own views of development.[132]

Although Heinrich Rickert and Wilhelm Windelband are frequently grouped together as leaders in the southwest German school of neo-Kantianism,[133] Troeltsch separated the two. Windelband may have had a great deal of insight into the category of the historical individual totality, Troeltsch felt, but his "concept of development was utterly ruined by generalities, contradictions, and uncertainties."[134] Rickert, on the other hand, did advance from the static concept of the individual totality towards the dynamic category of development, thereby approaching what Troeltsch called "the beating heart of history."[135] But however intellectually indebted he felt towards Rickert, in the final analysis Troeltsch thought that this neo-Kantian thinker unfortunately had not totally committed himself to the full meaning and implications of historical development. His critique of Rickert took on the ambivalence and complexity of a disciple's arguments with his master. Troeltsch's criticisms of Rickert were tantamount to a self-criticism of his own earlier neo-Kantian views held during his second decade on the Theological Faculty at Heidelberg, approximately 1903–1914.

Troeltsch had been attracted to Rickert's ideas to a large extent by the latter's rigorous, disciplined, logical mind.[136] But this great strength became, in Troeltsch's eyes, a great weakness, for it became rigid and unyielding when faced with the choice between the absolute values of a transhistorical realm and the relative values found in actual history. Rickert's systematic, dogmatic mind feared the apparently unpredictable and erratic flow of historical development. As Rickert himself expressed this apprehension: "Owing to thoughts of development, everything seems to become insecure and uncertain."[137] Against the seemingly Heraclitean flux of history, Rickert sought the stability of a "Parmenidian principle," explaining at one point: "The heterogeneous continuum of the flow of experience deserves no consideration."[138] He found his Parmenidian principle in a system of abstract, apriori values which he imposed upon history from without. Rickert ultimately was interested in historical development not for its own sake but as a realm for the materialization and reflection of suprahistorical, absolute values.

Troeltsch, of course, could not accept this solution, believing as he did that the imposition of an absolute system of values amounted to a denial of the genuine dynamics of life itself. In Troeltsch's view, Rickert's standard for judging historical things was "no standard growing out of history itself, but an extraneous one, floating above it, produced by pure reason."[139] Troeltsch objected that "for the historian, on the contrary, development is an inner movement of the object itself, into which one can and must be absorbed intuitively."[140] The meaning of historical development did not derive from its being judged in the light of eternity, but from the values intrinsic to the process of contingent development itself.

Troeltsch's own meaning of historical development becomes clearer when contrasted with equivalent or similar notions prevalent in the physical and biological sciences, in psychology, and in philosophy.

> *Physical* development treats the formation of relatively lasting and complicated systems of three-dimensional, corporeal processes, and measures their intensity of relations in terms of exten-

sion, stability, and harmony; *biological* development treats the continuity of living organisms and measures their intensity in terms of the results for the health and preservation of the species; *psychological* development treats the formation of the cohesive phenomena of consciousness of a body-ego, together with its subconscious presuppositions, and measures its intensity in terms of the degree to which it can serve in animals and humans as the mechanism and apparatus for higher spiritual abilities. *Historical* development, on the other hand, directly treats the growth and deployment of the higher spiritual abilities themselves—based first of all upon all these suppositions and completely breaking through for the first time in man himself—as well as the union and the continuous sequence of individual totalities of meaning in which these abilities operate, and it measures these formations in terms of an intricate system of standards or historical systems of values.[141]

Historical development, occurring in the realm of the spirit (*Geisteswelt*), far surpassed these other types of development in depth and profundity. It was possible to understand historical development (including, of course, the developing individual totality) only by immanent criticism. Based upon a variant of Ranke's notion that "every age is immediate to God," it was necessary for the historian, in Troeltsch's opinion, to immerse himself in the processes of history and judge these processes from within. This immanent criticism, akin to intuition and frequently called "*Verstehen*," "presupposes as unprejudiced as possible a sympathetic understanding [*Einfühlung*] of the alien historical totality of meaning, excluding all the special desires and ideals which the observer may have concerning life."[142] Unlike Rickert, Troeltsch insisted that the historian observing past totalities or developing totalities must respect the autonomous existence of inviolable, immanent values already in those totalities.

On the other hand, lest immanent criticism be misunderstood as pure mystical subjectivity, Troeltsch further insisted that "such thinking is separated from any fanciful Romanticism by its scholarly training."[143] Intuition was fine, even necessary, as Troeltsch indicated in his praise of Wilhelm Dilthey and other psychologizing philosophers of life: "Without question, [Dilthey's intuitive] method hits the nerve of the historical better than any of the others hitherto described. Especially with its immunity from theories has it felt the flow of history which can be grasped solely intuitively. . . . It is a philosophy of life which deems fitting that life can be understood by life." [144]

In the long run, however, Troeltsch objected to the "immunity from theories" of any presuppositionless intuition. Is presuppositionless immanent criticism, he asked, "really possible? Does this understanding, illustrating, and comprehending really ensue without logical categories, without transformation and modification of the materials through principles of selection, formation, and combination? Is the . . . relation of development to goals and to meaningful content really settled through mere empathy [*Einfühlung*]? Can there be a philosophy of life at all which comprehends life through life, and not through thought?" [145] The answer to these questions was clearly: No. At this point Troeltsch's eleven categories of the formal logic of history became operative, helping to refine and clarify the historian's intuitive, sympathetic understanding of history. Intuition went far, but without logic, not far enough. The categories of the formal logic of history were needed, in reciprocal relationship with immament criticism, to produce genuine historical understanding. [146]

Material Philosophy of History

In the midst of widespread relativity of values and cultural disorientation Troeltsch turned to what he called the material philosophy of history to supplement his emphasis on immanent criticism and the formal logic of history. The material philosophy of history (*die materiale Geschichtsphilosophie*), unlike mere historiography, was concerned not only with past history but with the present and the future. And it was action oriented. Noncontemplative in intent, the material philosophy of history was something of a hybrid or amphibian, a link (*Mittelglied, Mittelstellung*) between empirical history and ethics, with a foot in both camps. The tasks of the material philosophy of history were above all the practical tasks of life itself, centering upon "the problem of the further development of historical life out of the historically understood present." [147] Unlike those who thought the past could have no bearing upon present and future problems, Troeltsch insisted upon the relevancy of what had already happened to what was yet to come. [148] Part of this action-oriented concern was undoubtedly attributable to wartime and immediate post-war German problems that desperately needed solutions. The lengthy title of one of his articles in the journal *Der Kunstwart* sums up this aspiration: "Let the Governing Thought [Today] Be: Don't Quarrel over the Past, but Challenge the

Future."[149] The "purely contemplative investigation" of the past, employing the formal logic of history, led to a quietistic attitude towards history of which Troeltsch was wary.[150] It was necessary to go further. Historiography was oriented towards the past, but the philosophy of history was oriented towards past, present, and future, especially towards the present crisis in consciousness. Simply put, "the material philosophy of history is naturally teleological."[151]

The most prominent themes in Troeltsch's material philosophy of history were axiology (or the study of values), the need for a contemporary cultural synthesis, and the problems of universal history and of Europeanism. These themes overlap but for purposes of discussion will be treated analytically and separately.

As we have already seen in our examination of Troeltsch's views on religion, historicism, and the formal logic of history, he was virtually obsessed with the contemporary crisis of values.[152] In discussing axiology, or the question of value formation, Troeltsch even went so far as to remark that the problem of values "is the first important problem of all philosophy of history, after which all further [questions] come only in the second rank."[153] Friedrich Meinecke agreed that Troeltsch's concern with the problem of values in *Historicism and Its Problems* was "the central question of the book."[154] Meinecke further commented, alluding to the claim of Archimedes, that one could comprehend the thought of Troeltsch in six words, "$\pi\alpha\nu\tau\alpha$ $\rho\epsilon\hat{\iota}$, $\delta\acute{o}\varsigma$ $\mu o\iota$ $\pi o\grave{\upsilon}$ $\sigma\tau\hat{\omega}$," which loosely translated mean: "Everything is in flux, but give me a place to stand (and I will move the world)."[155]

The crux of the problem now became: What were the values which would give stability? What were their sources? How were they formed? The scope of these questions is immeasurably broad, for Troeltsch was seeking not merely personal sanity but stability for an entire civilization in a state of crisis.

In answering the questions, Troeltsch made a distinction of vital importance between what he called "formal values" and "cultural values": "As [formal values] lead us out of history into the sphere of the timelessly valid, so conversely [cultural values] conduct us back into history and development, and more particularly into the realm of the individual. Individuality bears an immeasurably greater significance in the latter than in the former."[156] Troeltsch did accept the existence of absolute values which were "purely formal . . . [and] outside time or history" and which could indeed "be developed into a timelessly valid and comprehensive system of precepts."[157] But he rejected "the realm of standards beyond the reach of time or history" as the solution to the problems of modern consciousness.[158] His basic conception we have already encountered: since history was the source of the problems of modern consciousness, history should also be the source of the solutions.

The preoccupation with gross formalism, such as in Rickert's neo-Kantian approach, Troeltsch repudiated as "not merely indifferent to history but directly opposed to the flow and the endlessness of becoming. . . . [It is] something thoroughly beyond history, indeed, hostile to history."[159] In an attempt to master history philosophically—to dam and control the historical stream of life, to borrow one of Troeltsch's most frequent metaphors—there was no room for "timelessness, eternity, universal validity, and absoluteness of standards."[160] Troeltsch was so convinced about this point that at times his impatience showed. For example, in *Historicism and Its Problems* he criticized the search for simplistic solutions, recommending instead less quickly attainable answers and "more intricate processes of thought than average thinking [*Durchschnittsdenken*] for the most part liked to have it."[161] In one of his last essays he remarked that in order to arrive at a satisfactory solution to the modern crisis in values one must shun guidelines set forth "by those who love simple ideas valid for all ages, irrespective of time and place, or hanker after utopian ideals to be realized only in a distant future."[162]

Scepticism, pessimism, and despair, however, were not Troeltsch's responses to this severe relativization of standards of value. He did admit that the inability in an era of historicism to fall back upon a firm foundation of solid absolutes "at first . . . is alarming,"[163] but he was most emphatic in insisting that the alternative to a denial of absolute values in history was not necessarily unbridled relativism: the "relativity of values, however, is not relativism, anarchy, chance, caprice."[164] Inclined "to accept the historical conditionality and complexity of the standards simply as a fact," Troeltsch nevertheless denied that the consequence of this position was an inevitable anarchy of values.[165] Rather, he took the stand that "there can be genuine and true validity which is not timeless and eternally immutable validity, but which suits the existence of the present time being, and, for that reason only, thus has general validity."[166]

With this sophisticated point of view, which frowned on an either-or dichotomy between absolutism and relativism, Troeltsch held that though historically conditioned values are relative, they are not arbi-

trary or capricious; though they are time-bound, within their time period they are obligatory; though they are products of history, they are,
nevertheless, absolutely binding within the particular situations in
which they obtain. This view is reminiscent of Troeltsch's concept of
polymorphous truth. Historically conditioned cultural values, though
not absolute, are not radically relative or subjective either but somehow partake of "a universal, more than accidental and more than individual validity." [167] How Troeltsch intended to use cultural values in his
material philosophy of history to help solve the problems of historicism is a question best investigated under the heading of another central theme of this philosophy, that is, what he called a contemporary
cultural synthesis.

The contemporary cultural synthesis (*die gegenwärtige Kultursynthese*) was an answer to the crisis in values of European civilization. "Here and here alone," Troeltsch remarked, "is the one possibility of a solution for our problem—the problem of damming and
controlling the historical stream of life." [168] The material philosophy of
history was naturally teleological, going beyond the analysis and judgment of the past to the additional task of evaluating the present. It was
certainly proper in the *formal* logic of history to judge the *past* by the
values of the *past*, but it was incumbent upon the *material* philosophy
of history to judge the *present*—with implications extending into the
future—by the values of the *past*. The aim of creating a contemporary
cultural synthesis was "thus the frank opposite of any purely contemplative attitude towards history." [169] It was instead intended to lead
towards a transfiguration of the present, "of engendering in the present
that which ought to be [*das Sein-Sollende*]." [170] As Troeltsch understood it, "criticism and creation are intrinsically connected"; an understanding of the past, aided by the formal logic of history, could be
teleologically channelled into constructing a new historical individual
totality, that is, a contemporary cultural synthesis. [171]

Rooted in the past, growing in the present, and bearing fruit in the
future, a cultural synthesis was not an artificial, ersatz concoction, but
an attempt "to mould the future organically out of the past." [172] In a
time of cultural turmoil and the questioning of traditional values,
Troeltsch's response was not to reject past historical values out of hand
but to reinvestigate them to see if they had any new relevance for
present, troubled times. A contemporary cultural synthesis based upon
past values, Troeltsch held, "is the something for which today we are
searching unceasingly in our modern world." [173] He cited as support

his Berlin colleague, Friedrich Meinecke, who had written that "in a time lacerated by problems and overburdened with the materials of civilization, modern man passionately desires spiritual bonds, simplified solutions, and bold and vigorous leaders who should certainly themselves experience all the complications of the present but who should also fuse these into an efficacious and impressive synthesis."[174] For these reasons, in Troeltsch's opinion, large-scale synthetic works, such as those by H. G. Wells and Oswald Spengler, had become popular in his time. Troeltsch thought that *An Outline of History, The Decline of the West*, and similar works provided suggestions of discernible patterns and meaning in one of those "decadent, chaotic periods, when all the contents of culture were overturned in confusion and there was no rudimentary formative tendency on hand."[175]

Wells and Spengler, however, although on the best-seller lists of their day, were seriously defective in Troeltsch's estimation. In *Historicism and Its Problems*, for example, Troeltsch remarked that "universal histories like those of Wells and Spengler actually veer away from historical realism entirely, although in opposite directions—the one into an ethical Spencerianism, the other into a neoromanticized organology, both of them into a world of letters [*Litteratentum*]."[176] Troeltsch was even more caustic elsewhere. In book reviews written for the *Historische Zeitschrift* he severely pilloried Spengler. After an itemized critique of specific passages from *The Decline of the West*, in which he repeatedly used phrases like "simply false. . . . pure fantasy. . . . an impossible explanation," Troeltsch summarized his review of Spengler's first volume: "It teems with incorrect allegations, fanciful contentions, and distorted analogies, and lacks almost every critical guarantee of data and accordingly any necessity. On this basis the book thus appears on second reading very much more distasteful, arbitrary, fantastic, and self-contradictory than on the first reading, when one was dazzled by deceptive trains of thought and lightly disregarded the 'evidence.'"[177] Reviewing Spengler's second volume several years later, Troeltsch called large sections of that book "confused rumor."[178] All in all, Troeltsch thought Spengler's works "creations of fancy" and Spengler himself a harmful dilettante bent on "hauling down the flag of life in the course of man's perpetual struggle to keep it flying."[179]

Neither Spengler nor Wells (nor anybody else for that matter) had yet created the contemporary cultural synthesis which the times demanded. Troeltsch had to admit that "there is no instruction, I confess, how one should create it and can create it." [180] He was fairly consistent, however, in his view that "such a specific and current synthesis of culture cannot be created without an extensive review of history and without questioning its prevailing values and formations." [181] Then the following questions had to be answered: How much of past history was relevant? How far back into the past was it necessary to go? And should one have a broad, ecumenical attitude towards all values or restrict one's focus to a more narrow range of cultural values?

In the widest sense, there were four "basic pillars" or "primeval forces" (*Grundpfeiler*, *Urgewalt*) upon which the contemporary cultural synthesis was to rest: the ancient Hebraic tradition, classical Greece, the Hellenistic-Roman period, and the Occidental Middle Ages. [182] This latter complex of cultural values—the most important of all the four sources—was itself an amalgamation of elements from Christianity, the Byzantine world, and the world of Islam. It was from these combined sources, Troeltsch maintained, that "the spiritual vigour of the future must be worked out." [183] More simply put, it was fair game for the contemporary cultural synthesis to draw upon "the totality of Occidental culture" for its completion. [184]

Elsewhere in *Historicism and Its Problems* Troeltsch suggested a briefer time span for historical sources; perhaps the most useful cultural values might be found in "the last two hundred years, or if need be, five hundred years of Occidental history." [185] Troeltsch had in mind that the eighteenth-century cultural synthesis was the last great coherent one in the history of Occidental civilization, and consequently the most crucial past synthesis towards which his own contemporaries should be attuned. In Troeltsch's view, the twentieth-century Occidental cultural circle to which he belonged was a product of the dissolution of the Enlightenment's cultural complex. And going back one step further, this eighteenth-century synthesis was itself the product of the dissolution of the Christian culture of the medieval period. This was consistent with Troeltsch's overall periodization of Western civilization: specifically, the modern history of Europe had two beginnings, "in a broad sense and in a narrower sense. In the former sense it begins with the fifteenth century and the new military and bureaucratic state opposed to the Church and the Empire, in the second sense it begins with the English Revolution and the Enlightenment." [186]

A viable cultural synthesis generally had a central cultural value as a "pivot of organization" around which all the other cultural values were arranged. The core value of the eighteenth-century Enlightenment, for example, was the idea of "humanity." In Troeltsch's opinion, however, the eighteenth century's own estimation of this concept was unfortunately in error insofar as it was regarded as absolute and universally binding. Troeltsch maintained to the contrary that this key idea was "a component of a quite specific, individual situation of European history, and not at all a rational and universal principle, just as indeed even the 'humanity' of Chinese and of Indian cultures was completely different." [187] As a practitioner of *Geistesgeschichte*, Troeltsch held that the European Enlightenment's concept of humanity was historically and sociologically conditioned. The *philosophes* may have considered their own cultural synthesis as timeless and definitive, but Troeltsch regarded it as an alleged "rationalistic system of absolute truths which was merely the secular transformation of ecclesiastical, dogmatic absolutism." [188]

Troeltsch regarded no cultural synthesis as permanently conclusive either for its own cultural circle (*Kulturkreis*) or as an export for other cultural circles in other places and times. Every cultural synthesis of necessity was unavoidably *zeitgebunden*, including the one which Troeltsch's own contemporaries urgently needed. No general formulae sufficed for all ages. This view was consistent with Troeltsch's broader conception that the aims of the philosophy of history did not include "the task of formulating ultimate, definitive, and universal goals for mankind, which could only become realized, indeed, in a perfect and universal community of the human race." [189] Rather, Troeltsch's aim for the material philosophy of history was more modest, that of helping to generate a cultural synthesis limited both in space and in time, a synthesis valid for present Europeans but not for non-Europeans or even for future Europeans. No cultural synthesis was permanently indispensable. Just as historiographic reconstructions of the past succeeded one another from age to age, so too did cultural syntheses. There was "no possibility of any limitation of the historical stream of life which is finally valid." [190]

Troeltsch felt an urgent need for a universal history in "a world living in grave social crises and spiritual and religious distress." [191] But he did not use the terms "universal history" or "world history" in a customary sense. Universal history for Troeltsch, as the backdrop for the creation of the contemporary cultural synthesis, was clearly more than the mere empirical record of the past. Endorsing "a return to a way of thinking, and a way of feeling about life, which was not merely 'historical,' but 'universal-historical,'" Troeltsch urged that "the image of Clio has to be made to face, once more, towards the great and universal problems of the future." [192] In his opinion, most contemporary historians were not sufficiently philosophically inclined but tended instead to immerse themselves in narrow, empirical monographic studies lacking theoretical, philosophical overviews. [193] Those contemporaries who did attempt to write universal history—such as Oswald Spengler and H. G. Wells—Troeltsch found grossly deficient.

It was not possible to write a universal history of mankind, in Troeltsch's opinion, because "mankind" or "humanity" never existed, either in the present or in the past. [194] Although Troeltsch did at times suggest that all men did have a common spiritual denominator which underlay cultural variations in time and place, [195] his more considered view seemed to be that "the truth is that there has never been any Common Spirit but that of a group, family, race, class, profession, school, or sect, and even the Church's attempt to comprehend all these, as it were, under a single dome remained, in the time of its real and complete domination, a work of force and diplomacy, a faith and a dream, contradicted in the actual life of the times by the eternal strife of ideas and interests." [196]

Writings based upon the unity of humanity Troeltsch tended to dismiss as "speculative soapbubbles and philosophically constructed castles in the air." [197] The feeble human intellect, in his opinion, was simply too weak to grasp the meaning of total humanity. "What do we know of humanity?" he asked; "of hundreds of thousands of years—or, as others say, millions of years which man has dwelled on our earth during the coming and going of glacial periods—we know tolerably the last six thousand years and within this period essentially only our own circle of culture and its presupposition. What does not belong to that circle of culture, we understand clumsily." [198] Even more devastating was his denial that mankind or humanity had a common history at all, his fundamental point being that "mankind as a whole has no spiritual unity [*geistige Einheit*] and therefore no unified development. Everything that one trots out as such are works of fiction, which tell metaphysical fairy tales about something that does not exist at all." [199] Troeltsch claimed that *development* could not occur unless an *individual totality* was already there to develop. Since humanity as a unified totality had not existed, it was consequently impossible to recognize a universal history of mankind. Troeltsch was intent on avoiding what he regarded as Hegel's error, that is, mistakenly viewing one's own contemporary world as the apogee of the unfolding development of all humanity.

The most satisfactory resolution of Troeltsch's sometimes apparently inconsistent views on universal history is found in statements made towards the end of his life to the effect that "for us there is only the universal history of European culture [*Universalgeschichte der europäischen Kultur*]." [200] In the final analysis, for Troeltsch it was individual historical totalities, more circumscribed in scope than humanity as a whole, that were immediate to God; thus the development of European culture was the only cultural circle fully intelligible to a good European. [201] "Humanity" had no common cultural values at all, and it was in specific cultural values—not in abstract formal values—that Troeltsch sought the origins of the contemporary cultural synthesis for his own age. As he put it, "the Occident, Near and Far East, civilized peoples, half-civilized peoples, and primitives are different to such an extent that a common content of culture for present-day humanity is still far out of the question, although certain extremely general and formal moral concepts of human dignity and justice, purity and goodness may be widely diffused to a certain extent." [202]

Again we see a recurrent leitmotif in Troeltsch's thought: systems of thought must reflect reality rather than be superimposed upon reality. In this context, Troeltsch's premise means that it is not possible to *write* a universal history of mankind because, existentially speaking, there *never was* such a universal history. Consequently, Troeltsch concluded that "*for us there is only a universal history of Europeanism* [*Weltgeschichte des Europäertums*]. *The old idea of universal history must assume new and more modest forms.*" [203]

The material philosophy of history—including the construction of a contemporary cultural synthesis and the specifics of a universal history—could rightly find meaning in the past only within a limited range of cultural values. A historically conscious European could find genuine meaning only in European values. How different, for example, from Hermann Hesse's Sinclair, who in finding that "Europe had conquered the whole world only to lose her own soul," thereupon turned to non-European cultures to understand life. [204] Troeltsch did not excessively object to incorporating vignettes of non-European history into an account of Europeanism, but he cautioned against their misuse. Making allowance for those who might want to "combine a few sideglances at the East . . . and into anthropology," he warned that such resultant mélanges belonged in the domain of the anthologist's compilations (that is, as *Buchbindersynthese*) and were not organic, natural syntheses. [205] Europeans might get some suggestions and ideas from foreign cultures, but nevertheless they could know fully only their own

reality, only their own cultural circle. "Chinese, Indian, Moham-
medan, Hellenic, Medieval, and Modern cultural atmospheres,"
Troeltsch stated, "are individual systems of thought, mysterious and
original. . . . [They contain] nothing timeless and universally valid."[206] His conclusion is humbling, almost dismal:

> We know, in fact, only ourselves and understand only our own
> being and hence only our own development. . . . One must have
> the courage to acknowledge one's own total historical fate, be-
> cause for all that we cannot get out of our own historical skin.
> . . . Everyone can from his own ground obtain the most spacious
> panorama and aspire to the highest heights, but nevertheless one
> thinks things out, argues, behaves, and creates only from one's
> own ground.[207]

I am reminded of the impasse between cultures in *Madame Butterfly*,
wherein Troeltsch's contemporary Giacomo Puccini gives his own version at the turn of the century of the inability of persons from one
culture to understand deeply alien values.

The creation of a contemporary cultural synthesis to help solve the
turn-of-the-century crisis in European consciousness had to accept this
impasse, however lamentable it seemed. One could only cultivate
one's own garden. Troeltsch did not endorse the vision of a global
unity, of an eventually uniform one-world culture with a common reservoir of values. Early in his career he had more idealistically leaned
towards a religiously oriented one-worldism—for example, in his
comment made in 1902 that "the Kingdom of God is . . . a wonderful
gift of God, something thoroughly objective, the community of men in
complete peace and complete love."[208] But in his later writings he
shifted from this more theoretical theology towards an increasing preoccupation with concrete phenomena. Burdened with the weight of
existential historical diversity, Troeltsch could no longer glibly foretell
a universal community of mankind or a global spiritual community.
Part of the context of this shift of emphasis certainly was the Great War
and the consequent widespread distress in Germany during the first
third of the Weimar Republic. To these political experiences I now
turn, examining them through Troeltsch's Berlin writings in his new-
found roles as wartime propagandist and as post-war political analyst.

5

An Intellectual in Politics

Der Mensch is zum Spielball des Schicksals geworden
und liegt nicht mehr in seiner eigenen Hand.

Troeltsch (1915)

Die Lage ist so dunkel wie in den hoffnugslosten
Zeiten des Krieges.

Troeltsch (1921)

The political crisis in Germany from 1914 through the early 1920s was extreme, even within the entire modern history of European nation-states. War, revolution, counterrevolution, economic deprivation, and personal trauma became part of the German way of life. In this context Ernst Troeltsch's political personality was expressed. These harsh experiences also had a marked impact upon the tone and emphases in his scholarly work on religious, historicist, and philosophic themes.

The immediate stimulus to Troeltsch's heightened political activities was the outbreak of the Great War of 1914–1918, the opening months of which coincided with his move to Berlin after two decades of an increasingly narrow life at Heidelberg.[1] Not only did Troeltsch leave behind in Bavaria the confining experiences of membership in the Theological Faculty, but, as his *Kunstwart* articles clearly reveal, his political attitudes had come remarkably to transcend a common type of narrow Bavarian patriotism.[2] More to the point, as Gerhard Ritter has observed, "war—and especially modern mass war—means an enormous intensification in political life."[3] Troeltsch's life was no exception to this dictum.

Before 1914 Troeltsch had not been entirely a stranger to politics. For eight years he was an elected representative to the Badenese Parliament from the University of Heidelberg, though his political participation in parliamentary debates was limited.[4] Furthermore, he had not written at length on political themes except within the context of church history or theology, in articles such as "The Separation of Church and State" (1906) and "The Church in the Life of the Present" (1911). With the outbreak of war, however, Troeltsch rapidly became "a person passionately interested in politics."[5] As he said, "the exciting situation of the war . . . laid claims for itself upon the pens of the scholars."[6]

Troeltsch's political activities at Berlin increased and diversified during the war and the first few years of the Weimar Republic. He became a member of a political circle including Walther Rathenau, Friedrich Naumann, and Max Weber, among others; helped form the *Volksbund für Freiheit und Vaterland*; became active in the Democratic party as a countermeasure against jingoist and annexationist elements in German politics; served as an elected representative in the Prussian Landtag; and became parliamentary undersecretary of state in the Prussian Ministry of Culture, where he helped influence the formulation of Prussian policies regarding education and the churches. Troeltsch had sufficient stature even to be mentioned as a possible candidate for the presidency of the Weimar Republic. His political connections provided him with valuable opportunities to "observe great historical events at least in part close by their points of origins"; he believed that such experience gave far deeper insights into "the nature of historical fortunes, development and catastrophes than could be obtained from merely the study of books and documents."[7]

During the war, Troeltsch delivered his share of patriotic addresses and essays, and in the subsequent early Weimar period contributed to the highly respected journal *Der Kunstwart* a series of more or less monthly articles which have been said to "rank among the most clear-headed political analyses of the day."[8] His first-hand exposure to political events in Berlin undoubtedly contributed to his acute remarks in essays such as "Democracy," "Aristocracy," "Socialism," and "Bolshevism," which Hermann Diehl described in 1921 as "an exceptionally perceptive introduction to the idea-world of the most important political and social tendencies of contemporary thought and action."[9] For the most part, however, Troeltsch remained an intellectual in politics, a political observer who did not relish being a *Tatmensch*, a man of action. As the pseudonym for many of his contributions to *Der Kunstwart* implies, he was a *"Spektator."*[10] Barely two months after Diehl's favorable judgment of his writings, for example, Troeltsch retired from his post in the Prussian Ministry of Culture, declaring: "I want to get out of politics and devote myself again to my studies."[11] Troeltsch regarded politics "much more as the art of compromise than as a struggle for power—he was a man of will, but not of power [*ein Willenmensch, aber kein Machtmensch*]."[12] He tended to lack appreciation for the delicate, personal handling of real political situations. Despite his excursions into active politics, he was a scholar primarily and a politician only secondarily. As Köhler has said, "he remained the academician . . . who preferred to discuss rather than lead."[13]

The Great War

The Great War, in which "an entire generation rotted on the battlefield," had a profound effect upon Germany, and upon Troeltsch.[14] Wartime censorship as well as his common sense proprieties about maintaining national morale severely curbed the public expression of Troeltsch's private doubts during the period 1914–1918, but even during hostilities he called the war an expression of a "straightforward conflict of interests, of bestial, brutish barbarity."[15] As a humanist he was grievously upset by "the absurd hell of destruction and hatred which the present war signifies."[16]

At the outbreak of the war, Troeltsch reacted instinctively in Augustinian terms. The essential contradiction between war and Christian values, "the antithesis of the wicked earthly world and the blessed heavenly world," deeply bothered him.[17] With the approach of the Christmas season in 1914, he seemed numbed that Christian themes in wartime Germany appeared like "an alien message from an alien world."[18] It was unsettling to him that there might be very few contemporary Christians who endorsed the themes of universal peace and love contained in the original Christmas experience. Troeltsch grieved that largely because of the war traditional Christian answers for contemporary problems had become "in part forgotten, in part relegated to school theories [*Schultheorien*] of barely any practical significance."[19] During the Quattrocentennial of the Protestant Reformation, he also regretfully observed that of those two early sixteenth-century contemporaries, Machiavelli and Luther, the ideas of the former had unfortunately grown stronger and richer.[20] With most of the leading peoples of the Christian world engaged among themselves in a fight for life or death, Troeltsch lamented that "for international Christianity—the religion of the white race—the war means a downright catastrophe."[21]

Never able to reconcile satisfactorily the values of Christianity and nationalism, Troeltsch did admit that flag-waving patriotism might have its proper place, but he insisted that men owed their ultimate allegiance to something greater than the national Fatherland. "Christianity has a higher loftiness," he felt, "than any national and political creed and the morality originating therein."[22] The Kingdom of God was not the kingdom of power politics, and men ultimately had greater ties to the universal kingdom of God than to any earthly country: "there is a higher world than the nation."[23]

And yet, despite his desire that all people love one another rather than die for the personification of any nation-state as divine reason upon earth, Troeltsch did respond patriotically to the theme of *la Patrie en danger!* As Raymond Aron and others have observed, the opening of World War I "was marked in all countries by an explosion of national fervor."[24] This explosion in Germany engulfed Troeltsch. Despite his repeated pre-war theological statements on the brotherhood of man, he became caught up in the wave of patriotic wartime polemics. This same scholarly theologian and church historian who yearned for universal peace and love among mankind could also resoundingly exhort his fellow countrymen: "*Be German, remain German, become German!*"[25]

On 1 August 1914, amid overtures of war made by Austria, Russia, Serbia, and Great Britain—including general mobilization by both Russia and Austria—Germany declared war against Russia and ordered general mobilization. The next day, in a representative "outburst of patriotic solidarity that bridged the cleavages inherent in the Wilhelmine structure of society,"[26] Troeltsch delivered a stirring speech to kindle war enthusiasm. On 2 August Germany sent an ultimatum to Belgium demanding the right to cross Belgian territory. War was declared on France the following day, and on 4 August German troops crossed the Belgian border. It was to the theme "Following the Declaration of Mobilization" that Troeltsch addressed himself in this the first of several dozen public wartime exhortations.

His remarks were not original and were undoubtedly reiterated during those early days of the war in hundreds of wartime rallies not only in Germany but in the homelands of all the war's participants. Yet they were needed at the time and exceedingly appropriate. In this speech the motif of unity was a central thought: "Prince and worker will join hands," Troeltsch exclaimed, and the nation will stand together as one man, united from the extreme right to the extreme left.[27] He felt Germany was entering into a struggle for its very life and continued existence as a nation against envy, hatred, and the spirit of revenge. In thus defending German values, Troeltsch urged, Germany was in effect fighting for the freedom and development of humanity itself.[28]

The magnitude of the present danger overwhelmed him: "Oh! If only the speaker this hour could turn every word into a bayonet, if only he could transform them into rifles, into cannon!"[29] But words should not be sneered at, he immediately added. People needed words in the present conflict—to inspire, uplift, clarify aims and ideas, and motivate great deeds—in the same way that Fichte, Arndt, and Schleiermacher had articulated a needed rationale for fighting in the 1813 War of Liberation against Napoleonic imperialism.[30] Be brave and valorous, do one's duty, trust and have confidence, believe, have faith, and pray, Troeltsch counselled. He was permissive in allowing his listeners a wide range of appropriate bases for their beliefs—be they "the metaphysical foundation of reality . . . the ethical order of the world . . . Providence . . . the Lord of Hosts . . . the Father in heaven"—but he insisted that "without faith there would be no victory."[31]

In the midst of this enthusiasm, however, he struck a sombre note that, in retrospect, seems the truer Troeltsch. Although he was able repeatedly to urge his countrymen, *"Zu den Waffen, zu den Waffen!"* ("To arms, to arms!"), he also recalled that Germany had never known more than fifty years of peace without the outbreak of another war. He dismally, almost fatalistically, mused: "The flames of irrationality and malice, of hatred and envy, the mysteries of dark conflicts of interests and the moods of the masses, knock the bottom out of everything and call our attention to the fact that all of human culture is a house built upon a volcano."[32]

Despite his pessimism about war, Troeltsch was liberal with praise for the German army itself. "God works through men," he declared, and the particular vehicle through which God was then working his greatness was "the Volksheer, the German army of 1914, an army of the people."[33] Herbert J. Muller, in discussing the paradoxical and deep ties between idealism and violence in World War I patriotism, has observed that "God and history were lined up behind every nation."[34] This certainly accurately describes the mentality of Troeltsch, who, with his sensitive religious temperament and more than two decades as a professional theologian, used a theological metaphor for the significance of the German military machine. "The army is flesh from our flesh and spirit from our spirit," he declared; "our salvation lies in its hands."[35] The German army—truly "the Volk in arms," the symbol of the nation's unity—was seen as the cutting edge of the German people in defensive action against foes poised to deny the country's life and existence. He told a wartime audience in the fall of 1914 that their boys were fighting on the western front for decent, lofty values—as expressed in that uplifting song, *"Deutschland, Deutschland, über Alles"*—against a motley horde of "Asiatic Indians, Negroes, Frenchmen, Englishmen, and Belgians . . . who possess no common ballad and are united with one another only by slanders and lies about 'German barbarians.' "[36] The Anglo-Saxon soldiers, especially, regarded war as merely a line of business where one got double wages for victory, Troeltsch scornfully asserted.[37]

Unfortunately for the German war effort, the confidence that Troeltsch displayed in his paean to the German army during the fall offensive of 1914 did not assure the expected immediate victory of the Schlieffen Plan. Although the public at large did not appreciate the significance of the long period of static trench warfare ushered in on the western front by mid-September, Troeltsch himself did sense during this fall offensive that contemporary conditions of warfare were unlike those of 1870 and that armed hostilities might drag on longer than had been widely expected. He lauded the intense ebullience and optimism seen "nowhere more beautifully today in Germany than at railroad stations when they teem with our soldiers," but he also prudently cautioned that "A Mighty Fortress Is Our God" might be a more appropriate motif for the season than railroad station nostalgia about fond farewells and imminent homecomings.[38] The German people's army would be ultimately invincible (*unüberwindlich*), but victory would take time.

Troeltsch did not have a simplistic mind, and in the early months of the conflict—as the war of mobility ground slowly down to a war of static positions—he recognized the complexities of the hostilities. Early in December 1914, barely four months after the war had begun, Troeltsch delivered a speech in Karlsruhe as a member of the Badenese Upper House, declaiming upon the tangled meaning of the war. "It is not a simple war," he observed, "but a bundle of wars thrown together."[39] He isolated five elements.

First, it was obviously a struggle between contending armies, although it would have remained a purely localized European war pitting Russia and France against Germany and Austria-Hungary had not England interfered and expanded the spheres of military operations. England repeatedly emerged as the chief culprit of the war in Troeltsch's writings, to be replaced in the immediate post-war period by a new chief villain, France.[40] Second, the dividing line between the armed combatant and the unarmed civilian was disappearing, with nonmilitary civilians increasingly feeling intense hostility towards the armed enemy, and vice versa. This was a step towards the twentieth-century phenomenon of "total war." Third, it was an economic and commercial hunger-war, a blockade to starve and weaken Germany into submission; as partial explanation for this effort Troeltsch cited the Entente powers' long resentment of Germany's economic ascendancy since Bismarck's time. Further, hostilities had also become a war of lies, a *Lugenkrieg*, concocted by Germany's enemies to inspire their own homefolk as well as unaligned neutrals against trumped-up German evils. And finally, the conflict had become a clash of cultures and spirits, a *Kulturkrieg* in which not only hack propagandists but also intellectual leaders and renowned writers were enlisting in a veritable crusade against the German spirit—a moral holy war against the essence of Germanness itself.[41]

Troeltsch was especially preoccupied with the *Lugenkrieg* and *Kulturkrieg* aspects, what he called "the war of the quill and the spirit."[42] He predicted these would be the greatest impediment to renewed mutual understanding in the post-war peace. Especially after the Marne offensive had failed in the fall of 1914, the Great War became transformed from one of soldiers and guns to a war of peoples and ideas.[43] As military mobility ground to a halt, the war of propaganda intensified.

Already during the early stages of armed hostilities Troeltsch observed what social psychologists in our own time have confirmed, that "participation of whole nations was more essential during World War I than during any previous war."[44] Troeltsch complained that the "atrocious campaign of suggestion" against the German nation involved "the most grotesque and crude" assertions; "the reader's flesh is made to creep by stories of Huns, barbarians, child-murderers, and cannibals."[45] French, Russian, and especially British propagandists were ingeniously manufacturing lies about the "culturally hostile, inhuman character of the Germans," cleverly but maliciously distorting Germany as

> a great antidemocratic, authoritarian, militaristic bugaboo. . . . [It is said to be] a land of reaction, of violence, of the apotheosis of the state and of anti-individualism, of inhuman political coer-

cion, of the official rubber-stamping of opinion, of class control, of hardly disguised princely absolutism, of a bound, ignoble, slavish mentality, of a constantly obsequious disposition, of crudeness and force, of non-commissioned officers and underling officials, of spiritual narrowness and coarseness, of hungry poverty and a constantly growing acquisitiveness, of unchristian attitudes and liberal theology, and of bad taste and rudeness. . . . All these abominable apparitions [are] concentrated in the horror of militarism, representing the enslavement of the individual, the glorification of power, and the principal menace to the world.[46]

"How could intelligent, experienced, and honorable men concoct such an ocean of lies and slanders?" Troeltsch vociferously demanded; "has the world become a madhouse, a monstrosity of malice and vileness? Is the devil himself loose in the world . . . deluding both clever and stupid alike?"[47]

Troeltsch found his answers in history. The elevation of the nation-state principle over many centuries to the level of absolute political dogma, together with the more or less concomitant democratization or politicization of the masses, had turned modern war into an ideological *Volkskrieg*. To an unprecedented degree, propaganda was required in order that participants in war would view their own war aims as righteous and just and their enemies' war aims as loathsome and insidious. Troeltsch charged (probably accurately, for the most part) that this veneer of propaganda was a fantasy world created for the masses, that whether the regimes of England, France, Russia, and Italy were monarchical or republican, actual political decisions lay in the hands of relatively small coteries. "The motivation of these affairs," he contended, "had to remain essentially a question of power politics."[48] Nevertheless, the facade of the *Kulturkrieg* remained—a stageshow to keep the masses involved and mobilized.

What was to be done against the anti-German *Lugenkrieg*? What should be done, Troeltsch asked, to combat the enemy's attempt to "disguise the power struggle as a spiritual and moral one?"[49] Gerhard Ritter is perhaps right when he suggests that "war propaganda develops virtuosos of lying."[50] Troeltsch, however, resisted this temptation. "We cannot return like for like," he admonished.[51] Despite Allied distortions and phoney propaganda, German morale-building efforts should be conducted "without the necessity of having to descend into regions of gradually disgusting polemics and abuses."[52] Besides, since "the days of August" Germany had become a land of brothers and required no artificial fomentation about alleged enemy evils to unite it.[53] Consequently, Troeltsch brought his learning to the defense of "the ideas of 1914," more intent on telling the truth about Germany than telling lies about the enemy. In an academic fashion he addressed himself to correcting those Entente conceptions of German culture which were distinguished by a curious mixture of "much misunderstanding and caricature" together with the erudite methodology and scientific method in which Germans themselves had pioneered.[54]

Troeltsch's statement of German war aims was simple: "We want only the free development of our individuality [as a nation], and we are fighting only against its strangulation, so we have no need of a *Kulturkrieg* against anyone else, whereas, on the contrary, our enemies are leading their peoples in a war of aggression, which they attempt to disguise as a defensive war through propaganda."[55] He exhorted his countrymen "to become more German than we were."[56] Germany's real strength, in fact, lay in its traditional beliefs and customs, not in its weapons of war.[57] "Become what you are," was his simple prescription.[58] No one—individual person or individual nation—could ever realize the full range of human values, so it was therefore incumbent to develop those values which arose in one's own particular historical conditions. As a variation on Voltaire's injunction to cultivate one's own garden, the requirement of the German nation as a whole should be *"taking stock of ourselves and deeply immersing ourselves in the essence of the German spirit."*[59]

The theme of Germany's not being "Western"—of "Western civilization" stopping at the Rhine—became exceptionally pronounced because of the war.[60] Troeltsch readily accepted the contention of Allied propaganda that Germany was different from the world of the French and the Anglo-Americans. As we have earlier seen in his philosophy of history, he maintained that not since the eighteenth-century Enlightenment had Europe enjoyed a semblance of spiritual unity.[61] During the war he delved beneath the surface of an assumed universal European culture, demonstrating the existence of a heterogeneity of various national subcultures. Troeltsch maintained not only that German values were distinct from those of Western Europe but also that between England and France there were radical cleavages of principle and temperament, with even Anglo-Saxon culture not a unified whole but a contradiction of opposites.[62]

Troeltsch's overriding preoccupation, however, was to explain that "the modern German world truly had its own special rudimentary principles and could not be subjected to foreign ones."[63] Typical of this scholarly correction of anti-German wartime caricatures was an essay incorporated into *Deutschland und der Weltkrieg*, an anthology of wartime pieces which included works by other eminent scholars such as Otto Hintze, Hans Delbrück, Gustav von Schmoller, Erich Marcks, and Friedrich Meinecke. In "The Spirit of German Culture" Troeltsch insisted that in order to characterize fairly a nation's way of life one could not look at a few randomly selected features but had to examine all important aspects of that culture. This he himself did in comprehensively commenting on German religion, art, music, philosophy, science, historical scholarship, literature, and poetry, all within the existential context of the prevailing economy, social and military structure, administration, educational system, and politics.[64] He offered this survey without contention or rancor, in the spirit that "the great national cultures all have their merits and their drawbacks, and the earth has room for them all."[65] Admittedly, he certainly did play up the attractiveness of German cultures, but in his comparisons of Germany with other nations this innately tolerant man of compromise did not, even in wartime, deride the uniqueness or worth of that which was non-German.[66]

One of Troeltsch's fundamental premises was the distinction between "*Kultur*" and "*Zivilisation*," which may be illustrated by comparing the German and Anglo-Saxon ways of life. Anglo-Saxon (and even French) "civilization" suggested "the natural right of the individual, and through it control of the state, freedom of the churches, the private character of personal beliefs, and the influence of public opinion on government and private life."[67] On the other hand, "*Kultur*" — which Troeltsch regretted as being "endlessly exposed to ridicule by the second-rate [Entente] press as '*Kultur* with a K' " — was rooted in the German world view and history, in Lutheranism and the national church, in German thought and feeling, implying "something romantically, individualistically irrational, the idea of self-development of the individual and the nation."[68] Decisive in determining the configurations of this German *Kultur* was a turbulent history, including chaos and desolation during the Thirty Years' War, the perpetual Austrian-led endorsement of political particularism, a burst of intellectual creativity since the eighteenth century, the ascendancy of Prussia culminating in the achievements of Bismarck, and the nineteenth-century disruptions of industrialization and social fomentation. Deep within, however, the "inner being of the German people" rested upon "an extraordinary instinct for order, combined with strict discipline and an earnest sense of duty."[69] The essence of German *Kultur* was the fact that "the German is by nature a metaphysician and melancholy brooder."[70] Given this, Troeltsch felt obligated, even in the midst of war, to explicate various German manifestations of *Kultur* that might seem far removed from armed hostilities.

This innate and crucial German metaphysical tendency revealed itself in many ways but especially in religion, which was intimately connected with the political state. Unlike the "Anglo-Saxon separation of politico-social civilization and private individual spiritual training," German culture tended to shun religious disestablishmentarianism and freedom of conscience as too atomistic and inorganic a way of life.[71] The sublime creations of German music likewise illustrated for Troeltsch "all that is unutterable and inexpressible in the German condition, simplicity and heroism, cheerfulness and melancholy, faith and struggle, ambiguity and intuition," all facets of the German term "*Kultur*," which itself was untranslatable into foreign modes of thinking.[72] German plastic art also, with its devotion to "substance, expression, [and] movement"—in the tradition of Dürer, Holbein, Grünewald, and Rembrandt—stood in marked contrast to those non-German artistic styles that emphasized "line, form, symmetry and delicacy."[73] German idealistic philosophy, too, as created by Leibniz, Kant, and Fichte, had an immense influence upon the German character. This idealism, often contemptuously criticized in anti-German war propaganda, actually was so well esteemed by the European intelligentsia, in Troeltsch's opinion, that "we had no need to go to war for the sake of our divergent philosophies."[74] And just as philosophy had been often misunderstood, so too had Germany's historical scholarship, with its focus upon the political state and opposition to "the democratic fiction that the state is an arrangement of individuals for their own security and happiness."[75] Anglo-French critics had failed to appreciate the merits of German historical scholarship because "they measure all foreign states by their private moral rules," assuming their own peculiar standards to be universally binding.[76] The most misunderstood feature of German *Kultur*, however, was the idea of freedom.

The Germans are said not to be a free people, Troeltsch observed, but that is a judgment made by foreign standards. "The world must get rid of the absolute tyranny of the concept of freedom of the western powers," he urged, contending that "the modern idea of freedom is no unequivocal dogma of reason but the result of modern political, social, and intellectual developments, and on that account quite certainly something originally different in all the great modern nations. It is thus really not so simple as today's propagandists claim."[77] Just as Troeltsch denied a universally binding "logic" or "reason," he denied that "freedom" was other than a variegated product of history. As a historicist, Troeltsch soundly repudiated the attitude that "freedom" was a monolithic dogmatic and moral ideal—as represented, for example, by the "*Gottin der Freiheit*," the Statue of Liberty in New York harbor—rather than a historically determined and culturally conditioned acquisition.[78]

Although it took the war to bring the German *Volk* to a political consciousness that German *Kultur* was so different from Western European civilization, the roots of this split went back to the breakup of the medieval synthesis and the subsequent different historical experiences of the various European nationalities.[79] The English idea of freedom, for example, had roots in medieval Anglo-Saxon history, Puritan ideas as well as the seventeenth-century Puritan Revolution, the parliamentary victories over the Stuarts, the philosophy of John Locke, the emergence of utilitarianism, and a strong British aristocratic tradition. The French idea of freedom, on the other hand, was rooted most specifically in the great revolution of 1789, which, with its slogans of *égalité*, *liberté*, and *fraternité*, was a violent overthrow of the abuses and injustices of the *ancien régime* including a bourgeois abolition of aristocratic privileges. Also important were a rationalistic Enlightenment, a strong anticlerical tradition, and a favorable bias towards scepticism.

German history and the German spirit, however, though sharing some European experiences, had given the German meaning of freedom different nuances. Some of the important influences were the devastation of the Thirty Years' War, a more religious Enlightenment than in the West, German idealistic philosophy and German romanticism, political upheavals in Germany during the Napoleonic period including the blossoming of German nationalism in the War of Liberation, and a late nineteenth-century form of developed industrial capitalism rather than an earlier Western European industrial capitalism or even the commercial capitalism of preceding centuries.[80] Made more self-conscious of their own national traditions by the *Lugenkrieg* directed against them, Germans had now become more aware of their peculiar concept of freedom as "an independent and conscious affirmation of, combined with an active sympathy towards, a supra-individual public spirit; the freedom of a voluntary commitment to the totality, and a personal living originality of the individual within this whole; the freedom of the common spirit and of discipline, both resting together on self-surrender to those ideas closely bound up with our entire ethical, religious nature, which is so deeply different from that of the English and the French."[81]

German freedom combined an emphasis on personal development and fulfillment with the growth and progress of the entire society and body politic. This freedom was not a rationalistically conceived *égalité*—an equality of atomistically independent individuals—but service by a unique individual to an organic whole. Self-actualization (*Selbstbildung*) occurred, in other words, not in separation from others but in the context of a web of human relationships, of which the ultimate whole was the state. And the state was not a bureaucratic, administrative structure but a living, organic entity with a mystical quality.[82]

Within this entity parliaments might play a limited role, but in Troeltsch's opinion "they are not the essence of freedom. The franchise and the collaboration of people in government breed a political maturity; but this is not the freedom which we have in mind. German freedom will never be purely political; it will always be bound up with the idealistic thought of duty and the romantic thought of individuality."[83] Parliamentary government was no universal categorical imperative but a bias of certain Western peoples given their own historical conditions.[84] The German idea of freedom had no need to rest upon "mere parliamentary institutions," nor could it be "that of a western style individualism, but rather only the freedom of empathy with an organic state."[85]

So important did Troeltsch consider the preservation and further development of this double-pronged German concept of freedom—the fulfillment of the individual as well as the state—that he cautioned against its dilution during war by a turn to "an idea-less realism, or even an idea-less 'patriotism.'"[86] Consider, then, how much more he must have resented the Allied propaganda effort, which portended an imposition of the Western style of freedom upon a defeated Germany. "Above all, we wish to gain and build up this freedom ourselves," Troeltsch told his countrymen, "and not receive it as a gift from foreigners—most certainly not as the result of defeat, as the hostile literature so often consolingly promises."[87] Because of powerful shared wartime experiences, not because of abstract theories and doctrines, the cherished German idea of freedom had become incorporated into "the ideas of 1914" for which Germany was fighting.[88] All Germany wanted to do, Troeltsch maintained, was to develop its own *Kultur* without interference from others.

> German freedom has no craving for world domination, either materially or spiritually. Germany wants freedom of coexistence for various peoples and not the extermination of different possibilities of development nor stereotyping in the name of some alleged law. In this sense, we believe that we are the people who are fighting for the true and genuine progress of mankind, which does violence to none and gives freedom to all.[89]

In contrast Troeltsch saw as the motive of the anti-German crusade the intent to ruin Germany, to repeat the devastation suffered during the Thirty Years' War. The Entente propagandized that they sought to liberate the nation of Goethe and Beethoven from the brutal hegemony of Prussian barbarism, but they did not realize, Troeltsch protested, that from the German viewpoint "the antithesis of Weimar and Potsdam, about which so many yarns have been spun, is really nonexistent."[90] "The empty space in the middle of Europe should once again be filled not with arms," Troeltsch informed a wartime audience, "but with thoughts—then all would be forgiven!"[91] He sarcastically rejected the view he detected in the British press that "the freedom of the world, insofar as it was possible, should be an English freedom, and that world peace should be a *Pax Britannica.*"[92] He was greatly upset that English Christians regarded themselves as a chosen people whose mission it was to save the world,[93] and when America entered the war Troeltsch's distress increased. He told the assembly in the Abgeordnetenhaus in Berlin in May 1917 that the American propagandists were reiterating the moralistic lies of the English—that the crusade against Germany stood for "freedom, justice, and humanity, for democracy, world peace, and anti-militarism."[94] With the litany of lies raised against Germany expanded to include the self-righteous war aims of the Americans, Troeltsch believed the insanity of the *Lugenkrieg* had reached a peak.

As the conflict dragged on over the years, the war-weary Troeltsch expressed the hopes of his countrymen for an end to hostilities, for a "peace of self-determination" and for a "Germany warmed and enlightened by a free and independent place in the sun."[95] But these hopes were rudely shattered. The German people woke up in the early days of November 1918 to a series of abrupt shocks. Germany had lost the war. An internal political revolution had overthrown the monarchy, abolishing the German Empire and the Bismarckian constitution. And soon the infamous *Diktat* was imposed upon a defeated German nation.

Weimar Politics

Troeltsch greeted the Armistice of 11 November 1918 with both relief and uneasiness. Certainly glad that the fighting was over, he was understandably distraught at the conditions in which Germany now found itself. "The collapse of Germany is today an accomplished fact," he regretfully recognized.[96] The army had collapsed. The allies in the field had collapsed. Germany's very political system had collapsed. "Defeat and revolution have thus become our fate," he sadly announced; "we no longer hold our fate in our own hands."[97]

The outstanding result immediately clear to this "most perceptive of contemporary observers" in November 1918 was that the "exceptional position" of militarism as a way of life in Germany was dead.[98] "The construction of the state and society on the hitherto prevailing Prussian military frame of mind and its corresponding spirit" had been shattered by the war beyond possible resuscitation.[99] In other words, "German militarism . . . [as] a political institution, a decisive element in the constitution of the state," was now a thing of the past.[100] Troeltsch appeared convinced that the war had so damaged the institution of German militarism that a restoration of the *status quo ante bellum*, with its militaristic-aristocratic foundation, was impossible.[101]

During the war, as we have previously noted, Troeltsch had patriotically rejected as a fiction the "two Germanies" concept of a regnant Prussian militarism barbarizing an otherwise decent Germany. Within the week after the Armistice, however, with the need to maintain wartime morale gone and his satiation with the horrors of the war at a peak, his latent antipathy towards the military establishment surfaced. He criticized sharply the General Staff's usurpation of political power, the orientation of the officer corps towards self-seeking glory and prestige, and the tendency of German militarism to have become an end in itself.[102] "With Ludendorff, a Napoleonic spirit stormed incredibly brilliantly through the world," he noted, "but without any trace of the political competence and knowledge of a Napoleon."[103] In the wake of the Armistice, Troeltsch publicly decried the bankruptcy of the "foolhardy policies of the adventurer and the cadet" [*verwegene Abenteuer- und Kadetenpolitik*], the politics of militarism pursued by Ludendorff and the General Staff and hidden "behind a hundred masks."[104]

Almost simultaneously with his acquiescence in the collapse of German militarism, however, Troeltsch uneasily perceived a paradox about war's end, namely, that "this Armistice was a veiled capitulation, and no armistice."[105] Repeatedly over the months ahead, he retracted his premature impression that the war was actually over. For example, in January 1919 he stated that although actual military operations might have come to a halt, "the 'end of the war' was really an illusion."[106] In March he reiterated that real peace had not yet been attained; and during the summer of 1919 he still complained that despite the German people's longing for peace—even despite Germany's recent signing of the Peace of Versailles—there really was no peace.[107] By now he had come to put the word "Peace" consistently in quotation marks. Again, in October 1919, nearly a year after the Armistice had been signed and four months after the signing of the "Versailles 'Peace,'" Troeltsch expressed his unmistakably disillusioned view that "the war is [still] convulsing all over and has really not ended."[108]

Rather than attributing this extension of "the insanity of the world" to impersonal "historical forces," Troeltsch placed the blame squarely upon the shoulders of the Entente powers.[109] Germany itself was not responsible for the current miseries and chaos. The constant harassment of Germany by its enemies (Troeltsch did not mince words by calling them "former enemies") was the single most important factor to be eliminated in contemporary politics before relative harmony and normalcy could be restored. "The policies of the Entente," Troeltsch insisted, "are diabolical; there is no more trace of . . . humanitarian platitudes" such as those mouthed by the American President Wilson during the last months of the war.[110]

If the terms of the Armistice had stunned the Germans, the terms of the Treaty of Versailles crushed beyond all measure their hopes for a just peace. Troeltsch would have totally disagreed with the recently expressed judgment that "intrinsically there was nothing wrong with the Treaty of Versailles. It was neither unjust nor unworkable."[111] He himself spoke of the Versailles Treaty as "the work of the devil," as intending the "helotization of Germany."[112] It was, in his impassioned view—which was probably shared by most of his countrymen—"a peace of revenge, of deceit, of force."[113] Someone has said that each new peace treaty in world history but creates the conditions for the next war. Similarly, Troeltsch cited approvingly a pamphlet appearing in Switzerland in February 1919 that claimed "even stupid men realize that there is no peace, and clever men know that each present hour is only an unpleasant pause between the great storm which departs and the yet greater storm which approaches."[114] Adding his own rhetorical postscript, Troeltsch remarked: "Will this second, greater storm actually come?"[115]

The so-called War Guilt Question was the aspect of the treaty that most bothered Troeltsch.[116] "The dogma of German [war] guilt is established as fact in the modern court of inquisition," he bitterly complained, "as strongly as medieval courts of inquisition were certain of the existence of the devil."[117] It was simply a matter of faith, to be accepted and not disputed, and in Troeltsch's opinion, a patently sham pretext to shift the blame for a horrendous war exclusively onto the Germans.[118] He recommended that no political speech should close without criticism of the *Schuldfrage* and urged the German press to constantly remind the public about it, to "hammer it in."[119]

Despite the harsh, unacceptable terms of the Versailles Treaty, Troeltsch did acquiesce in its signing because it was a "decision between peace or a new war."[120] The Weimar government simply lacked support from the people for Brockdorff-Rantzau's obstructionist policies of brinksmanship. "An absolute need for peace impregnates the masses," Troeltsch felt at the time; "the people are physically and spiritually broken by all the suffering and turmoil of the recent past, especially by this period of the armistice which was utilized by the Entente in a masterly manner to spiritually wear down Germany and enhance confusion."[121] The need for a return to a day-to-day normalcy was immense. With the signing of the Versailles Treaty Troeltsch clearly saw that "world power politics is now at an end for us, for a long time and probably altogether."[122] Panoramically surveying past German catastrophes from medieval times to the present, he fatalistically concluded that "with each great attempt to create our state we have been rebuffed."[123] The present catastrophes in Germany were not unique; the Germans in their history had been consistently disaster prone.

Troeltsch's dismal outlook was no personal quirk. Germany was truly in desperate condition after the war. During the winter of 1918–1919 and into the coming year the domestic situation was horrendous. In late winter of 1919 Troeltsch accurately summarized conditions with his remark that "Germany is physically and morally exhausted, weary, and confused."[124] Outlining the dimensions of the ominous gloom into which Germany had been cast, he vividly described daily sights in post-war Berlin, portraying the city as

> filthy, surfeited with scrap paper, the ground-level parts of buildings pasted with all manner of placards, soldiers on the streets playing barrel-organs or trying to peddle odds and ends, the faces of most people full of apprehension, a delirious search for pleasure on the faces of others, numerous window-shutters closed for fear of plundering, other stores converted into makeshift living quarters, and everywhere soaring prices together with the depreciation of paper money. In the midst of everything, motor cars roar back and forth with masses of soldiers, protective units of youthful, smoking soldiers on patrol, who garrison military barracks whose justification and continued existence occupy their thoughts more than anything else. In this atmosphere are generated repeated disturbances and outbreaks of violence, offering to clever politicians the readily available means and the masses for a new revolution. Such misery is precisely the prerequisite for trouble.[125]

That spring, in discussing the significance of the normally joyous Easter season, Troeltsch remained gloomy: "This Pentecost which lies just behind us was the most cheerless Pentecost in a hundred years, perhaps the most cheerless in all of German history. The future is completely unclear and murky, and not even the recent past is generally understood."[126] What especially impressed him about the German domestic situation were the frantic fluctuations and oscillations of events and trends, which he tried to depict in his regular contributions to *Der Kunstwart*—twenty-eight articles in 1919 alone. At one point he offhandedly remarked that "these letters never really have been very cheerful."[127] This is indeed an understatement. Typical of the prevailing mood of "widespread disillusionment, a longing for the good—or at any rate, the better—old days" was a remark he overheard concerning the colors of the new national flag, the same as those of the 1848 experiment in democracy: "Red stands for the present, black for the future, but gold for the past."[128]

The 1848 flag had come from revolution. The 1919 flag likewise, but the revolution was strange indeed. True, the Kaiser had abdicated, the government and the empire itself had fallen, and a republic had been declared. Nevertheless, it was not uncommon then, nor is it rare now, to hear these events culminating in 9 November 1918 described as the "so-called revolution," or the "pseudo-revolution." Certainly Troeltsch himself was of this persuasion.

"No man dead for Kaiser and Reich!"[129] This casual remark, which he made in recollecting his personal experiences during the November Revolution, forcefully expresses the ease with which the old order had been toppled. It had simply not seemed worth defending. The revolutionaries themselves, moreover, were not impelled by coherent ideology and planning; this had been "a revolution which was not born out of ideas."[130] The November events were not comparable, in his judgment, to the well-known English and French revolutions, which had been replete with social, religious, philosophical, and ethical overtones, although the German Revolution did have a parallel in the recent Russian Revolution of 1917 insofar as both directly emanated from faulty war policies and their consequences.[131] At any rate, Troeltsch thought that the German Revolution "was a great misfortune," especially to have occurred when it did, for "the revolution broke the backbone of the Reich in the most horrible moment of its history."[132]

Troeltsch placed exceptional emphasis upon the National Assembly, which was to provide Germany with a new, republican constitution. Comparing the current post-war complexities with those discussed in Bismarck's *Gedanken und Erinnerungen*, Troeltsch made the striking contrast that present problems were not to be solved largely by one man but that "the National Assembly should be today's new Bismarck."[133] And the ideology behind the solutions was to be democracy. Thus, in this double emphasis upon parliament and democracy, Troeltsch performed one of the most remarkable of the several significant reversals in thought of his career.[134]

One needs only to recall some of his typical antidemocratic, antiparliamentary wartime statements to appreciate this *volte-face*. For example, in his article on "The Spirit of German *Kultur*" published in 1915, Troeltsch had emphasized that

> the Germans are above all a monarchical people. . . . Only under monarchical leadership can the work of unification and consolidation of a nation confronted with difficult dangers be carried out. . . . No parliamentary majority can accomplish that. As great as the advantages of a parliamentary form of government

may be for the discovery and training of political talent as well as for the political development of a people in general, it is hazardous for the determinations of the military leadership of a youthful state. Consequently, the demand for parliamentary government is not very great in Germany, completely aside from the legal and historical difficulties of such a form of government in a confederation of states.[135]

An antipathy towards parliamentary, democratic forms of government was also evident in his belief that "German historical scholarship opposes by all means, as emphatically as Plato had done in his day, the democratic fiction that the state is an arrangement of individuals for the purpose of their own security and prosperity."[136]

In 1919, however, though not necessarily unequivocally rejecting the view that "we Germans are not cut out for democracy, generally not [even] for politics," Troeltsch assured his countrymen that the experiment should be made, that Germany should try democracy.[137] "We will learn it," he urged, "even though it means unpleasantness and pains and much confusion."[138] No more striking contrast could be found to his own wartime strictures against the "assault of western democracy" than the advice he now gave in the summer of 1919 that

> if something should really give us again freedom and dignity, order and soundness, and economic and spiritual expansiveness, it could only be the National Constituent Assembly, and therefore democracy. We have unalterably come to democracy. . . . We *must* learn how to deal with this political form, and above all we must have the *will* to do so.
>
> Now that certainly means a fundamental transformation of the whole situation, especially our intellectual reappraisal regarding the state and society.[139]

Was Troeltsch a true democrat? It seems likely that he was a sane, concerned patriot intent on helping to solve his country's problems and that democracy seemed to him the best currently available means. Instinctively, Troeltsch rejected the dynamics of what today's social psychologists call "the self-fulfilling prophecy," whereby by believing something will happen—in this case, that democracy would not work —one unconsciously and inadvertently acts in ways that guarantee the anticipated result—here, democracy's failure.[140] It is true that this scholar who insisted within the week following the November Revolution and the signing of the Armistice that "our deliverance will happen only through the fundamental principles of pure democracy," does appear in subsequent writings to be a typical *Vernunftrepublikaner*, that is, merely a "rational republican" whose heart and soul are not fully committed to democratic institutions and processes in a republican Germany. He himself recognized this, suggesting in the fall of 1919 that there was some validity in the often heard remark that Germans were a people long accustomed to authoritarian rule, that they were not gifted for self-governing, that fundamentally Germany had now become "a democracy without democrats, a republic without republicans."[141] But his basic common sense, together with his historical understanding and increased political insight, persuaded him that glumly proclaiming that Germany lacked a solid democratic tradition would only make matters worse.

Rather than regarding democracy as an alien imposition upon a defeated Germany, Troeltsch now suggested that it could be considered as "the natural consequence" of various historical forces extending back a hundred years or more, including the steep demographic increase during the past century, the economic and social processes of modern industrialization, a growing system of mass education and the partially resulting politicization of unprecedented numbers of people, universal mass conscription and compulsory military service, and so forth.[142] All these historical forces and trends had ineluctably brought Germany to the point in its history where democracy had to be accepted as a fact of life. "Though today's constitution and laws might be temporary," Troeltsch wrote at the end of 1919, "German democracy itself is irreversible."[143]

Heroically he now attempted to convince his countrymen that democracy was indeed compatible with German traditions and not a historical aberration. Admitting that "democratization brings new problems for the spirit and intellect," he maintained that these problems were merely "those of the organization and promulgation" of this largely untried life-style in Germany and not radical problems regarding the essence of German *Kultur* itself.[144] "Does this fundamental upheaval [of becoming democratic] signify a revolution of the German spirit and of German *Kultur*?" he candidly asked; was democracy an alien imposition against the course of German history and traditions?[145] The answer he gave was: Not necessarily. Democracy in Germany in 1919 could be either an alien form superimposed by foreign influences, or, if managed correctly, it could be a less radical change within German *Kultur* itself, utilizing and rearranging innate ingredients. We can learn, he suggested, from "the greatest and soundest democracy in the world, that of North America. . . . There, democracy is conservative."[146] He even enlarged the examples of "conservative democracies" to include England and France.[147] Endorsing Viscount James Bryce's contention in *Modern Democracies* that the democratic form of government need not be revolutionary and drastically innovative but rather could be a conservative, historically hallowed organization of a nation's human resources, Troeltsch recommended that Germany "set up the ideal of a conservative democracy."[148] It was possible to create a conservative style of democracy peculiarly German, linked to German historical traditions in a way whereby "spirit and *Kultur* retain a depth of soul exactly as formerly. The spiritual content remains afterwards as before united to historical substance and tradition."[149]

In this articulation of what might be called the German idea of democracy, Troeltsch emphasized that "political thought must be closely tied to social knowledge and ideas of social reform; for a merely political democracy, which embodies only basic principles and forms, has entirely no meaning and no efficacy."[150] Consequently, German democracy had to take into account social forces as old as aristocracy and as new as socialism. The aristocracy, challenged as the foundation of German society by recent economic and political pressures, had come to appear anachronistic in a rapidly modernizing world. An emerging aristocracy of talent, however, would be indispensable in the viability of modern German democracy.[151] Further, although in Troeltsch's opinion there were no logical or historical reasons why democracy and socialism had to be linked, he thought that in the present circumstances it would be appropriate to do so, bluntly stating that "German democracy must be socialistic."[152] A democratic Germany was being led towards socialism not by theory or enthusiasm but by economic necessity, by "the world situation of the modern economy, the chaos of shattered German production, and the psychology of . . . the working masses."[153] In addition to including both aristocratic and socialistic elements in its fabric, Troeltsch gave the future German style of democracy several further mandates: to place a positive emphasis on the idea of the *Völkerbund* and a negative emphasis on militarism; to acknowledge that the Prussian bureaucracy and army as foundations of the former Bismarckian state had been demolished; and to construct the new democratic state not out of theoretical doctrines or dogmas, as had been the tendency in 1948, but in the context of the current situation in Germany.[154]

Unfortunately, Troeltsch's lofty, idealistic hopes for a smooth implementation of German democracy were not fulfilled—though they were not abruptly dashed to the ground as had been the hopes of the participants in the Frankfort National Assembly seventy years earlier. The new National Constituent Assembly convened at Weimar on 6 February 1919, eventually producing a constitution promulgated on 11 August 1919. It survived for fourteen years, until the beginning of the Hitler period in 1933. Within this framework of a democratic republic, however, a myriad of forces contended against the republic itself and against its democratic search for order.

At the start of its career, the Weimar Republic was confronted by a host of complex, bewildering problems, with economic ones clearly the most immediately pressing.[155] "The financial situation of the Reich is in convulsions," Troeltsch wrote early in 1919, and a year later he could still insist that of all the great governmental problems "the first and most difficult task is the ordering of finances."[156] Economic miseries begun during the war, when Germany had become a "closed commercial state," increasingly mounted, while debates over solutions accomplished little or nothing.[157] Troeltsch's prediction made in the spring of 1917 came true; the bread-ration card—the symbol of austere wartime economic conditions—was around long after peace had come.[158]

What the economy needed most was a generally enhanced productivity, but everywhere Troeltsch saw instead a terribly shrunken interest in production, an *Arbeitsunwilligkeit*.[159] There were widespread transportation problems, industrial coal shortages, threats of strikes and work stoppages, and misunderstandings between the food-producing rural areas and the food-consuming urban centers. But more important, beneath all these relatively measurable economic factors lurked a disastrous attitude, what Troeltsch called "work-timidity" or "work-aversion" (*Arbeitsscheu*).[160] The old European system with its productive work ethic had placed a positive emphasis on the meaning of work, whether that of the soldier, the artist, the bureaucrat, or the intellectual.[161] Now, however, four years of war had changed values radically. Troeltsch made a gloomy diagnosis. With Germany's apparently irreparable loss of a thriving economy, a viable political system, and an unfettered optimistic belief in the possibilities of progress, he saw the will to work (*Arbeitswillen*) also destroyed.[162] Because of the war this old work ethic had been more disrupted in Germany than in most countries, certainly least of all in America.[163]

Paradoxically, despite this economic morass and widespread work-aversion, Troeltsch also detected an almost neurotic preoccupation with material things. "Interests have completely turned from spiritual to material concerns," he regretfully noted, although he certainly did appreciate the people's reasons.[164] Under severe economic depriva-tions, it would be hard to imagine their top priority being spiritual regeneration. And yet, Troeltsch exhorted, "the task of the moral and spiritual recovery of our people" was a mandatory responsibility of the present German leadership, despite—or perhaps because of—the fact that life had virtually become "a struggle for existence, a groping from descent to descent, a prospectless and thoughtless desperation."[165] Al-though the government might not be able comprehensively to change the spiritual atmosphere, Troeltsch insisted that needed changes could be effected in certain specific areas, such as educational policies (in-cluding university reforms) or church organization and church-state relations.[166]

Numerous other responsibilities and tasks faced the government, such as ordering the relationships between the Reich and the regions, most notably clarifying Prussia's truncated role in the Weimar system vis-à-vis Prussia's former status of decisive leadership in the period of Bismarck and William II.[167] Further, the government had to create a militia, satisfactorily resolving the dilemma of being caught, on the one hand, without adequate armed forces for protection and of facing, on the other hand, the fear that reconstructed armed units might be used in a counterrevolution. And at least initially there was the sensi-tive task of returning the workers' and soldiers' councils to merely advisory and supervisory functions, devoid of any real political deci-sion-making powers. The tasks of government were legion, with "each day having its own problems."[168]

Constant foreign harassment aggravated the difficulties of returning Germany to some semblance of normalcy. Troeltsch's political writ-ings unquestionably support Ranke's dictum that domestic politics are significantly linked to foreign affairs.[169] "These restraints and aggrava-tions from outside are indeed the essential reasons for the frightfully difficult development and settlement of the German Revolution," Troeltsch asserted.[170]

It should be emphasized that Troeltsch continued to speak of the November Revolution in the present tense. It was for him an ongoing affair, not restricted to a day or a month in the past, but a continuous process whereby Germany sought to rehabilitate itself and find a stable, acceptable order. In general, however, the government seemed to muddle along undistinguishedly; its occasional minor accomplishments were not sufficient to extinguish ever-persistent public criticisms of the administration, its personnel, and more radically the parliamentary, republican system itself.[171] Troeltsch was continuously preoccupied with counterrevolutionary tendencies, especially the daily, piecemeal, bit-by-bit accumulation of incidents and events that wore at and eroded the very foundation of the new democratic republic.

There was no question that post-war Germany needed a national restoration. The German *Volk* had become so tired and exhausted from constant wartime and post-war crises that the "mere organization" of parliamentary democracy was not sufficient aid.[172] Yet that was the main fare Germans were offered. To Troeltsch this was a shallow solution, and he lamented that "the great moralistic upswing which many expected is missing."[173] The democratic republic he had finally endorsed was not working as a system. Consequently, throughout the *Kunstwart* articles one finds repeatedly the tensions and ambiguities of a mind which endorsed the *idea* of the new system of Weimar politics but which also frequently rejected the *realities* of the idea's implementation.[174]

Probably the most irritating element of the domestic political scene for Troeltsch was the insidiousness of partisan politics.[175] He readily admitted that given the present system "it is not possible to govern without parties," that "there must be parties. They are the only means of forming a government."[176] Popular self-government in large states required a parliamentary system of government, and parliamentary government meant, in turn, party government. But the perfervid splintering of political parties in Weimar politics was an unhealthy situation, a manifestation of the *Zerrissenheit* condition of Germany, its lack of deep-seated unity. That dozens of parties were at any point in Weimar political history vying for or sharing in political power was an unfortunate updating of the long-standing German phenomenon of *Partikularismus*. For hundreds of years, German politics had been particularistic, generally rooted in territorially based local traditions; the contemporary variation on this theme added the harsh new notes of allegiance to competing and mutually hostile political ideologies, party platforms, and visions of the ideal Germany.

Fractional politics in itself was bad enough, but as Gerhard Ritter has suggested in surveying the post-war European political scene, naturally "there was trouble between extremists and moderates in all the belligerent countries; but only in Germany, unlike the Western countries, did this lead to the formal organization of mutually hostile mass groups, permanently polluting the political atmosphere."[177] Troeltsch acknowledged that although a few large parties might be more desirable than a multitude of splinter groupings, "one cannot create parties at one's pleasure," and the multiplicity of parties in Weimar politics reflected distressingly the many divergencies within the society as a whole.[178] As an ideologically eclectic German Democrat, Troeltsch was willing to support the programs of almost any middle-of-the-road party working for the interests of Germany as a whole, including the moderate demands of the majority socialists—although, as he quipped, this endorsement was hardly very daring because "outside of coal and electricity there was nothing which could be socialized except hunger and misery."[179]

Within this system of Weimar politics—"actually a government of fragmented political parties"—Troeltsch did not find much evidence of the strong leadership Germany needed.[180] He excoriated Weimar political institutions with their "ridiculous and troublesome controls of factional parties" as drawing into government "little men" with "psychological inhibitions" against thinking big.[181] Troeltsch did have some genuine praise for influential politicians like Matthias Erzberger, but his overwhelming opinion was that Erzberger "lives in the horizon of the small man."[182] To his credit, however, Troeltsch did not go so far as many other critics did in *"Der Kampf um die Person Erzberger"* in using this controversial figure as a convenient scapegoat for Germany's woes.[183] In Troeltsch's analysis of the Weimar political process, persons of limited political vision and little or no political experience became members of parties; then coalitions of these motley parties, the *Fraktionen*, governed. In the midst of the extraordinary crises post-war Germany faced, how could things be improved, he mused, when one took a group of former petty shopkeepers, dignified them with new parliamentary titles, and then expected them to run the country.

Faced with persistent foreign harassment and enormous domestic problems, the new parliamentary government—not universally accepted, in addition to its deficiencies in talent—tried to steer a middle-of-the-road course. Constant threats from the extremes of both right and left did not enhance the probabilities of success. Partly systematically, partly instinctively, the foundations of counterrevolution were emerging, as protests against Weimar and what it represented swelled.[184] Regardless of the fundamental lack of homogeneity in the motley "bond between independents, Bolsheviks, literateurs, ideologues, and conservatives," these groupings—and others, such as Pangermans, heavy industrialists, and nationalists—were united in what they opposed.[185] Even if disunited in views about the proper form of German government, the anti-Weimar opposition forces acted in temporary, inadvertent collusion to pull down the edifice of the democratic, parliamentary republic. Apprehensive of this troublesome state of affairs Troeltsch regretfully observed that "the insanities of the right and the left were precipitating crisis after crisis in constantly new ways."[186] Germany was not becoming a democracy, he admonished, "but a spawning ground of revolution."[187]

On the left, radicals clamored that the events triggered by the November Revolution had not yet gone far enough towards the proper goals. The Spartacist uprising and the careers of Karl Liebnecht and Rosa Luxembourg are typical cases in point. Troeltsch felt that Communists were continually trying to bring the masses to the boiling point, as were those socialists who split from the revisionists, "declaring majority rule and democracy to be nonsense."[188] Exceptionally scornful of the pseudo-intellectual left, Troeltsch regarded the combination of "Marx, anarchism, communism, and the unavoidably present Nietzsche"—all melded together in protest against Weimar institutions and values—as "simply nonsensical and self-contradictory rigamarole."[189]

Troeltsch took the threats from the right much more seriously. The growing swell of its agitation was such a persistent theme in early Weimar politics (and one of the most repeated subjects in the *Kunstwart* articles) that by the end of 1919 Troeltsch could remark that it was almost no longer news.[190] "The *Bürgerkrieg* from the right, the 'White Terror,'" had stronger possibilities, in his opinion, than any successful left-wing counterrevolution.[191] Conditions in immediate post-war Germany seemed to him ripe for a conservative counterrevolution and what he called "the time of the dictator."[192]

In his diagnosis of right wing strength, Troeltsch delineated numerous, overlapping political and sociological categories of support—for example, in the German National Party and the German People's Party (the latter containing the remnants of the *Vaterlandspartei*); among Weimar bureaucrats obstructing or even sabotaging the system from within; among East Prussian groupings plotting to secede from what they called the "socialist republic" to set up their own monarchical German state; among the great proprietary landed interests; among farmers (who tended to distrust any politicians currently in power); among Protestant church groups; even among certain urbanites and professional academic circles, and certainly among the students.[193] Unlike the kaleidoscope of ideas and interests which loosely united left-wing agitators against the republic, the right's ideas were relatively simpler: "All misery comes from the Revolution, which has no national conviction and morale, and which forced a fickle Jewish democracy on Germany."[194] Further, the unquestioned dogma at the heart of the rightist cause was "the great historical myth upon which the entire reaction rests, that a victorious army had been treacherously stabbed in the back by unpatriotic comrades on the homefront."[195]

The Jewish question (a "daily growing anti-Semitism") was a major rightist theme.[196] Right-wing forces in early Weimar Germany said so much with such exaggeration about the Jews that Troeltsch was astonished: "What one can hear in private conversations borders on the incredible."[197] Readily admitting (and providing documentation) that the role of Judaism in Germany was exceptionally enhanced because of the November Revolution, Troeltsch proceeded to consol his countrymen that "the real ascendancy of Judaism is probably only a temporary appearance."[198] He admonished his readers that "the whole notion of a consciously induced take-over by 'Judaism' is altogether a fairy tale, which only political children like the Germans could believe and cultivate with the total fervor of their headstrong and near-sighted quarrelsomeness."[199]

Troeltsch's own position on the Jews was ambivalent, to say the least. The attitude which emerges in his article on "The Predominance of Judaism?," for example, reminds one of the "some-of-my-best-friends-are" remarks heard in the United States in the wake of the historic 1954 Supreme Court desegregation decision. One finds Troeltsch suggesting that Jews are not all alike, that some of them are remarkably like the rest of us—even the best of us. After all, a Jew who could discuss Goethe and Beethoven could not be all bad.[200] But on the other hand, Troeltsch was bothered that some Jews still harbored feelings of revenge against alleged oppressors. Although he stressed the desperate need for Germany to rebuild a national culture, he was unwilling to let Jews take the lead, proscribing any disproportionate Jewish influence on the course of German national renewal by casting this "sociological minority" into the role of "not the spiritual leaders, but the zealous commentators and clever transcribers of German leadership."[201]

The long-anticipated right-wing counterrevolution finally came in March 1920—a blow to the state by "praetorians, Junkers, and Pangermans," which is now called simply the Kapp Putsch.[202] Ineptly planned and poorly executed, in Troeltsch's opinion, the Kapp takeover of Berlin's central government seemed to vindicate his remark made sixteen months before that "under no circumstances can there be a Restoration [of the old order] by means of the military."[203] Troeltsch took the ultimate failure of the Putsch as yet another example of the typical German's political ineptness and inability for long-range, detailed political planning. As an example he recounted the incident when Kapp was asked who his new cabinet ministers would be; Kapp replied that he had not yet had time to think about it but would probably have an answer in eight days![204] As events transpired, most of the Reich and the overwhelming portion of the Reichswehr did not participate in the Putsch; the bureaucracy tended to remain loyal to the Republic; a general strike paralyzed Berlin; military support for the takeover collapsed; and Kapp and his fellow-conspirators fled after only five days in power. Perhaps the only gain that could be derived from the Kapp fiasco, Troeltsch speculated, was that its failure might generate a favorable impression abroad that the German people really wanted no part of a reactionary, anti-republican regime.[205]

But even though the counterrevolution was put down, the long-standing problems of the Weimar Republic had not been solved and now seemed even more irritating than before. The Kapp Putsch had been no isolated Berlin episode but a violent trauma that sent shock waves throughout the entire nation. Class divisiveness and the lack of ideological unity among the German people visibly heightened, and critiques of the parliamentary system intensified.[206] New elections were called for, and during the election campaign of May 1920, which he described as "dirty politics," Troeltsch sensed the importance of a vote for the future of the republic itself.[207] As the balloting neared, in an election which presumably would decide whether future Weimar politics followed or repudiated the constitution, Troeltsch ominously noted the evident popularity of the right.[208]

The election results of 6 June 1920 proved Troeltsch's pre-election diagnosis correct. The swing of German politics to the right was unmistakable, with losses most notably suffered by the Social Democrats, Centrists, and German Democrats.[209] So significant was this

"Rechtsbewegung" to Troeltsch that he regarded the election as the symbolic watershed separating two major phases of the German Revolution. "With this summer," he stated, "the German Revolution has entered its second phase."[210] Troeltsch was unconsoled by the insight that revolutionary activities everywhere have a similar logic and structure and that "the history of all revolutions" shows that elements of the reactionary right frequently successfully regroup their forces.[211] From his own viewpoint, writing not as a dispassionate political observer but as a nationalist deeply perturbed over his country's ills, he termed "the demolition of the middle-of-the-road support for the new constitution" a "catastrophe—for that is in truth what it is."[212] Proponents of moderate politics had indeed made mistakes, and no one had been quicker to criticize them than Troeltsch himself, but insofar as the moderates had supported democratic republicanism, "the destruction of the middle therefore signified the endangerment of the Constitution and the Reich."[213]

Repeatedly, in his several dozen remaining *Kunstwart* articles from mid-1920 through the fall of 1922, Troeltsch pressed the point that although "the present constitution is surely not the last word," it was nevertheless the most reasonable one offered so far.[214] His plea for a pledge of allegiance to the republic was neither an endorsement of any current regime nor of the details of the existing system, but an endorsement of the *principle* of a democratic republic.[215] In his view, Germany *needed* a united front which stood for the republic; Germany *needed* to develop a new national feeling of unity; and Germany *needed* to pursue compromise ("the essence of all politics") and to put aside the "bloodthirsty abuses of the election campaign and the beerhalls."[216]

But this was his diagnosis of Germany's needs. The actualities of German politics were something else. Although even the blind could see that "the restoration of the center is in any case the great problem," he admonished that fractional, partisan politics sometimes conditioned one to be "blinder than the blind."[217] Because internal German politics continued to be characterized by divisiveness, moral righteousness, and hatred, by the spring of 1921 Troeltsch became willing to concede "the complete impossibility of the parliamentary-democratic system."[218] He thought the system had simply evolved into an absurdity and openly wondered whether the German people might be suited only for a militaristic monarchy. He interpreted the assassination of Erzberger as a symptom of a widespread poisonous atmosphere in German politics and even anticipated the growth of "a German fascism. . . .

[and] an era of political murders."[219] Walther Rathenau's assassination by right-wing agitators a year later was further compelling evidence of the disastrous internal German instability, as well as an additional sign to foreigners of the methods of "German barbarism" in solving political problems.[220] This chaotic political situation was complicated by the government's continued ineptness in resolving the economic and financial vicissitudes of the day and by the inability to quell the growing mood of distress and disillusionment.[221] The course of the German democratic revolution was going "as wretchedly as it was possible to do so."[222]

These domestic misfortunes were complicated by foreign pressures, by what Troeltsch called "all-consuming bloodsuckers, constant vexations, and perpetual intimidation."[223] In international relations generally he detected harmony only in occasional rhetorical outbursts which in practice were universally denied or contradicted. In such a "sick world," he felt (writing in 1921), there could be no more than ten more years of peace, beyond which no one could dare speculate.[224]

Since the Armistice and the Versailles settlement it had become increasingly clear that "a new system of great world powers" had emerged.[225] Real power was now polarized between the block of Entente states in the West (England, France, the United States) and Russia in the East,[226] with this East-West dichotomy given a new ideological dimension by the institutionalization of Bolshevism in Russia since 1917. On the Western front, real power in international affairs now resided in an "Anglo-Saxon dyarchy," with America—the new "policeman of the world"—the obviously stronger partner.[227] In the East, Troeltsch saw Russia as a gradually diminished threat to Germany because "the pure ideology of communism had . . . lost its spell" in light of the transformation of Bolshevik Russia into "a new feudalism" dominated by a "communist oligarchy."[228]

By the spring of 1921, Troeltsch judged the greatest threats to Germany to be France and England, with the chief culprit, in his view, "the new French Napoleonism," which was principally the French press's resuscitation of the *Kulturkrieg* of 1914–1918 with all the old hackneyed anti-German biases and stereotypes.[229] Behind the "moral mask" of the war-guilt clause—legalizing foreign "peace time" abuses towards Germany—the precipitating factor in French policies was really aggrandizement of power and the quest for European continental hegemony in the spirit of Richelieu and Napoleon.[230] Hostility towards Germany was being generated, Troeltsch complained, not only against an alleged "German criminality" but against German scholarship and *Kultur* itself.[231] The question of "guilt" had become a question of "guilts," with Germany judged in the wrong whatever its actions or ideas.[232] In the face of this moral, demagogic offensive—led by France and her not always willing allies and cloaked with puny motives of "reparations" and "indemnities"—Troeltsch could but conclude that "the World War continues." There was "no peace, but an unbloody extension of the war."[233]

From without, a moral war against Germany's continued existence; from within, vicious and persistent attacks against the system of parliamentary, democratic republicanism: such was Weimar Germany's predicament in the early 1920s.[234] Troeltsch was consistently hesitant in predicting the future—"who knows how things will stand in even four weeks?"—but he was also consistently gloomy in his forebodings that things would probably not go well.[235] "One thing only is clear," he remarked in the spring of 1921, "in these past two years in international politics we have not been getting along very well, and in internal affairs . . . we are sliding into increasingly difficult predicaments, with the outlook as dark as it was in the most hopeless period of the war."[236] Nightmares had been turned into realities. Illusions and hopes were at an end. World crises and transformations had become so profound and radical that "the entire world now stands helplessly facing the chaos without any guidelines and without any common ideas based upon experience and precedent."[237] Troeltsch's last articles in *Der Kunstwart* were portraits of crises and despair.[238]

Early in 1923, after a brief illness, Troeltsch died. His death symbolized the death of a system. He did not live to see the superficial semblance of a return to normalcy in the middle years of the Weimar Republic, the so-called "golden twenties." Nor did he live to see Germany plunge once more into the depths, in the last third of the Weimar Republic from 1929 to 1933. The system he defended did outlive him by ten years, but when the Weimar Republic itself died, it was nevertheless the death of an adolescent which had not reached full maturity, which had not been allowed to come of age despite the pleas of clear-headed thinkers like Ernst Troeltsch.

6

Epilogue

*Troeltsch was a complex man and lived
in a complex time.*

H. Richard Niebuhr

*Troeltsch posed all the critical problems
which are still present.*

Clark M. Williamson

From my examination of Ernst Troeltsch's writings, his contributions in areas of thought including theology, church history, historicism, philosophy of history, and political analysis are clear. It remains only to ruminate a bit over some loose ends and to evaluate Troeltsch as a whole.

Geoffrey Barraclough, in his thought-provoking *Introduction to Contemporary History*, convincingly argues that at least by the early twentieth century Western civilization was entering a new phase; to the tripartite division of "ancient-medieval-modern" he adds a fourth phase, a post-modern or "contemporary" period. Barraclough believes that "We live today in a world different, in almost all its basic preconditions, from the world in which Bismarck lived and died. . . . A person living today [1967] who was suddenly put back into the world of 1900 would find himself on familiar ground, whereas if he returned to 1870 . . . the differences would probably be more striking than the similarities."[1] Ernst Troeltsch flourished during this transition from modern to contemporary periods and in so doing personally and professionally embodied the crisis in consciousness which was the hallmark of intellectual history during these times.

"Everything is tottering!" Upon this theme, expressed by Troeltsch near the beginning of his career, I have focused throughout this book in examining the spectrum of his writings. And against the pervasiveness of this theme, as Western civilization passed from one phase to the next, Troeltsch must be judged. As Fritz Ringer properly characterizes

131

him, Troeltsch was an eminent example of that group of turn-of-the-century German and European mandarin intellectuals who "by the early 1920's . . . were deeply convinced that they were living through a profound crisis, a 'crisis of culture,' of 'learning,' of 'values,' or of the 'spirit.' " [2]

Did Troeltsch meet this crisis successfully? Did he overcome or help surmount the anarchy of values which he so eloquently diagnosed? Did he provide viable cures or solutions? In his own words, did he give his contemporaries the "new spiritual freshness, power, concentration, and discipline, which have everywhere to be formed against the crudity, shallowness, and vulgarity of a trivialized or caricatured, increasingly disintegrated and desolate civilization?" [3]

The answer is ambiguous. Although I have written sympathetically at length about Troeltsch, I cannot permit myself to assert or even imply that he was totally successful in all his exploits. But I must likewise reject the extreme interpretation of Benjamin Reist that "the record of Troeltsch's steps is the outline of a ruin." [4] The conventional judgment of past decades that Troeltsch was an unqualified failure now meets with increasing dissent. He was too complex a thinker, reflecting too turbulent a time, to dismiss out of hand. It is simplistic to judge cavalierly that "the problem was clearer in his mind than the solution." [5]

Might one conclude, with fairness, that he died too soon to be adequately judged? Did not his premature death, before he had definitively expressed his views, cut off in midstream a promised synthesis? Should we not sympathize with Georg Wünsch's observation "that the final consummation was not granted to him. His death at 57 came too early." [6]

One must appreciate that the unfinished character of Troeltsch's work was deliberate. Hans-Georg Drescher accurately notes in this regard that Troeltsch's "whole response consisted of hints about interconnections, indications of where the problems lie and suggestions about where the solutions are to be sought, rather than aiming at the real outline of a system." [7] Even though Troeltsch had planned to write a two-volume philosophy of history that would itself be a prelude or introduction to a philosophy of religion, [8] his corpus of writings remains unsystematized not only because of his early death but because he eschewed definitiveness as a matter of principle. As Bornhausen has correctly observed, each of Troeltsch's publications seemed to raise new problems, making each finished production but a preliminary to some future work.[9] Hugh Quigley has similarly commented: "The whole tendency of his work was not completion of one idea before attacking another, but rather retention of all ideas in a state of flux until a final expression could be reached."[10]

Although Troeltsch's critics have generally agreed that his works are characterized by this quality of incompleteness, they have not agreed on what this incompleteness means. On the negative side, for example, H. Stuart Hughes harshly described Troeltsch as not "a particularly coherent historical thinker. . . . [he] was frankly confused and never attained to a full mastery of his materials."[11] Others see Troeltsch differently. Oesterreich, for example, using almost the same language as Hughes, remarked that "his works are distinguished by an extraordinary mastery of materials."[12] Rather than seeing Troeltsch as confused, his sympathizers have cautioned that "the reader must always remember that Troeltsch had a growing mind."[13] He could never be fairly accused of that foolish consistency which is the hobgoblin of small minds. His eclectic nature and his tendency towards compromise, his desire to strive towards syntheses of disparate elements without seeking the definitive stance (which he considered always unattainable), have been interpreted by his followers to be the highly desirable virtues of a perpetually open mind.[14] Albrecht Dietrich, one of Troeltsch's chief Berlin disciples, spoke of Troeltsch this way: "Always ready to learn and to relearn, he recoiled from nothing more than from airs of having spoken the last word."[15]

Troeltsch himself maintained that he was nonsystematic not by default but by design. For example, when asked to contribute an autobiographical sketch on his philosophical position to the anthology *Die Philosophie der Gegenwart in Selbstdarstellungen*, he declined writing about any philosophical "system" because he denied having one.[16] He would write instead only about "My Books," that is, the succession of topics and themes which he had treated during the previous three decades. In this 1922 essay he stated:

> I have no particular system, and that is how I differ from most other German philosophers. Naturally, I have certain preconceptions in the back of my mind, but only that these might be constantly corrected in the course of my work. Thus I cannot show a system in such a state of incompleteness, but only comment on the sequence of my books, which to a systematically oriented person is nevertheless a sort of system.[17]

Adolf von Harnack, with whom Troeltsch had his disputes on professional matters, nevertheless praised this nonsystematic attitude in
Troeltsch's character, speaking of "the respect and sensitivity with
which he regarded each object, each living thing. He detested the violence of the rationalist and the bad habits of the systematizer, and felt
himself divorced by a deep chasm from all those who are not content
until they have transformed each living object into an unequivocal,
petrified thing, and robbed it not only of all mellowness but also of life
itself, with its tensions and contradictions."[18]

Troeltsch pursued this nondogmatic approach not only in his research and writing but in the classroom as well, where he had a marked
success almost despite his desire not to seek popularity.[19] Harnack
spoke of Troeltsch's method of lecturing as "completely original and
exciting at the same time. He did not formulate rigorously and exactly,
but pitched an observation or an idea to and fro with ever renewed
efforts and with a bubbling eloquence which was profusely, too profusely, at his disposal, assaulted it from all sides and placed it in ever
new relations, until it appeared purified and intelligible. His mind
worked like a powerful centrifugal machine or like a rotating drum
which shakes an object until it is cleansed of all foreign elements and
shines in its own singularity."[20] As to the impact Troeltsch had upon his
students, Sleigh maintained that

> as a lecturer he was very influential. . . . His effect upon his
> students as they crowded round him was almost electrical. He
> was greeted with the utmost enthusiasm when he entered the
> classroom, and he left it amid a storm of applause. He came in
> with all the hurry of a man bent on the most urgent of business,
> and lectured with amazing vigour, his grey eyes dancing with
> vivacity and all his body in perpetual motion. As a professor he
> did not come to his students with solutions on various topics
> which they were only required to take up. Rather he strove to get
> their minds to work for themselves and contented himself in
> pointing to the sources where the necessary material might be
> had for the formation of a sound judgment.[21]

Georg Wünsch reiterated that when it came to providing research topics for his students, Troeltsch "did not like to furnish dissertation
themes, because he held the viewpoint that the university professor
should not be a 'doctor factory'; the student should on the contrary

come to problems and seek to solve them through his own work."[22]

A dominant trait of Troeltsch's mind was his unprejudiced, open pursuit of truth wherever it might lie. Just as he preferred not to impose views upon his students, he preferred in his own research and publications not to prove pet theses but to investigate problems in whichever direction they might lead, however unexpected the results might be. Thus, in the opening pages of *Historicism and Its Problems*, for example, Troeltsch remarked that "how I think about the solution of the crisis [in contemporary thought], so far as I am concerned, can be formulated only as the *consequence* of these pages."[23] Further, in the "Foreword" to his *Social Teachings* Troeltsch wrote that "the results have been summarized in the concluding section. They are genuine *results* which have been gained from the process of research, *not theses* which the book was written to support. This is why they are placed at the end and not at the beginning."[24] H. Richard Niebuhr agreed that Troeltsch's conclusions in the *Social Teachings* which "he summarizes at the end . . . are the actual results of the studies that precede and not propositions he had set out to illuminate and defend. The work is more like a river, flowing towards junction with other streams on their way to the sea, than like a house built according to planned specifications. To read it in the way in which it was written is to accompany the author to his effort to understand a mass of historical data and to seek with him solutions of some intellectual and practical problems."[25]

Similar imagery was used by Adolf von Harnack in describing Troeltsch's thoughts as flowing "through the lifeworks of great philosophers and thinkers" and assimilating diverse material into his own viewpoint.[26] Troeltsch did not have the answers to his problems before he began investigating them. He went on a quest, knowing, through his constant *Referieren*, something of the direction but not the destination. And he was cut down before the end of his journey. In describing Troeltsch's work during his last years, one commentator intriguingly speculates that "this may well have been a passing phase."[27]

To withhold evaluation of Troeltsch on the grounds of his untimely death or unsystematic nature might be derelict, however. His work may be unfinished and lack a classified systematic program, but a large volume is available to us—although the body of his writings has repeatedly been called an incomplete torso.[28] In these works, one must cautiously balance two factors. First, there is Troeltsch's "astonishing intellectual equipment,"[29] his unmistakable scholarly capacities and his conscientiousness. Second, there is an element resembling over-kill, as Macintosh noted: "Encyclopaedic in learning, he often appears to know too much. His books now and then leave the impression that the author has emptied out the contents of his notebooks into the printed page without too much regard for form or clarity."[30]

Troeltsch had an ecumenical largesse with which he tried to tolerate and appreciate diverse and clashing viewpoints. Convinced that beneath the surface of conflicting views there could be found common denominators, if properly searched for, he had a thoroughgoing esteem for "compromise." His personal philosophy of life was the basis for this scholarly attitude. "Life has at all times consisted in battle and strife," he wrote to Hügel in 1912; "life remains a *compromise* between a thousand tendencies and their countless inter-crossings."[31] Eleven years later, shortly before his death, Troeltsch reiterated that "all intransigence breaks down in practice, and can only end in disaster. . . . In the last resort life itself . . . consists in a constant, persistently precarious *compromise* between its respective constituent elements. . . . And if *the whole course of history is thus characterized by compromise, it is not likely that the thinker can escape it.* He, too, must confess to a *compromise.*"[32]

Unequivocally Troeltsch rejected the view that compromise was "the lowest and most despicable means to which a thinker can have resort."[33] "The desire for theoretical simplicity is deep-rooted in human nature," he wrote, "and where men stand before a choice between alternatives, the simpler proposition is always preferred. Men can endure multiplicity in practical life, but not in their theoretical systems."[34] Not so, however, with Troeltsch himself. Eschewing the uncomplicated and easy, his scholarly writings were eminently eclectic, borrowing freely from the systems of others. The drawback of this unfettered eclecticism and pursuit of "compromise" was that it tended in the long run to be a mere juxtaposition of diverse elements of thought, an unstable compromise but hardly any durable synthesis. As one of his contemporaries remarked about Troeltsch's desire to seek "middle ways" rather than extreme positions, "in his synthesis of the various mystical, romantic, philosophic, and scientific tendencies of his *milieu*, it soon became apparent that he did not quite agree with anybody."[35]

On the other hand, despite the unmistakable contradictions and inconsistencies in his body of works, one must acknowledge the nobleness of Troeltsch's goals in attempting to solve the problems of his age.

Facing what he regarded as a major crisis in consciousness, Troeltsch
was perpetually "dissatisfied with [his] achievements and under the
influence of new stimuli and ideas."[36] Troeltsch epitomizes the self-
consciousness of a generation living through an age of dissolving certainties. His was a "restless program."[37] He may at times have indicated the direction in which solutions might be reached, but he could
not stand still. He invariably found other disturbing problems. In undogmatic fashion, rejecting as illusory the search for absolutely permanent solutions within history, Troeltsch argued that the problems of the
age demanded not one final solution but a series of successively re-
placeable syntheses none of which was indispensable or permanent.
He endorsed the view of Lessing that "the search for truth was preferable to the unsought possession of it."[38]

Insofar as the awareness and subsequent formulation of problems is
at times more difficult to achieve than their solutions, Troeltsch scores
very high. He did not shun difficulties, even when he knew he could
not personally surmount them. Troeltsch was a representative figure by
the very fact that he did not ultimately succeed in all his ventures. Had
he been consistently successful, he would be anomalous to an age of
crisis.[39] Troeltsch eminently represented an important phase of history
in which "there was a general consciousness of the end of an era."[40]

Although Troeltsch never fully consummated his major intellectual
concerns, he ranks with pivotal thinkers of the past such as Schleiermacher, Hegel, and Ritschl. Some of his particular solutions—like
some of theirs—may be inappropriate today, but Troeltsch's lucid clar-
ifications of important problems still haunt us and are relevant to our
own times. Troeltsch has challenged us to reappraise traditional, ecclesiastical religion and to investigate anew the nature of Christianity and
even religion in general. We are still struggling to dam and control the
raging currents of historical life, an obsession of Troeltsch seen both in
his scholarly religious and philosophic writings as well as in his en-
gagements in a turbulent political arena.

Throughout three decades of learned scholarship and five hundred
publications Troeltsch struggled with the theme of crisis. His vision
that "everything was tottering" left him no rest. Walter Bodenstein at
one point described *Historismus und seine Probleme* in words sug-
gestive of Troeltsch's lifework as a whole: it is "a great question mark,
as striking in its negatively critical statements as in its prevailing
strength, and therefore the most important and in its way the most
splendidly impressive example of the spiritual atmosphere of Germany

at that time."[41] In both his posing and clarification of important questions and his ambivalent solutions to them, Troeltsch was significantly typical of German thought in his period. Not despite his lack of consistent success but because of it, Troeltsch admirably represents the profound crisis in consciousness experienced by the European mind at the turn of the century.

Notes

If the first citation of a source is in shortened form, full publishing information for that source is located in the bibliography.

Preface

1. James Luther Adams, "Why the Troeltsch Revival?," pp. 4 ff.
2. Adams, "Ernst Troeltsch as Analyst of Religion," p. 98; Emil Spiess, *Die Religionstheorie von Ernst Troeltsch*, p. viii; and Kurt Kesseler, "Ernst Troeltsch als Geschichtsphilosoph," p. 87.
3. For example, Roland N. Stromberg, *An Intellectual History of Modern Europe*, 2nd ed. (Englewood Cliffs, New Jersey: Prentice-Hall, 1975), and Golo Mann, *Deutsche Geschichte des neunzehnten und zwanzigsten Jahrhunderts* (Frankfurt am Main: S. Fischer, 1960).
4. Walther Köhler, *Ernst Troeltsch*, p. v.
5. Robert Morgan, "Troeltsch and Christian Theology," p. 208.
6. Wolfhart Pannenberg, quoted in Karl-Ernst Apfelbacher, *Frömmigkeit und Wissenschaft*, p. 33. The phrase "pluralistic context of contemporary theology" is borrowed from a chapter title in David Tracy's attempted synthesis of Troeltsch and Catholicism, *Blessed Rage for Order*.
7. Jacob Klapwijk, *Tussen Historisme en Relativisme*; Arrigo Rapp, *Il Problema della Germania*; Apfelbacher, *Frömmigkeit und Wissenschaft*; and John Powell Clayton, ed., *Ernst Troeltsch and the Future of Theology*.
8. Hans-Georg Drescher, "Ernst Troeltsch's intellectual development," in Clayton, *Ernst Troeltsch*, pp. 31–32. Cf. J. B. Metz and T. Rendtorff, eds., *Die Theologie in der interdisziplinären Forschung* (Düsseldorf: Bertelsmann Universitätsverlag, 1971).
9. Thomas W. Ogletree, *Christian Faith and History*; Benjamin A. Reist, *Toward a Theology of Involvement*; and Robert S. Sleigh, *The Sufficiency of Christianity*.
10. See, for example, Robert J. Rubanowice, "Intellectual History and the Organization of Knowledge," *Journal of Library History: Philosophy and Comparative Librarianship* 10 (July 1975):264–71, reprinted in Bill Katz, ed., *Library Lit. 6—The Best of 1975*, pp. 111–19.
11. See, for example, Drescher, "Troeltsch's intellectual development," pp. 14–15, and Drescher, "Das Problem der Geschichte," p. 195, n. 2.
12. Friedrich Nietzsche, "Von den Gelehrten," *Also Sprach Zarathustra* (Munich: Goldmann, 1900), p. 97.
13. Troeltsch, "Die christliche Weltanschauung und ihre Gegenströmungen" (1894), reprinted in his *Zur religiösen Lage*, p. 238. In subsequent footnotes where authorship is not indicated, the author is Troeltsch.

Chapter 1

1. Charles Péguy (1909), quoted in René Sedillot, *L'Histoire n'a pas de sens* (Paris: Libraire A. Fayard, 1965), p. 167.
2. Roland N. Stromberg, *An Intellectual History of Modern Europe*, 2nd ed. (Englewood Cliffs, New Jersey: Prentice-Hall, 1975), p. 363.
3. Gerhard Masur, *Prophets of Yesterday*, p. 37; Egon Friedell, *Kulturgeschichte der Neuzeit: Die Krisis der europäischen Seele von der schwarzen Pest bis zum ersten Weltkrieg* (Ungekürzte Sonderausgabe in einem Band; München: C. H. Beck, 1965), "Epilog," pp. 1493 ff. (the epilogue portion of this originally multivolume study was first published in 1931); and H. Stuart Hughes, *Consciousness and Society*, p. 33.
4. See, for example, Melvin Kranzberg and Carroll W. Pursell, Jr., eds., *Technology in*

140 *Notes*

Western Civilization, vol. 1: *The Emergence of Modern Industrial Society: Earliest Times to 1900*
(New York: Oxford University Press, 1967), passim.

5. See, for example, Carleton J. Hayes' book in the Rise of Modern Europe series, still
valuable in portraying this period of prosperity: *A Generation of Materialism: 1871–1900* (New
York: Harper & Row, 1941), especially chaps. 3, 9.

6. See, for example, Lewis Mumford, *Technics and Civilization* (New York: Harcourt,
Brace, 1934), passim.

7. Kenneth E. Boulding, *The Meaning of the Twentieth Century: The Great Transition* (New
York: Harper & Row, 1964), p. 180. Cf. Lynn White, Jr., *Machina Ex Deo: Essays in the
Dynamism of Western Culture* (Cambridge, Massachusetts: M.I.T. Press, 1968), p. 11.

8. The view that technological advancements provide the "promise of utopia in our time" is
examined by Emmanuel G. Mesthene in *Technological Change: Its Impact on Man and Society*
(New York: New American Library, 1970), pp. 16 ff. and passim.

9. Page Smith, *The Historian and History* (New York: Random House, 1966), p. 102.
Troeltsch himself noted the swelling symptoms of a crisis in values throughout the preceding
centuries. See, for example, Troeltsch, "Die christliche Weltanschauung und ihre Gegenströmungen" (1894), reprinted in his *Zur religiösen Lage*, pp. 230 ff.; "Die Restaurationsepoche am
Anfang des 19. Jahrhunderts" (1913), reprinted in his *Aufsätze zur Geistesgeschichte und Religionssoziologie*, p. 590; "Renaissance und Reformation" (1913), *Gesammelte schriften* (hereafter, *G.S.*) IV:294–95; and "Die geistige Revolution," *Der Kunstwart*, 34 (Jan. 1921): 227–33.

10. Georg G. Iggers, "The Idea of Progress: A Critical Reassessment," *American Historical
Review* 71 (Oct. 1965): 1. Although I tend to agree with Leonard Krieger's remark that "any
historian worth his salt can find a cultural crisis wherever he has a mind to find it," I do believe
that the cultural crisis of Troeltsch's period was one of extreme proportions. See Krieger, *Kings
and Philosophers: 1689–1789* (New York: Norton, 1970), p. 139.

11. William Butler Yeats, "The Second Coming," in *The Variorum Edition of the Poems of
W. B. Yeats* (New York: Macmillan, 1957), p. 402.

12. George L. Mosse, *The Culture of Western Europe: The Nineteenth and Twentieth Centuries* (Chicago: Rand McNally, 1961), pp. 213 ff.

13. Samuel Smiles, *Self-help* (1859), quoted in Franklin Le Van Baumer, *Main Currents of
Western Thought*, 2nd ed., rev. (New York; Knopf, 1965), p. 498.

14. See, for example, Mosse, *Culture of Western Europe*, pp. 214–22.

15. Pitirim A. Sorokin, *The Crisis of Our Age: The Social and Cultural Outlook* (New York:
E. P. Dutton, 1941), p. 315.

16. See, for example, "Das neunzehnte Jahrhundert" (1913), *G.S.* IV:642 ff.

17. Matthew Arnold, "Dover Beach," in Jonathan Middlebrook, ed., *Dover Beach* (Columbus, Ohio: Merrill, 1970), pp. 9–10.

18. Hardly more than a decade after Nietzsche's death in 1900, Troeltsch could already remark that a "Nietzsche cult was in vogue for the masses." "Die Kirche in Leben der Gegenwart"
(1911), *G.S.* II:97.

19. "Das neunzehnte Jahrhundert," p. 642.

20. Sigmund Freud, *Civilization and its Discontents*, trans. James Strachey (New York: Norton, 1962), pp. 62, 91–92.

21. Carl Gustav Jung, *Modern Man in Search of a Soul*, trans. W. S. Dell and Cary F. Baynes
(New York: Harcourt, 1933), pp. 204, 211.

22. Georges Sorel, *The Illusions of Progress*, trans. John and Charlotte Stanley (Berkeley
and Los Angeles: University of California Press, 1969), p. xiv.

23. Karl Jaspers, *Man in the Modern Age*, trans. Eden and Cedar Paul (Garden City, New
York: Doubleday, 1957), pp. 1–2.

24. Carl F. H. Henry, *Remaking the Modern Mind*, 2nd ed. (Grand Rapids, Michigan: Eerdmans, 1946), p. 265.

25. Werner Heisenberg, *Physics and Philosophy: The Revolution in Modern Science* (New
York: Harper & Row, 1958), p. 201.

26. Max Planck, *Scientific Autobiography, and Other Papers*, trans. Franck Gaynor (New
York: Philosophical Library, 1949), p. 81.

27. Desmond Morris, *The Naked Ape* (New York: Dell, 1967).

28. Thomas Wolfe, *Look Homeward Angel* (New York: Charles Scribner's Sons, 1952), p. 1.

29. Jean-Paul Sartre, *No Exit and Three Other Plays*, trans. Stuart Gilbert (New York: Vintage, 1960), p. 47.

30. Jack Roth, "Conclusion," in Roth, ed., *World War I: A Turning Point in Modern History* (New York: Knopf, 1967), p. 107. I treat further the impact of the Great War in Chapter 5.

31. Some have argued that even the initial appearances of socialism in the early nineteenth century emerged "out of a crisis in classical liberalism." Albert Fried and Ronald Sanders, eds., *Socialist Thought: A Documentary History* (Garden City, New York: Doubleday, 1964), p. 3 and passim.

32. See, for example, Carl J. Friedrich and Zbigniew K. Brzezinski, *Totalitarian Dictatorship and Autocracy*, 2nd ed., rev. (New York: Praeger, 1968), p. xi.

33. J. Robert Oppenheimer, *The Open Mind* (New York: Simon and Schuster, 1955), p. 141.

34. Alvin Toffler, *Future Shock* (New York: Random House, 1970).

35. Malcolm Bradbury, *Eating People Is Wrong* (New York: Knopf, 1960), p. 133.

36. The phrase is borrowed from Michael Harrington, *The Accidental Century* (Baltimore: Penguin Books, 1965).

37. "Das neunzehnte Jahrhundert," p. 631.

38. "The Morality of the Personality and of the Conscience" (1923), *Christian Thought* (1957), p. 68. See also Troeltsch's *Die wissenschaftliche Lage und ihre Anforderungen an die Theologie* (Tübingen: J. C. B. Mohr, 1900), pp. 4–5.

39. "The Common Spirit" (1923), *Christian Thought*, p. 129. See also "Moderne Geschichtsphilosophie" (1904), *G.S.* II:678; and "Die geistige Revolution," pp. 227–33.

40. "Morality of the Personality," p. 67.

41. Walther Köhler, *Ernst Troeltsch*, p. 1. The phase Troeltsch used was *"Es wackelt alles!"* For Troeltsch's sensitivity to crisis as representative of the academic profession generally, see further Fritz K. Ringer, *The Decline of the German Mandarins*.

42. *Die wissenschaftliche Lage*, p. 5.

43. "The Common Spirit," p. 143.

44. "The Place of Christianity Among the World Religions" (1923), *Christian Thought*, p. 38.

45. William Barrett, *Irrational Man: A Study in Existential Philosophy* (Garden City, New York: Doubleday, 1962), p. 20.

46. Robert S. Sleigh, *The Sufficiency of Christianity*, pp. 19, 18.

47. Ibid., pp. 19, 24–25.

48. Leicester C. Lewis, "Troeltsch vs. Ritschl," pp. 42–43, 48–49, 52, 57. On this subterranean crisis that had not yet "percolated through to the masses," cf. further Troeltsch's "Die christliche Weltanschauung," especially pp. 324–27, and "Moderne Geschichtsphilosophie," p. 678.

49. The most complete published bibliography of Troeltsch's works is still the chronological listing compiled by Hans Baron, "Bibliographie der von Troeltsch im Druck erschienen Schriften," in *G.S.* IV:863–72. Although not definitive, it is the best currently available. See the note preceding my own bibliography for further related information.

50. Hugh T. Kerr, ed., *Readings in Christian Thought* (Nashville, Tennessee: Abingdon Press, 1966), p. 262.

51. "Place of Christianity," p. 37. For overviews of Troeltsch's intellectual development see further: Robert Morgan, "Introduction: Ernst Troeltsch on Theology and Religion"; Hans-Georg Drescher, "Ernst Troeltsch's intellectual development"; and Emil Spiess, *Die Religionstheorie von Ernst Troeltsch*.

52. "Meine Bücher" (1922), *G.S.* IV:3.

53. Ibid.; and "Place of Christianity," p. 36.

54. "Meine Bücher," pp. 3–4.

55. Ibid., p. 4. For the record, Troeltsch claimed that he "never regretted the years devoted to theology. Entirely the opposite."

56. Adolf von Harnack, "Rede am Sarge Ernst Troeltschs," p. 102.

57. A 1905 letter to Baron Friedrich von Hügel, quoted in Hügel, "Ernst Troeltsch" (letter to the editor), *The Times Literary Supplement* (London), March 29, 1923, p. 216.

58. A 1913 letter, quoted ibid. Apropos to Troeltsch's religious temperament, R. S. Sleigh insists that "there was, notwithstanding his sunniness and vivacity, a definite streak of melan-

choly in his make-up which shot itself through all his work." Sleigh, *Sufficiency of Christianity*, p. 21.

59. Taken from the special preface to the English edition of *Protestantism and Progress*, trans. W. Montgomery (1958), pp. vi–vii, x. The original work is *Die Bedeutung des Protestantismus für die Entstehung der modernen Welt*. Troeltsch also illustrated that the presence of religiosity in itself need not be an insuperable barrier to the development of a disinterested historical temper by citing elsewhere the accomplishments of the seventeenth-century French Benedictine monastic congregation, the Maurists. *Der Historismus und seine Probleme*, 1:16.

60. "Meine Bücher," p. 6.

61. Wilhelm Pauck, *Harnack and Troeltsch*, pp. 56–57.

62. *Vernunft und Offenbarung*, passim.

63. Pauck, *Harnack and Troeltsch*, p. 57.

64. Hughes, *Consciousness and Society*, p. 231. Cf. "Meine Bücher," pp. 12–13. A similar narrow concept of the role of theologian is contained in Walter Bodenstein, *Neige des Historismus*, p. 97.

65. "Meine Bücher," p. 13.

66. Hughes, *Consciousness and Society*, p. 374.

Chapter 2

1. Benjamin A. Reist, *Theology of Involvement*, p. 19.

2. Robert Morgan and Michael Pye, trans. and eds., *Ernst Troeltsch*, p. vii.

3. Pannenberg's suggestion is cited by James Luther Adams in "Why the Troeltsch Revival?," p. 5. See also Adams's Introduction to Troeltsch's *The Absoluteness of Christianity and the History of Religions*, trans. David Reid, pp. 7, 15. An abstract of this work first appeared in the form of fourteen concise theses in *Die Christliche Welt*, 15 (26 Sept. 1901): 923–25. Troeltsch's final version was *Die Absolutheit des Christentums und die Religionsgeschichte: Vortrag gehalten auf der Versammlung der Freunde der Christlichen Welt zu Mühlacker am 3. Oktober 1901*. Subsequent citations are to the conveniently available Reid translation.

4. W. Warren Wagar, *The City of Man: Prophecies of a World Civilization in Twentieth-Century Thought* (Baltimore: Penguin Books, 1967), p. 53. Cf. Troeltsch's "Die Zukunftsmöglichkeiten des Christentums im Verhältnis zur modernen Philosophie" (1910), *Gesammelte Schriften* (hereafter, *G.S.*) II:841.

5. William Robert Miller, *The New Christianity* (New York: Delacorte, 1967). Cf. Troeltsch's "Religion und Kirche" (1897), *G.S.* II:146.

6. Cf. W. Richard Comstock, "Naturalism and Theology," *The Heythrop Journal*, 8 (April 1967):181 ff.

7. Carleton J. Hayes, *A Generation of Materialism: 1871–1900* (New York: Harper & Row, 1941), pp. 125–26.

8. Søren Kierkegaard, quoted in Walter Lowrie, *A Short Life of Kierkegaard* (Princeton, New Jersey: Princeton University Press, 1942), p. 246.

9. William Barrett, *Irrational Man: A Study in Existential Philosophy* (Garden City, New York: Doubleday, 1962), p. 24.

10. James R. Kelley, "Relativism and Institutional Religion," *Journal for the Scientific Study of Religion*, 9 (Winter 1970):281.

11. See, for example, Hans Meyer, *Abendländische Weltanschauung* (Paderborn: Schöningh, 1949), 5:316–21.

12. "Das Wesen des modernen Geistes" (1907), *G.S.* IV:329. See also "Die Religion im deutschen Staate" (1912), *G.S.* II:73; and "Religion und Kirche," p. 182.

13. "Das Wesen des modernen Geistes," p. 327.

14. *Absoluteness of Christianity*, p. 102.

15. *Protestantism and Progress* (1958), p. 26.

16. *The Social Teaching of the Christian Churches*, trans. Olive Wyon (1960), 1:34. This important work was translated in 1931 from *Die Soziallehren der christlichen Kirchen und Gruppen*.

17. "Das Wesen des modernen Geistes," p. 333. See also *Protestantism and Progress*, p. 181.
18. "Das Wesen des modernen Geistes," pp. 327–29.
19. *Protestantism and Progress*, p. 186.
20. *G.S.* III:717. See also, "Renaissance und Reformation" (1913), *G.S.* IV:295–96; and "Die theologische und religiöse Lage der Gegenwart" (1903), *G.S.* III:1.
21. *Protestantism and Progress*, p. 3.
22. See, for example, *G.S.* III:701.
23. See, for example, *Protestantism and Progress*, pp. 11–27. On Troeltsch's view of the complexity of the Middle Ages, see further "Renaissance und Reformation," pp. 282–85, as well as *Social Teachings*, passim.
24. "Religionswissenschaft und Theologie des 18. Jahrhunderts," *Preussische Jahrbücher*, 114:32.
25. "Das Wesen des modernen Geistes," p. 329.
26. *Protestantism and Progress*, p. 40. See further H. Fischer, "Luther und seine Reformation in der Sicht Ernst Troeltschs," *Neue Zeitschrift für Systematische Theologie und Religionsphilosophie*, 5 (1963):132–72.
27. *Protestantism and Progress*, pp. 45, 59, 85. Troeltsch repeated this line of interpretation elsewhere, for example, in "Renaissance und Reformation" and in "Protestantisches Christentum und Kirche in der Neuzeit" (1906; 1909), the latter a chapter in Paul Hinneberg, ed., *Die Kultur der Gegenwart*, Teil I, Abteilung IV, I, 2nd ed. (Berlin and Leipzig: B. G. Teubner, 1909). Rebuttals of this view have been frequent and heated. See, for example, the argument in F. Strich's own "Renaissance und Reformation," *Deutsche Vierteljahrsschrift für Literaturwissenschaft und Geistesgeschichte*, 1 (1923):582–612.
28. *Protestantism and Progress*, p. 52.
29. "Renaissance und Reformation," pp. 267–68.
30. Ibid., pp. 277, 273.
31. Ronald Gregor Smith, *The Whole Man: Studies in Christian Anthropology* (Philadelphia: Westminster, 1969), p. 47, n. 4. Cf. Larry Shiner, "The Concept of Secularization in Empirical Research," *Journal for the Scientific Study of Religion*, 6 (Fall 1967):207–20.
32. *Protestantism and Progress*, pp. 85–86. More than a decade after these remarks, Troeltsch persisted in his downgrading of the Renaissance in notes written in 1907, reprinted in "Zusätze und handschriftliche Erweiterungen," *G.S.* IV:830–32.
33. "Renaissance und Reformation," p. 286. See also *Protestantism and Progress*, pp. 66–67. On Troeltsch's view of the Renaissance and Reformation as antagonistic, not complementary movements—unlike the interpretation of his contemporary Wilhelm Dilthey—see further Wallace K. Ferguson, *The Renaissance in Historical Thought: Five Centuries of Interpretation* (Cambridge, Massachusetts: Houghton Mifflin, 1948), pp. 284–89.
34. *Protestantism and Progress*, p. 87. See also, "Die englischen Moralisten des 17. und 18. Jahrhunderts" (1903), *G.S.* IV:380 ff.
35. *Protestantism and Progress*, p. 22.
36. Ibid., p. 24.
37. "Renaissance und Reformation," p. 279. Troeltsch's tendency sometimes to gloss over differences among varieties of early Protestantism is today occasionally disputed, as in Robert D. Preus, *The Theology of Post-Reformation Lutheranism: A Study of Theological Prolegomena* (St. Louis, Missouri: Concordia, 1970), pp. 243–44.
38. "Renaissance und Reformation," p. 277.
39. Ibid., p. 279.
40. Ibid., p. 280. See also *Protestantism and Progress*, pp. 176 ff.; and cf. Erich Kahler, *Man the Measure* (New York: Pantheon, 1943), pp. 241 ff. For Christianity in general as "one of the important sources of Western profanation," see, for example, Pierre Burgelin, "On the Transition from the Sacred to the Profane," *Diogenes*, 33 (1961):126.
41. "Die Aufklärung" (1897), *G.S.* IV:338. See also "Die wissenschaftliche Lage" and *G.S.* III:763–64.
42. "Die Aufklärung," p. 339. See also "Religiöser Individualismus und Kirche" (1911), *G.S.* II:117 and "Christentum und Religionsgeschichte" (1897), *G.S.* II:330 ff.

43. "Die Aufklärung," p. 339.

44. Ibid., p. 343. For the development of the autonomy of ethics, see "Die englischen Moralisten," passim. Fritz K. Ringer properly suggests that "the German *Aufklärer* were not so much critics as modernizers of Protestant Christianity." Ringer, *The Decline of the German Mandarins*, p. 83.

45. "Die Aufklärung," p. 342.

46. Ibid., pp. 344–45.

47. See especially ibid., pp. 346–74; and also "Christentum und Religionsgeschichte," p. 335.

48. "Der Deismus" (1898), *G.S.* IV:429–30; and "Zusätze und handschriftliche Erweiterungen," p. 845.

49. "Der Deismus," p. 434. See also *Encyclopaedia of Religion and Ethics*, 1924 ed., s.v. "Free-Thought"; and "Religionswissenschaft und Theologie des 18. Jahrhunderts," pp. 37 ff., where Troeltsch maintained that the psychological point of view came to replace a dogmatic one.

50. "Der Deismus," p. 40, and "Religionswissenschaft und Theologie des 18. Jahrhunderts," pp. 40 ff.

51. See, for example, "Religionswissenschaft und Theologie des 18. Jahrhunderts," p. 52; and "Das neunzehnte Jahrhundert" (1913), *G.S.* IV:617–18.

52. "Das neunzehnte Jahrhundert," p. 617.

53. "Die Restaurationsepoche am Anfang des 19. Jahrhunderts" (1913), *G.S.* IV:604.

54. Ibid., p. 588. See also Troeltsch's "Schleiermacher und die Kirche" in Friedrich Naumann, ed., *Schleiermacher: Der Philosoph des Glaubens* (Berlin: Bücherverlag der "Hilfe," 1910).

55. *Absoluteness of Christianity*, p. 60. This flowering was due largely to the fruitful influence of German idealistic philosophy, for which see, for example, "Religionswissenschaft und Theologie des 18. Jahrhunderts," p. 56. On the revival of religion vis-à-vis the Romantic movement, see "Der deutsche Idealismus" (1900), *G.S.* IV:571; and "Die Restaurationsepoche," p. 592. For a brief systematic approach to the church-state question see Troeltsch's prorectorial address at the University of Heidelberg, November 22, 1906: *Die Trennung von Staat und Kirche, der staatliche Religionsunterricht und die theologischen Fakultäten* (Tübingen: J. C. B. Mohr, 1907).

56. "Die Restaurationsepoche," p. 611.

57. Ibid., p. 613.

58. "Das neunzehnte Jahrhundert," p. 647.

59. *Die wissenschaftliche Lage und ihre Anforderungen an die Theologie* (Tübingen: J. C. B. Mohr, 1900), pp. 3–4.

60. "Die Restaurationsepoche," pp. 612–13. See also "Das neunzehnte Jahrhundert," p. 646.

61. *Die Trennung*, pp. 56–57.

62. Ibid., p. 29, and passim. For the medieval period, see ibid., pp. 13 ff.; for sixteenth-century Protestantism, ibid., pp. 7, 19–20, *Protestantism and Progress*, pp. 66–69, and "Renaissance und Reformation," p. 286; for the seventeenth century, *Protestantism and Progress*, pp. 45–46, 50, 125–26; for the eighteenth-century "modern toleration-state" (*Toleranzstaat*), "Die Aufklärung," p. 343, and "Religionswissenschaft und Theologie des 18. Jahrhunderts," pp. 50–51.

63. "Das Wesen des modernen Geistes," p. 328.

64. *Die Trennung*, p. 57.

65. "Ernst Gedanken zum Reformations-Jubiläum," *Kunstwart*, 31 (Nov. 1917):91.

66. "Das neunzehnte Jahrhundert," p. 645. This appeal was principally found among writers and intellectuals, whereas rural people and the burghers of small towns still tended to support the church-type organization and countless numbers of Europeans showed sheer indifference to the churches. The wave of the future lay with the writers and intellectuals. "Die Kirche im Leben der Gegenwart" (1911), *G.S.* II:94. See also "Das neunzehnte Jahrhundert," p. 648.

67. "Christentum und Religionsgeschichte," p. 328.

68. "Das Wesen des modernen Geistes," p. 327; and "Der Modernismus" (1909), *G.S.* II:57, 65.

69. *Social Teachings*, 1:381; and "Das Wesen des modernen Geistes," p. 328. See also *Social Teachings*, II:1008; and *Die Trennung*, p. 26.
70. "Die Kirche im Leben der Gegenwart," p. 91.
71. "Religiöser Individualismus und Kirche," p. 111. Cf. "Rückblick auf ein halbes Jahrhundert der theologischen Wissenschaft" (1909), *G.S.* II:195–97, where Troeltsch noted that in the fifty years prior to 1908 scientific theology had grown increasingly apathetic towards churchly or ecclesiastical problems.
72. "Religion und Kirche," p. 160.
73. "Religionswissenschaft und Theologie des 18. Jahrhunderts," p. 47.
74. "Religion und Kirche," p. 148. For an update, cf. Dietrich Bonhoeffer, *Letters and Papers from Prison*, ed. Eberhard Bethge, trans. Reginald Fuller, rev. ed. (New York: Macmillan, 1967); Malcolm Boyd, ed., *The Underground Church* (Baltimore, Maryland: Penguin Books, 1969); and David Poling, *The Last Years of the Church* (Garden City, New York: Doubleday, 1969).
75. "Religiöser Individualismus und Kirche," p. 112. See also ibid., p. 126, and *Die Trennung*, p. 60. For background on the church-religion distinction—in terms of the comparative study of the religious phenomena of Greco-Roman antiquity, Buddhism, Judaism, Islam, and early Christianity—see further "Religion und Kirche," pp. 150–64, 178–80.
76. "Aus der religiösen Bewegung der Gegenwart" (1910), *G.S.* II:23.
77. "Leibniz und die Anfänge des Pietismus" (1902), *G.S.* IV:520.
78. Ibid. See also "Religionswissenschaft und Theologie des 18. Jahrhunderts," pp. 50–51.
79. "Die theologische und religiöse Lage," p. 21. See also "Die Kirche im Leben der Gegenwart," p. 95.
80. "Das Wesen des modernen Geistes," p. 328. See also "Aus der religiösen Bewegung der Gegenwart," p. 23. On the point that this profusion has continued to our own time, see Jacob Needleman and George Baker, eds., *Understanding the New Religions* (New York: Seabury, 1978).
81. See, e.g., "Religiöse Individualismus und Kirche," p. 115; and cf. "Die Kirche im Leben der Gegenwart," p. 105.
82. "Religion und Kirche," p. 148.
83. Ibid.
84. Carlo Antoni, *From History to Sociology*, p. 73.
85. W. Warren Wagar, *Science, Faith, and Man: European Thought Since 1914* (New York: Walker, 1968), p. 5.
86. A. C. Bouquet, *Is Christianity the Final Religion?* (London: Macmillan, 1921), p. 241; Adams, Introduction to the *Absoluteness of Christianity*, p. 8. See further Richard Pipes, *Europe Since 1815* (New York: Harper & Row, 1970), pp. 367–68.
87. See the full citation in n. 3., Chap. 2.
88. Jacket comment, *Absoluteness of Christianity*.
89. Ibid.
90. Hugh Ross Mackintosh, *Types of Modern Theology*, p. 138. Mackintosh's eventual judgment about Ritschl was somewhat less flattering, though similar to Troeltsch's own evaluation of Ritschl. Ibid., p. 179.
91. Gustav Krüger, "The 'Theology of Crisis,'" *Harvard Theological Review*, 19 (July 1926):227.
92. *Social Teachings*, 1:19. For a broad introductory overview to Ritschl see, for example, David L. Mueller, *An Introduction to the Theology of Albrecht Ritschl* (Philadelphia: Westminster, 1969).
93. John R. Van Pelt, "Ritschl and After," *Methodist Review*, p. 47.
94. "Geschichte und Metaphysik," *Zeitschrift für Theologie und Kirche*, 8 (1898):52, n. 1. See also Hans-Georg Drescher, "Ernst Troeltsch's intellectual development," pp. 5–6.
95. *Vernunft und Offenbarung*, p. 213.
96. Ibid., p. 206. A recent book exploring Troeltsch's "historical method" in theology is George Rupp's *Culture-Protestantism*. As both his text and footnotes indicate, Rupp's essay unsatisfactorily blends Troeltsch's participation in political activities with his involvement with culture-protestantism.

97. Horst Stephan, *Geschichte der Deutschen Evangelischen Theologie seit dem Deutschen Idealismus*, 2nd ed. (Berlin: A. Töpelmann, 1960). Robert Morgan has recently argued persuasively "for Christian intellectuals to develop the 'extensive' type of theology represented by Troeltsch." Morgan, "Troeltsch and Christian Theology," pp. 210 ff.

98. "Die christliche Weltanschauung," pp. 319, 321. See also "Christentum und Religionsgeschichte," pp. 354, 358.

99. "Die Selbständigkeit der Religion," *Zeitschrift für Theologie und Kirche*, 6 (1896):200. The full citation for this several part essay is ibid., 5 (1895):361–436, and 6 (1896):71–110, 167–218.

100. Ibid., 6:209–10.

101. Ibid., 5:373.

102. "Geschichte und Metaphysik," p. 2. See also Kaftan's reply, *Zeitschrift für Theologie und Kirche*, 8 (1898):70–96. This exchange was part of an ongoing theological disputation, with Troeltsch's "Geschichte und Metaphysik" itself a reply to an earlier article of Kaftan's, which in turn had been a response to Troeltsch's "Selbständigkeit der Religion" of 1895–1896.

103. "Geschichte und Metaphysik," pp. 3–4.

104. Ibid., p. 9. Further on Troeltsch's phenomenological approach to religion, see Gotthold Müller, "Die Selbstauflösung der Dogmatik bei Ernst Troeltsch," pp. 334–46.

105. See the footnote in "Geschichte und Metaphysik," pp. 52–53, for an unmistakably clear statement of Troeltsch's opposition to the Ritschlian system.

106. Ibid., pp. 68–69.

107. Ibid., p. 69.

108. "Ueber historische und dogmatische Methode in der Theologie" (1900), *G.S.* II:738; and "Geschichte und Metaphysik," p. 69.

109. *Absoluteness of Christianity*, pp. 111–12.

110. Ibid., p. 126.

111. Ibid., p. 131.

112. Ibid., p. 47.

113. Ibid., p. 85. For a recent attempt in comparative hermeneutics in the spirit of Troeltsch, see Michael Pye and Robert Morgan, eds., *The Cardinal Meaning*.

114. *Absoluteness of Christianity*, pp. 106, 76.

115. Ibid., p. 45.

116. Ibid., p. 122.

117. Ibid., p. 90.

118. Ibid., p. 122.

119. "Die Mission in der modernen Welt" (1906), reprinted in revised (1907) form in *G.S.* II:796–97.

120. Ibid., pp. 789–90.

121. *G.S.* III:165. For another perspective on Troeltsch's views of non-Christian religions, see Michael Pye, "Ernst Troeltsch and the end of the problem about 'other' religions," in Clayton, *Ernst Troeltsch*, pp. 172–95.

122. "Die Mission in der modernen Welt," p. 804.

123. Troeltsch's inclination to compromise and conciliation notwithstanding, he was on occasion severely criticized for his revisionism. See, for example, Mackintosh, *Types of Modern Theology*, p. 214.

124. See further B. A. Gerrish, "Jesus, Myth, and History," pp. 13–35; as well as Thomas Warren Ogletree, *Christian Faith and History*, p. 62; and George Edgar Wolfe, "Troeltsch's Conception of the Significance of Jesus," *American Journal of Theology*, 20 (1916):179–204.

125. *Die Bedeutung der Geschichtlichkeit Jesu für den Glauben* (Tübingen: J. C. B. Mohr, 1911), p. 4.

126. Ibid., p. 33.

127. "Rückblick auf ein halbes Jahrhundert," p. 211. See also "Die christliche Weltanschauung," p. 324, n. 20.

128. *Die Bedeutung der Geschichlichkeit Jesu*, p. 33.

129. Ibid., p. 51.

130. *Absoluteness of Christianity*, p. 132.

131. Ibid., p. 119.

132. Heinz Zahrnt, *The Historical Jesus*, trans. J. S. Bowden (New York: Harper & Row, 1963), p. 13.

133. Hubert Cunliffe-Jones, *Christian Theology Since 1600* (London: Duckworth, 1970), p. 119.

134. Ibid.

135. Brunner (1927), quoted by Robert Morgan, "Ernst Troeltsch and the dialectical theology," in Clayton, *Ernst Troeltsch*, p. 50.

136. Morgan, ibid., p. 71.

137. A. O. Dyson, "Ernst Troeltsch and the possibility of a systematic theology," in Clayton, *Ernst Troeltsch*, p. 81.

138. James D. Smart, *The Divided Mind of Modern Theology: Karl Barth and Rudolf Bultmann, 1908–1933* (Philadelphia: Westminster Press, 1967), p. 13.

139. S. W. Sykes, "Ernst Troeltsch and Christianity's essence," in Clayton, *Ernst Troeltsch*, p. 141.

140. Heinz Zahrnt, *The Question of God: Protestant Theology in the Twentieth Century*, trans. R. A. Wilson (New York, Harcourt, Brace & World, 1969), p. 20.

141. Morgan, "Troeltsch and Christian Theology," p. 212. The reference is to the picture of Troeltsch in Gertrud von Le Fort's novel, *Der Kranz der Engel* (Munich: Ehrenwirth, 1950).

142. Morgan, "Ernst Troeltsch and the dialectical theology," pp. 72, 74.

143. Libertus A. Hoedemaker, *The Theology of H. Richard Niebuhr* (Philadelphia: Pilgrim, 1970), p. 13.

144. Morgan, "Introduction," in Morgan and Pye, *Ernst Troeltsch*, p. 5.

Chapter 3

1. Van Austin Harvey, *The Historian and the Believer: The Morality of Historical Knowledge and Christian Belief* (New York: Macmillan, 1966), pp. 4, 17. Harvey's Chapter I treats the status of history in contemporary theology, with frequent allusions to Troeltsch. Cf. Hans W. Frei, "The Relation of Faith and History in the Thought of Ernst Troeltsch," in Paul Ramsey, ed., *Faith and Ethics: The Theology of H. Richard Niebuhr* (New York: Harper, 1957), pp. 53–64.

2. John B. Cobb, Jr., "From Crisis Theology to the Post-Modern World," in Bernard Murchland, ed., *The Meaning of the Death of God: Protestant, Jewish, and Catholic Scholars Explore Atheistic Theology* (New York: Random House, 1967), p. 142.

3. See, for example, Gerhard Ebeling, *The Problem of Historicity*, trans. Grover Foley (Philadelphia: Fortress, 1967); as well as Heinz Zahrnt: "There can be no serious theology worthy of credence which disregards the problems of history," *The Historical Jesus*, trans. J. S. Bowden (New York: Harper & Row, 1963), p. 23.

4. *Protestantism and Progress* (1958), p. 34.

5. Nietzsche, quoted in Gerhard Masur, *Prophets of Yesterday*, p. 93.

6. "Christentum und Religionsgeschichte" (1897), *Gesammelte Schriften* (hereafter, *G.S.*) II:331–35, 362–63. See also "Die Aufklärung" (1897), *G.S.* IV:343 and passim; and cf. "Das neunzehnte Jahrhundert (1913), *G.S.* IV:649.

7. "Die Dogmatik der 'religionsgeschichtliche Schule,'" p. 500, n. 35. This is an expanded though fundamentally unrevised version of the English translation appearing earlier that same year as "The Dogmatics of the 'Religionsgeschichtliche Schule.'" On the theological context in which the *religionsgeschichtliche Schule* had its origin, see the section on "Die Krisis des deutschen Protestantismus," in Emil Spiess, *Die Religionstheorie von Ernst Troeltsch*, pp. 1–10.

8. "Die Dogmatik," p. 507.

9. Ibid., pp. 500–501, 508. For the views of Troeltsch's colleagues on this subject, see Gerhard Wolfgang Ittel, "Die Hauptgedanken der 'religionsgeschichtliche Schule,'" pp. 61–78.

10. *The Absoluteness of Christianity and the History of Religions*, p. 131. This example illustrates excellently the conception of intellectual history represented by H. Stuart Hughes as dealing "with ideas that have still to win their way." Hughes, *Consciousness and Society*, p. 10.

11. "Die Dogmatik," pp. 504–5.

12. Ibid., p. 509.

13. Ibid., pp. 507, 510. Cf. Harvey, *The Historian and the Believer*, p. 246.

14. "Die Dogmatik," pp. 510–11, 519; emphasis mine. Compare Adolf von Harnack, *What*

148 *Notes*

is Christianity?, trans. Thomas Bailey Saunders, intro. Rudolf Bultmann (New York: Harper, 1957), with Troeltsch's own critical essay on this theme, "Was heisst 'Wesen des Christentums'?" (1903), *G.S.* II:386–451. On the critical differences between the original six-instalment publication of Troeltsch's latter article and the revised version of 1913, see S. W. Sikes, "Ernst Troeltsch and Christianity's essence," in John Powell Clayton, *Ernst Troeltsch*, esp. pp. 143, 148, 153. Sikes also suggests that the differences between Troeltsch and Harnack were not as great as is sometimes presumed. Ibid., pp. 145–46.

    15. "Die Dogmatik," p. 518.
    16. Ibid., p. 503.
    17. Ibid., p. 519.
    18. Ibid., p. 517.
    19. Ibid., p. 516. Troeltsch's rationalization of his relativistic theological dogmatics illustrates the principle of "polymorphous truth," which is discussed in detail in the last section of this chapter.
    20. On Troeltsch as sociologist of religion, see further James Luther Adams, "Ernst Troeltsch as Analyst of Religion," pp. 102–6.
    21. *The Social Teaching of the Christian Churches* (1960), 1:34.
    22. Roland H. Bainton, "Ernst Troeltsch—Thirty Years Later," p. 70.
    23. Ibid., pp. 71–72.
    24. *Social Teachings*, 1:20–21.
    25. *G.S.* III:369, n. 190.
    26. Benjamin A. Reist, *Toward a Theology of Involvement*, p. 39.
    27. "Max Weber" (1920), in *Deutscher Geist und Westeuropa*, p. 249.
    28. "Meine Bücher" (1922), *G.S.* IV:11.
    29. H. H. Gerth and C. Wright Mills, eds. and trans., *From Max Weber: Essays in Sociology* (New York: Oxford University Press, 1958), p. 11. See also Bainton, "Ernst Troeltsch," p. 70.
    30. J. P. Mayer, *Max Weber and German Politics: A Study in Political Sociology*, 2nd ed., rev. (London: Faber and Faber, 1956), p. 48. On comparisons between Troeltsch and Weber, see further, for example, H. Herring, "Max Weber und Ernst Troeltsch als Geschichtsdenker," pp. 410–34; and Julius Jakob Schaff, *Geschichte und Begriff.*
    31. Max Weber, " 'Objectivity' in Social Science and Social Policy" (1904), in *The Methodology of the Social Sciences*, trans. and ed. Edward A. Shils and Henry A. Finch (New York: Free Press, 1949), pp. 90, 93.
    32. Ibid., p. 90. See further Rolf E. Rogers, *Max Weber's Ideal Type Theory* (New York: Philosophical Library, 1969).
    33. Weber, "Objectivity," p. 90.
    34. Ibid., p. 94.
    35. Reinhard Bendix, *Max Weber: An Intellectual Portrait* (Garden City, New York: Doubleday, 1962), p. 70, n. 1. See also Ephraim Fischoff, "The Protestant Ethic and the Spirit of Capitalism: The History of a Controversy," in S. N. Eisenstadt, ed., *The Protestant Ethic and Modernization: A Comparative View* (New York: Basic Books, 1968), pp. 68–69.
    36. *Social Teachings*, 2:993.
    37. J. Milton Yinger, *Religion, Society, and the Individual: An Introduction to the Sociology of Religion* (New York: Macmillan, 1957), p. 416. Cf. Benton Johnson, "Church and Sect Revisited," *Journal for the Scientific Study of Religion*, 10 (Summer, 1971): 124–37; and on an alleged misfortune of the "Troeltschian syndrome," see further William H. Swatos, Jr., "Weber or Troeltsch," pp. 129–44. The *J.S.S.R.* has frequent articles on these paradigms. See also the entire issue of *Sociological Analysis*, 36 (1975), containing six articles on the general theme of "Church, Sect, Mysticism."
    38. *Social Teachings*, 2:991–92.
    39. Summary-critiques of Troeltsch's *Social Teachings* abound, especially in English-language circles. See, for example, Bainton, "Ernst Troeltsch," pp. 70–96; Franklin H. Littel, "Church and Sect," pp. 262–76; M. C. D'Arcy, "Ernst Troeltsch," pp. 13–30; and Francis A. Christie, "Spiritual Values in the Work of Ernst Troeltsch," pp. 415–23; as well as the appropriate passages in Thomas Warren Ogletree, *Christian Faith*, and Reist, *Toward a Theology of Involvement.*
    40. Talcott Parsons, ed., *Theories of Society: Foundations of Modern Sociological Theory*

(New York: Free Press, 1961), I:646. Cf. J. Milton Yinger, "The Sociology of Religion of Ernst Troeltsch," pp. 309–15.

41. *G.S.* III:178, 66. See also ibid., p. 715, where Troeltsch again refers to sociology as an "auxiliary science" (*Hilfswissenschaft*).

42. Ibid., p. 63.

43. Peter Gay, *Weimar Culture* (New York: Harper & Row, 1970), p. 89.

44. *G.S.* III:45–46.

45. In addition to the widely used term "historicism," which I use, the original German word "*Historismus*" has been also variously interpreted as "historism" (E. N. Anderson, P. Geyl, D. E. Miller), "historical standpoint" (F. von Hügel), "historical spirit" (G. G. Iggers), "science of history" (B. Croce), "historical relativism" (H. A. Hodges, B. Reist), and occasionally loosely the broad term "historical movement." There have also been suggestions that the term "historicism" was derived initially not from the German "*Historismus*" but from the Italian "*storicismo.*" See Dwight E. Lee and Robert N. Beck, "The Meaning of 'Historicism,' " p. 568, n. 1; and Georg G. Iggers, *The German Conception of History*, p. 288, n. 1.

46. Calvin G. Rand, "Two Meanings of Historicism in the Writings of Dilthey, Troeltsch and Meinecke," p. 504. See also Karl Heussi's similar remarks, *Die Krisis des Historismus*, pp. 5–6; and Ernst Cassirer, *The Logic of the Humanities*, trans. C. S. Howe (New Haven: Yale University Press, 1961), p. 88.

47. Walther Hofer, *Geschichtschreibung und Weltanschauung: Betrachtungen zum Werk Friedrich Meineckes* (Munich: R. Oldenbourg, 1950), p. 327. On the mutual crossfertilization of ideas between Troeltsch and Meinecke during Troeltsch's Berlin period, see further: Iggers, *The German Conception*, p. 175; Friedrich Meinecke, "Hintze, Troeltsch und der Spaziergang," *Autobiographische Schriften, Werke*, Bd. VIII (Munich: R. Oldenbourg, 1969):232 ff.; Meinecke, "Ernst Troeltsch und das Problem des Historismus," p. 368; but cf. Otto Hintze, "Troeltsch und die Probleme des Historismus," p. 331.

48. Hofer, *Geschichtschreibung*, p. 322. See also Erich Rothacker, "Das Wort 'Historismus,' " *Zeitschrift für deutsche Wortforschung*, 16 (1960):3–6.

49. John Lukacs, *Historical Consciousness: Or, the Remembered Past* (New York: Harper & Row, 1968), p. 19, n. 15.

50. Rand, "Two Meanings of Historicism," p. 505. Sometimes the word "historicism" is used in ways outside even the broad spectrum of meanings in academic historical circles, such as in the concern over a new form of literary criticism shown by Roy Harvey Pearce in his *Historicism Once More: Problems and Occasions for the American Scholar* (Princeton, New Jersey: Princeton University Press, 1969).

51. Meinecke, *Die Entstehung des Historismus, Werke*, vol. 3 (Munich: R. Oldenbourg, 1959):1, 4.

52. Ibid., pp. 2–3. Cf. Karl Mannheim, *Essays on the Sociology of Knowledge*, p. 85. In an article critical of Meinecke's " 'catastrophic' theory, which posits a great intellectual divide at Leibniz's generation," George Huppert has suggested that the roots of historicism extended back even into the Renaissance. Huppert, "The Renaissance Background of Historicism," *History and Theory*, 5 (1966):48–60. Carlo Antoni speculated that it might be proper to "identify in historicism a constant of the human spirit, with the same claim as mysticism or intellectualism." Antoni, *Lo Storicismo* (Rome: Edizione Radio Italiana, 1957), p. 1.

53. This emphasis is clear in Troeltsch's later writings especially. See, for example, "Naturrecht und Humanität in der Weltpolitik" (1922), reprinted in *Deutscher Geist und Westeuropa*, pp. 3–27.

54. "Die Krisis des Historismus," p. 573. Cf. the similar definitions given in his *G.S.* III:9, 102. On Troeltsch's views of historicism in context, see further: Jacob Klapwijk, *Tussen Historisme en Relativisme*; and Anthony Oakley Dyson's *The Immortality of the Past*, as well as his earlier 1968 Oxford doctoral dissertation, "History in the Philosophy and Theology of Ernst Troeltsch." On the nineteenth-century development of historicism, see further: Friedrich Engel-Janosi, *The Growth of German Historicism* (Baltimore, Maryland: Johns Hopkins Press, 1944); Hans Meyerhoff, Introduction to *The Philosophy of History in Our Time* (Garden City, New York: Doubleday, 1959), pp. 1–25; Heinrich Ritter von Srbik, *Geist und Geschichte vom deutschen Humanismus bis zur Gegenwart*, 2 vols. (Munich: F. Bruckmann, 1950–1951); Carlo Antoni, *Dallo Storicismo alla Sociologia* (Florence: E. C. Sansoni, 1940), trans. Hayden V. White as

From History to Sociology; and Pietro Rossi, *Lo Storicismo Tedesco Contemporaneo*. For the twentieth century, see further: Georg G. Iggers, "The Dissolution of German Historism [*sic*]," pp. 288–329; Eugene N. Anderson, "Meinecke's *Ideengeschichte* and the Crisis in Historical Thinking," in James Lea Cate and Eugene N. Anderson, eds., *Medieval and Historiographical Essays in Honor of James Westfall Thompson* (Chicago: University of Chicago Press, 1938), pp. 361–96; Alfred Stern, *Philosophy of History and the Problem of Values* (The Hague: Mouton, 1962); Geoffrey Barraclough, *History in a Changing World* (Oxford: Blackwell, 1956); and Wolfgang Müller-Lauter, "Konsequenzen des Historismus in der Philosophie der Gegenwart," pp. 226–55.

55. Paul Tillich, *Perspectives on 19th and 20th Century Protestant Theology*, ed. Carl E. Braaten (New York: Harper & Row, 1967), p. 232. Tillich appears to err when he comments that "Troeltsch's philosophy of history is rooted in a negative attitude toward what he calls 'historism,' or perhaps in English one might call it 'historicism,'" as well as when he suggests that Troeltsch remained a rationalistic Ritschlian throughout his life. Ibid., pp. 232, 234.

56. *Absoluteness of Christianity*, p. 85.

57. *G.S.* III:211.

58. Ibid., p. 68.

59. "Die Krisis des Historismus," p. 572. I take a closer look at Troeltsch's meaning of values later in this chapter and throughout Chapter 4.

60. "The Common Spirit," *Christian Thought* (1957), p. 126. See also Edward C. Thaden, "Natural Law and Historicism in the Social Sciences," *Social Science*, 32 (1957):33.

61. *G.S.* III:102.

62. Karl R. Popper, *The Poverty of Historicism* (Boston: Beacon, 1957), pp. ix, xi. See also Popper, "Prediction and Prophecy in the Social Sciences" (1948), published for the first time in Patrick Gardiner, ed., *Theories of History* (Glencoe, Illinois: Free Press, 1959), pp. 276–85.

63. Cf. Lee and Beck, "The Meaning of 'Historicism,'" pp. 574–77; and Meyerhoff, *The Philosophy of History in Our Times*, pp. 299–300. The polemics at times reached ridiculous extremes, such as the following remarks about romanticism, one of the antecedent ingredients of historicism: "Hitlerism was certainly an extreme formulation of the ideas of romanticism. . . . There was at least symbolic truth in the allegation of allied war propaganda that German [*sic*] represented barbarism as opposed to the civilization of Western Europe." Thaden, "Natural Law and Historicism," pp. 33, 35.

64. *G.S.* III:67.

65. But cf. Antoni, *From History to Sociology*, pp. 75–76.

66. *G.S.* III:104.

67. Ibid.

68. Ibid., p. 105.

69. Ibid., p. 106.

70. Ibid., pp. 104, 103. See also "Das neunzehnte Jahrhundert," pp. 623 ff.

71. *G.S.* III. Carl Sagan's recent best-selling *Dragons of Eden: Speculations on the Evolution of Human Intelligence* (New York: Random House, 1977) vindicates Troeltsch's imaginative vision.

72. Goethe, quoted in ibid., p. 85.

73. *G.S.* III:99–100. Although current scholarship tends to date the beginning of the Neolithic period at approximately 10,000 B.C., with the emergence of "civilization" in the fourth millenium B.C., this contemporary chronological revision does not invalidate Troeltsch's main point.

74. Ibid.

75. Ibid., pp. 100–101. See also *Glaubenslehre* (Munich and Leipzig: Duncker & Humblot, 1925), pp. 94, 292.

76. *G.S.* III:86. Troeltsch seemed to think that this doctrine of the plurality of worlds was an expression of a perennial human impulse which took various forms such as the pre-Copernican belief in angels or the spiritual animation of stars and other celestial bodies.

77. Also cf. Lee and Beck, "The Meaning of 'Historicism,'" p. 570; and Geoffrey Barraclough, review of I. S. Kohn's *Die Geschichtsphilosophie des 20. Jahrhunderts*, appearing in *History and Theory*, 6 (1967):230.

78. "Die Dogmatik," pp. 520–21. These particular citations were part of the material not included in the English-language version of this article. *Supra*, Chap. 3, n. 7.

79. "The Place of Christianity Among the World's Religions" (1923), *Christian Thought*, pp. 52–53.

80. "Meine Bücher," p. 14.

81. "Geschichte und Metaphysik," *Zeitschrift für Theologie und Kirche*, 8 (1898):69. In this essay, Troeltsch used the term *"Historismus"* no less than half a dozen times in the last two pages alone.

82. Compare the reverse tendency in the later Arnold Toynbee. Whereas Troeltsch had come to explain religion in terms of the nonreligious, Toynbee as a mature writer "now . . . explained civilization in terms of religion." Page Smith, *The Historian and History* (New York: Random House, 1966), p. 103.

83. George L. Mosse, *The Culture of Western Europe: The Nineteenth and Twentieth Centuries* (Chicago: Rand McNally, 1961), p. 142.

84. "Place of Christianity," p. 53.

85. *G.S.* III:718, n. 384.

86. John Saltmarsh (1646), quoted *sic* in Wilhelm Schenk, "Ernst Troeltsch's Conception of History," p. 27.

87. With this consistent emphasis in his writings, Troeltsch helped lay the foundation for the discipline of the sociology of knowledge. See, for example, Max Scheler, "Ernst Troeltsch als Soziologe," pp. 7–21.

88. "Place of Christianity," p. 63.

89. *G.S.* III:134. This important conception of polymorphous truth appeared as early as 1906 in *Die Trennung von Staat und Kirche* (see note 55, chapter 2), where it is applied to differentiations within Christianity itself.

90. "The Ethics of Cultural Values" (1923), *Christian Thought*, pp. 120–121; emphasis mine. As a corrective to certain European-American stereotypes regarding the inscrutable Orient see John M. Steadman, *The Myth of Asia* (New York: Simon and Schuster, 1969).

91. *G.S.* III:183. Cf. the similar view of Troeltsch's contemporary, Hermann Hesse, in *Der Steppenwolf* (Frankfort am Main: Suhrkamp Verlag, 1970), pp. 208–9.

92. *G.S.* III:187.

93. Cf. Troeltsch's criticisms of Heinrich Rickert, *supra*.

94. "Das neunzehnte Jahrhundert," p. 645.

95. *G.S.* III:187.

96. "Place of Christianity," p. 55. See also "Ostern," *Kunstwart*, 31 (Apr. 1918):4, where Troeltsch also spoke of Christianity as the essential European religion: "We remain in truth bound to our fate, and our fate is Christianity."

97. "Place of Christianity," pp. 55–56; all emphases mine except where otherwise noted.

98. *G.S.* III:695.

99. Ibid., p. 215.

100. Ibid., pp. 695–96.

101. For historical intuition and the categories of the formal logic of history, see *supra*.

102. Edward Hallett Carr, *What is History?* (New York: Random House, 1961), pp. 30–31.

103. *Absoluteness of Christianity*, p. 72.

104. *G.S.* III:10.

105. Friedrich Meinecke, letter to W. Hofer (17 July 1946), quoted in Klaus Epstein's review of Meinecke's *Ausgewählter Briefwechsel*, appearing in *History and Theory*, 4 (1964):87. See also ibid., pp. 94–95; as well as Meinecke, "Kausalitäten und Werte in der Geschichte" (1933), quoted in Fritz Stern, ed., *The Varieties of History: From Voltaire to the Present* (Cleveland, Ohio: World, 1956), p. 411, n. 12; and Friedrich Meinecke, *Aphorismen und Skizzen zur Geschichte*, 2nd ed., rev. (Stuttgart: K. F. Koehler, 1948).

106. *G.S.* III:4.

107. Herbert J. Muller has commented in *Freedom in the Modern World* (New York: Harper & Row, 1966), p. 224. that "much more historical research was carried on [in the nineteenth century] than had been in all the previous centuries of Europe put together." Troeltsch himself praised these nineteenth-century undertakings as admirable accomplishments.

108. *G.S.* III:10. See also ibid., p. 719.
109. Leszek Kolakowski, "Historical Undertaking and the Intelligibility of History," *Tri-Quarterly*, 22 (Fall 1971):115.
110. *G.S.* III:723. See also the similar remark made much earlier at Heidelberg in *Protestantism and Progress*, p. 79.

Chapter 4

1. *Gesammelte Schriften* (hereafter, *G.S.*) III:110.
2. Friedrich Meinecke, "Ernst Troeltsch und das Problem des Historismus," p. 370.
3. Kurt Kesseler, "Ernst Troeltsch als Geschichtsphilosoph," p. 87.
4. This preference for the currently fashionable *Referieren* undoubtedly contributed towards Troeltsch's turgid prose, about which Hugh T. Kerr expresses a typical sentiment: "His literary style was heavy and wooden; German students sometimes joked that they preferred to read him in the more lucid French translations." Kerr, ed., *Readings in Christian Thought* (Nashville, Tennessee: Abingdon Press, 1966), p. 262. On Troeltsch's literary style, see further, for example, Clarence E. Craig, "Ernst Troeltsch," p. 259; M. C. D'Arcy, "Ernst Troeltsch," p. 13; Benjamin A. Reist, *Toward a Theology of Involvement*, p. 11; and John Baillie, review of *Die Soziallehren* in *Review of Theology and Philosophy*, 10 (July 1914–June 1915):609, 617.
5. *G.S.* III:viii; 110, n. 47.
6. Troeltsch did not consider seriously non-Occidental philosophies of history. His attitude becomes understandable, though perhaps not completely acceptable, for a complex of reasons that hinges on his meaning of "Europeanism," developed especially in *G.S.* III, which I examine later in this chapter.
7. *G.S.* III:12.
8. Ibid.; emphasis mine.
9. Ernst Laslowski, "Probleme des Historismus," *Historisches Jahrbuch*, 62–63 (1949): 593.
10. Regarding Troeltsch's esteem for the contingent, see "Die Bedeutung des Begriffs der Kontingenz" (1910), *G.S.* II:769–78.
11. *G.S.* III:13. Cf. Norman Austin, "Greek Historiography," *The Greek Historians* (New York: Van Nostrand–Reinhold, 1969), pp. 1–75.
12. See *Augustin, die christliche Antike und das Mittelalter* (Munich and Berlin: R. Oldenbourg, 1915). Cf. Emil Brunner, *Man in Revolt: A Christian Anthropology*, trans. Olive Wyon (Philadelphia: Westminster, 1947), pp. 435, n. 1; 451, n. 1.
13. *G.S.* III:14: "Diese Geschichte keine Geschichte ist."
14. Ibid.
15. *The Social Teaching of the Christian Churches* (1960), 1:64 ff.
16. *G.S.*III:15.
17. Ibid.
18. "Renaissance und Reformation" (1913), *G.S.* IV:267–68.
19. Ibid., p. 273. Cf. Peter Burke, *The Renaissance Sense of the Past* (New York: St. Martin's, 1969).
20. *Protestantism and Progress* (1958), p. 156.
21. Ibid., p. 130.
22. Ibid., pp. 158–59. Troeltsch elsewhere suggested that the Protestantism of the Reformation era lacked any integral connections with nonreligious scholarship; for example, "zur Wissenschaft hat der Altprotestantismus eine innere Beziehung nicht bessessen." "Das Verhältnis des Protestantismus zur Kultur" (1913), *G.S.* IV:201.
23. *Protestantism and Progress*, p. 86.
24. *G.S.* III:597.
25. Ibid., p. 105.
26. Ibid., pp. 105–106.
27. Ibid., p. 16.
28. Cf. Harry Elmer Barnes, *A History of Historical Writing*, 2nd ed., rev. (New York: Dover, 1962), p. 192; or Elizabeth Farquhar Flower, "Philosophies of History," in Vergilius Ferm, ed., *A History of Philosophical Systems* (New York: Philosophical Library, 1950), p. 578.

29. *G.S.* III:18, 104, n. 45. Cf. Ernst Cassirer, *The Logic of the Humanities*, trans. C. S. Howe (New Haven: Yale University Press, 1961), pp. 52 ff.

30. *G.S.* III:11.

31. "Die Aufklärung" (1897), *G.S.* IV:353.

32. Ibid., p. 351.

33. *G.S.* III:17.

34. See, for example, ibid., p. 24.

35. Ibid., p. 16. See further "Das stoisch-christliche Naturrecht und das moderne profane Naturrecht" (1911), *G.S.* IV:166–91.

36. For example: "Aus diesem Zusammentreffen entstand die histoire philosophique oder philosophie de l'histoire, wie sie Voltaire geschaffen hat, . . . die Umbindung der katholischen Geschichtsphilosophie Bossuets in völlig moderne Probleme." *G.S.* III:17. Dating the origin of the philosophy of history from Voltaire is not uncommon. See, for example, Fritz Stern, ed., *The Varieties of History: From Voltaire to the Present* (Cleveland, Ohio: World, 1956); as well as an essay published within the decade of Troeltsch's own "Die Aufklärung" by Paul Sakmann: "Die Probleme der historischen Methodik und der Geschichtsphilosophie bei Voltaire," *Historische Zeitschrift*, 97 (1906):327–79, appearing in translation in *History and Theory*, Beiheft 11 (1971):24–59.

37. *G.S.* III:18–19. On Rousseau's greater impact in Germany than in his homeland, see "Der Deismus" (1898), *G.S.* IV:487. Apropos to Troeltsch's sympathetic handling of Rousseau and his evident antipathy towards Enlightenment rationalism, one might note that at the time of Troeltsch's death the Romantic-influenced concept of the historical individual totality (*die historisch-individuelle Totalität*) was central to his thought, a state of mind his friend, Friedrich von Hügel, among others, lamented as undesirable "excessive individualism." Hügel, Introduction to Troeltsch's *Christian Thought*, p. 17.

38. "Der deutsch Idealismus" (1900), *G.S.* IV:532–87. See also "Der Geist der deutschen Kultur," in Otto Hintze et al., eds., *Deutschland und der Weltkrieg* (Berlin and Leipzig: Teubner, 1915), pp. 82–83.

39. *Encyclopaedia of Religion and Ethics*, 1924 ed., s.v. "Idealism."

40. Troeltsch noted that idealism was not confined solely to Germany either, citing examples of it in France in Cousin, Renouvier, and Maine de Biran, and in Britain in Coleridge, T. H. Green, Hutchinson Sterling, the Cairds, and the Seths. Ibid., p. 93.

41. *Encyclopaedia of Religion and Ethics*, s.v. "Kant."

42. *G.S.* III:127, 23.

43. Ibid., pp. 129–30. See also ibid., pp. 541 ff.

44. Ibid., p. 132.

45. Ibid., p. 770, n. 417. See also ibid., pp. 253–54.

46. Ibid., p. 132.

47. Ibid., p. 130.

48. Ibid., p. 263.

49. "Naturrecht und Humanität in der Weltpolitik" (1922), reprinted in *Deutscher Geist*, p. 22.

50. *G.S.* III:26. See also ibid., p. 167.

51. See, for example, ibid., pp. 132, 255.

52. Ibid., p. 282.

53. In contrast, that is, to strictly political-military-diplomatic historical accounts. Ibid., p. 294.

54. "Die Restaurationsepoche am Anfang des 19. Jahrhunderts" (1913), *G.S.* IV:607. Other German organological thinkers included Savigny, Eichhorn, Jacob Grimm, Böckh, Adam Müller, and the Prussian school including Droysen.

55. *G.S.* III:287.

56. "Der deutsche Idealismus," p. 581.

57. *G.S.* III:309.

58. Ibid., p. 138.

59. Ibid., p. 707.

60. Ibid., p. 21.

61. Ibid., pp. 20–21.

154 *Notes*

62. "Naturrecht und Humanität in der Weltpolitik," p. 17.
63. *G.S.* III: 149. Donald E. Miller has called Troeltsch's treatment of Marx "one of the most perceptive and illuminating analyses of the theories of Karl Marx available in any language." Miller, "Troeltsch's Critique of Karl Marx," p. 117. See also Michael Pye, "Troeltsch and the Science of Religion," pp. 243–47.
64. *G.S.* III: 342.
65. Ibid., pp. 337–38.
66. Ibid., p. 345.
67. Regarding Troeltsch's indebtedness to Marx, it is inconceivable that Troeltsch could have pioneered as he did in the sociology of religion, and the sociology of knowledge generally, without leaning (at least indirectly) on Marx's earlier labors. On this point see, for example, Hans Bosse, *Marx, Weber, Troeltsch*, passim.
68. *Encyclopaedia of Religion and Ethics*, s.v. "Idealism."
69. *G.S.* III: 421, n. 216.
70. Ibid., pp. 391–92.
71. Ibid., pp. 406–7. By 1922 Troeltsch had resolved satisfactorily for himself the problem posed over two decades earlier: "Wenn Jedermann zugiebt, dass die Wissenschaft völlig frei und doch wieder überall an Voraussetzungen irgendwie gebunden sein müsse, dann ist die Frage nicht so einfach zu entscheiden." "Voraussetzungslose Wissenschaft," *Die Christliche Welt*, 15. Jg., Nr. 50 (13 Dez. 1901): 1179. This article is incorrectly cited as an 1897 publication in *G.S.* II: 183.
72. *G.S.* III: 143, 144. See further Troeltsch's critical review of Wells originally appearing in the *Historische Zeitschrift* in 1922 and reprinted in *G.S.* IV: 699–705.
73. John Higham, *History* (Englewood Cliffs, New Jersey: Prentice-Hall, 1965), p. 98.
74. *G.S.* III: 10.
75. Ibid., p. 22.
76. Ibid., p. 493.
77. Ibid., p. 494.
78. Ibid., pp. 26; 505, n. 264.
79. Ibid., pp. 504. 139–40.
80. Ibid., p. 499.
81. "Das neunzehnte Jahrhundert" (1913), *G.S.* IV: 642.
82. *G.S.* III: 578.
83. Georg Simmel, quoted ibid., p. 577.
84. *G.S.* III: 632.
85. Ibid., p. 634.
86. Ibid., p. 646. See also ibid., p. 141.
87. *Encyclopaedia of Religion and Ethics*, s.v. "Idealism." Troeltsch pointed out that though Bergson owed much to German neo-Kantianism, he "never accentuated, as did Croce, his connection with German thought," *G.S.* III: 634, n. 355. Troeltsch's own "immanent criticism," a central feature of his historical epistemology, was remarkably similar to Bergson's stress on intuition.
88. *G.S.* III: 162.
89. Ibid., p. vii.
90. Ibid., p. 17.
91. Ibid. p. 110, n. 47. Although Troeltsch endorsed the view that viability in this pursuit was a sometime thing, with the "necessary relativity of the philosophy of history" a fact of life, he also was convinced that the absolute could be more or less grasped. *Encyclopaedia of Religion and Ethics*, 1915 ed., s.v. "Historiography."
92. Jean R. de Salis, "La théorie de l'histoire selon Ernst Troeltsch," p. 5.
93. For example, *G.S.* III: 26. On this distinction between "critical philosophy of history" and "speculative philosophy of history," see further W. H. Walsh, *Philosophy of History: An Introduction* (New York: Harper, 1960), pp. 13 ff.
94. *G.S.* III: vii.
95. Ibid., p. 27.
96. Ibid., p. 23.
97. Ibid., p. 24. Among those philosophers of history who helped establish a firm foundation

for the formal logic of history Troeltsch cited Lotze, Sigwart, Wundt, Dilthey, Rickert, Windel-band, Lask, Simmel, Max Weber, Spranger, H. Maier, Ed. Mayer, Xenopol, Schuppe, and Bergson.

98. Ibid., p. 28, n. 14. See also ibid., p. 111.

99. See, for example, s.v. "Historiography," *Encyclopaedia of Religion and Ethics.*

100. *G.S.* III:29.

101. This charge occurs, for example, in Hans Meyerhoff's discussion of the ideas of Charles A. Beard. Meyerhoff, *Philosophy of History in Our Time* (Garden City, New York: Doubleday, 1959), p. 139.

102. *G.S.* III:29.

103. "The Place of Christianity Among the World's Religions" (1923), *Christian Thought* (1957), p. 44.

104. Ibid.

105. S.v. "Historiography," ibid.

106. *G.S.* III:33. See also ibid., p. 120.

107. Ibid., p. 35.

108. See, for example, *Encyclopaedia of Religion and Ethics*, 1912 ed., s.v. "Contin-gency"; and *G.S.* III:182.

109. *G.S.* III:236. See also "Meine Bücher" (1922), *G.S.* IV:10. Troeltsch did not totally ignore the role of the nomothetic generalization in history, as James Luther Adams points out in "Ernst Troeltsch as Analyst of Religion," p. 107. Troeltsch's nomothetic-ideographic dichotomy was in the nature of a polar contrast of ideal-types, the extreme ends of a seven-staged continuum of the sciences (*Wissenschaften*) and not a simplistic classification (*G.S.* III:80, n. 34), with this scheme allowing for various "descriptive sciences" where both ideographic and nomothetic ele-ments were mixed together (*G.S.* III:229). Further on neo-Kantianism in Troeltsch, see Eckhard Lessing, *Die Geschichtsphilosophie Ernst Troeltschs*, pp. 57–112.

110. S.v. "Contingency," ibid.

111. *G.S.* III:32.

112. Ibid., p. 39.

113. Ibid., p. 40.

114. Ibid., p. 42.

115. Ibid., p. 43.

116. Ibid., p. 44.

117. Ibid.

118. Ibid., p. 46.

119. Ibid., p. 47.

120. Ibid., p. 46.

121. Ibid., p. 48.

122. S.v. "Historiography," ibid.

123. *G.S.* III:49, n. 21. Troeltsch likewise rejected the antithetical view of normal creative development endorsed by Bergson whereby the world of natural science was made to appear as the aberration.

124. "Die Aufklärung," pp. 339–40.

125. *G.S.* III:50. See also s.v. "Contingency," ibid.

126. *G.S.* III:51. Despite his stance against determinism in history, Troeltsch somehow man-aged to retain his endorsement of theological predestination. See ibid., pp. 101–2.

127. Ibid., p. 51.

128. Ibid., p. 53.

129. Ibid., p. 312.

130. Ibid., p. 54.

131. Ibid., p. 241.

132. See, for example, Troeltsch's own acknowledgement in ibid., p. 238, n. 102. Troeltsch also used Rickert's position as a framework for his views on the category of the individual totality, the concept of universal history, and axiology or the study of values.

133. See, for example, Gottfried Martin, "A Lifetime's Study of Kant," *Synthese*, 23 (Au-gust 1971):2–17.

134. *G.S.* III:559.

135. Ibid. See Troeltsch's substantial quotes from Rickert, ibid., p. 237.

136. See, for example, "Meine Bücher," p. 9.

137. Heinrich Rickert, quoted in *G.S.* III:564, n. 307.

138. Rickert again quoted ibid., p. 563.

139. *G.S.* III:156.

140. Ibid., p. 235.

141. Ibid., p. 222; emphases mine.

142. Ibid., p. 119.

143. Ibid., p. 176.

144. Ibid., p. 531. R. G. Collingwood concurred about the importance of Dilthey's emphasis on the historian's inward experiencing (*Erlebnis*) of historical objects: "This conception of the historian as living in the object, or rather making his object live in him, is a great advance on anything achieved by Dilthey's German contemporaries." Collingwood, *The Idea of History* (New York: Oxford University Press, 1946), p. 172.

145. *G.S.* III:531.

146. Troeltsch acknowledged that in Dilthey's later works he sought to modify this imbalance neglected in works like the *Einleitung in die Geisteswissenschaften*. *G.S.* III:522.

147. Ibid., p. 79. In a symposium on the theme, "What is Philosophy of History?," one of Troeltsch's critics, Maurice Mandelbaum, suggested in principle (somewhat unconvincingly) the plausibility of "a rejection of the belief in the adequacy of any material philosophy of history." *Journal of Philosophy*, 49 (May 1952):361.

148. See, for example, *G.S.* III:26.

149. "Nicht um Vergangenes rechten, sondern Zukunftiges fordern," *Kunstwart*, 32 (Aug. 1919):169. In this activist orientation Troeltsch shows the influence of Paul de Lagarde, who had written: "Shame on the man who, while his neighbor's house is ablaze, pursues learned studies about the nature of fire, instead of extinguishing the fire. Pure theology is worth nothing; today's world is basically evil and immoral; to improve it must be the chief goal of our lives and labors." Lagarde, quoted in Fritz Stern, *The Politics of Cultural Despair: A Study in the Rise of the Germanic Ideology* (Garden City, New York: Doubleday, 1965), p. 61.

150. *G.S.* III:67.

151. Ibid., p. 112.

152. See also my initial stress in Chap. 1 on Troeltsch's persistent awareness that "everything is tottering!"

153. *G.S.* III:201.

154. Friedrich Meinecke, "Ernst Troeltsch und das Problem des Historismus," p. 375.

155. Ibid., p. 369. Meinecke's own translation is: "Alles fliesst, gib mir den Punkt, wo ich stehen kann."

156. "The Ethics of Cultural Values (1923), *Christian Thought*, p. 105.

157. Ibid., pp. 102–3.

158. Ibid., p. 95.

159. *G.S.* III:152. Troeltsch similarly criticized a follower of Rickert, Georg Mehlis, whose method he described as "the manipulation of history as illustrative material for a rational system of values." Ibid., p. 160.

160. Ibid., p. 182. See also ibid., p. 169, and "The Morality of the Personality and of the Conscience" (1923), p. 92.

161. *G.S.* III:116.

162. "The Ethics of Cultural Values," p. 109.

163. *G.S.* III:122.

164. Ibid., p. 211.

165. "Morality of the Personality," pp. 73–74.

166. *G.S.* III:183.

167. "The Ethics of Cultural Values," p. 95.

168. Ibid., p. 115.

169. *G.S.* III:113.

170. Ibid., p. 200. In this regard, Rolf Schroeter appears to err when he remarks that "the cultural synthesis is not a formation of present and future but a mode of thinking about the past." Schroeter, "Geschichte und Geschichtlichkeit in der deutschen Philosophie der Gegenwart"

(Ph.D. dissertation, Cologne University, 1937), p. 19. In contrast (*G.S.* III:221): "The material philosophy of history tends towards a cultural synthesis which is obliged to shape the present and future out of a disciplined historical illumination of the past."

171. *G.S.* III:169.

172. Ibid., p. 26. See also ibid., p. 167; and cf. Rickert, whose system eliminated the need for such a synthesis of culture: "The past can play no role whatsoever as the stage of a realization of value." Rickert, quoted ibid., p. 157.

173. "The Ethics of Cultural Values," p. 117. See also *G.S.* III:697–98.

174. Friedrich Meinecke, quoted in *G.S.* III:697, n. 370.

175. *G.S.* III:52.

176. Ibid., p. 654.

177. Review of Oswald Spengler's *Der Untergang des Abendlandes*, vol. 1, originally in *Historische Zeitschrift* (1919), reprinted in *G.S.* IV:680.

178. Review of Oswald Spengler's *Der Untergang des Abendlandes*, vol. 2, originally in *Historische Zeitschrift* (1923), reprinted in *G.S.* IV:687.

179. *G.S.* III:709; and "The Idea of Natural Law and Humanity in World Politics" (1923), *Christian Thought*, p. 221.

180. *G.S.* III:771. See also "Die Aussichten der Weltrevolution und die Zersetzung der Sozialdemokratie," *Kunstwart*, 32 (Sept. 1919):211.

181. *G.S.* III:113.

182. Ibid., pp. 765 ff.

183. Ibid., p. 767.

184. Ibid., p. 167. Troeltsch regarded ancient Hebraic ethics, the only pre-Grecian source he considered useful, as having become detached from its original milieu and now "a revealed or even a rational ethics of mankind." Ibid., p. 768.

185. Ibid., p. 171. See also ibid., p. 770.

186. Ibid., p. 763.

187. Ibid., p. 195.

188. Ibid., p. 192.

189. Ibid., p. 198–99.

190. "Morality of the Personality," p. 92.

191. *G.S.* III:692.

192. "Idea of Natural Law," p. 218.

193. See, for example, *G.S.* III:649 ff., and 690–91; as well as "Das neunzehnte Jahrhundert," p. 625.

194. *G.S.* III:186, 705–7.

195. See, for example, "The Common Spirit" (1923), *Christian Thought*, pp. 123 ff.

196. "The Common Spirit," p. 136.

197. *G.S.* III:703.

198. Ibid., p. 186.

199. Ibid., pp. 706–7.

200. Ibid., p. 710.

201. See, for example, ibid., p. 188.

202. Ibid., pp. 705–6. See also "The Common Spirit," pp. 143–44.

203. *G.S.* III:708; emphasis mine.

204. Hermann Hesse, *Demian*, trans. Michael Roloff and Michael Lebeck (New York: Harper & Row, 1965), p. 123.

205. *G.S.* III:707, 711.

206. "The Ethics of Cultural Values," p. 106. See also "Politics, Patriotism, Religion" (1923), *Christian Thought*, p. 154.

207. *G.S.* III:708–10.

208. "Grundprobleme der Ethik" (1902), *G.S.* II:552.

Chapter 5

1. On the transformation of Berlin itself from a regional center to the national capital of Germany, see Gerhard Masur, *Imperial Berlin* (New York: Basic Books, 1970). For introductions

158   Notes

to Troeltsch's political thought and activities see further: Arrigo Rapp, *Il Problema della Germania*; Gustav Schmidt, *Deutscher Historismus und der Übergang zur parlamentarischen Demokratie*; Eric C. Kollman, "Eine Diagnose der Weimarer Republik," pp. 291–319; and G. M. Schwarz, "Deutschland und Westeuropa bei Ernst Troeltsch," pp. 510–47.

2. On the political atmosphere in Bavaria, see, for example, the opening pages of Harold J. Gordon, Jr., *Hitler and the Beer Hall Putsch* (Princeton, New Jersey: Princeton University Press, 1972); and Troeltsch, "Die Verfassungskrise," *Kunstwart*, 35 (Okt. 1921): 29–30.

3. Gerhard Ritter, *The Sword and the Scepter: The Problem of Militarism in Germany*, vol. 3: *The Tragedy of Statesmanship: Bethmann Hollweg as War Chancellor (1914–1917)*, trans. Heinz Norden (Coral Gables, Florida: University of Miami Press, 1972), p. 1.

4. Kollman, "Eine Diagnose," p. 293.

5. Ibid., p. 313.

6. "Meine Bücher" (1922), *Gesammelte Schriften* (hereafter, *G.S.*) IV: 174.

7. Ibid., p. 175.

8. *International Encyclopedia of the Social Sciences*, 1968 ed., s.v. "Troeltsch, Ernst," by Thomas F. O'Dea.

9. Hermann Diehl, "Zeitschriften-Umschau," *Die Christliche Welt*, 35 (27 Jan. 1921): 68. In his periodic essays Troeltsch generally focused upon topical themes and major developments, leaving detailed reporting on daily developments to the more frequently appearing newspapers.

10. Troeltsch contributed at least sixty-nine signed articles to *Der Kunstwart* (of which only thirty-two bore the pseudonym *"Spektator"*) which have been anthologized by Hans Baron as *Spektator-Briefe*. The selections have been judiciously made, but because several dozen articles were omitted entirely and because more than forty of the selections have been included only in part, for the sake of consistency all references in subsequent footnotes here will be to the original articles and not to the more conveniently available but incomplete anthology.

11. Troeltsch, quoted in Walther Köhler, *Ernst Troeltsch*, p. 293.

12. Kollman, "Eine Diagnose," p. 314.

13. Köhler, *Ernst Troeltsch*, p. 292. Köhler also remarks that in light of Troeltsch's basically apolitical nature it was fortunate that the possibility of Troeltsch's candidacy for president of the Weimar Republic never materialized.

14. Felix Gilbert, *The End of the European Era: 1890 to the Present* (New York: Norton, 1970), p. 129. The material dealing with the impact of the war on Germany is enormous.

15. *Nach Erklärung der Mobilmachung* (Heidelberg: Carl Winters Universitätsbuchhandlung, 1914), p. 4. See also "Wahnsinn oder Entwicklung?," *Kunstwart*, 32 (Feb. 1919): 81.

16. "Imperialismus," *Die neue Rundschau*, 16 (Jan. 1915): 2.

17. "Friede auf Erden," *Die Hilfe*, 51 (17 Dez. 1914): 833.

18. Ibid., p. 834.

19. "Der Völkerkrieg und das Christentum," *Die Christliche Welt*, 39 (15 Apr. 1915): 298.

20. "Ernst Gedanken zum Reformations-Jubiläum," p. 87.

21. "Der Völkerkrieg und das Christentum," p. 295. For comments on Troeltsch's alleged overreaction to the crisis of Christianity during the war, see Ludwig Heitmann, "Der Völkerkrieg und das Christentum: Eine Erwiderung," *Die Christliche Welt*, 39 (6 Mai 1915): 360–64; as well as Theodor Häring, "Bemerkung zu Troeltschs Artikel 'Der Weltkrieg und das Christentum,'" ibid., pp. 358–60.

22. *Deutscher Glaube und deutsche Sitte in unserem grossen Kriege* (Berlin: Verlag Kameradschaft, 1914), p. 26. On the dilemma of Christianity and war see further ibid., pp. 15–16, 24–30; as well as "Privatmoral und Staatsmoral," *Die neue Rundschau*, 27 (Feb. 1916): passim, esp. 146, 167–68.

23. "Friede auf Erden," p. 834.

24. Raymond Aron, *The Century of Total War* (Garden City, New York: Doubleday, 1954), p. 25.

25. *Das Wesen des Deutschen* (Heidelberg: Carl Winters Universitätsbuchhandlung, 1915), p. 32.

26. Klaus Epstein, *Matthias Erzberger and the Dilemma of German Democracy* (Princeton, New Jersey: Princeton University Press, 1959), p. 96.

27. *Nach Erklärung der Mobilmachung*, p. 10.

28. A. J. P. Taylor has remarked that during the war "every nation thought it was defending

its existence." This aspiration certainly was true for Troeltsch, at least at the beginning of the war. Taylor, *A History of the First World War* (New York: Capricorn, 1969), p. 16.

29. *Nach Erklärung der Mobilmachung*, p. 6.

30. See, for example, *Das Wesen des Deutschen*, pp. 20–22; and cf. "Die Ideen von 1914," *Die neue Rundschau*, 27 (Mai 1916):607–9, where Troeltsch contrasted the more complicated conditions of war in the twentieth century with those of the Napoleonic period.

31. *Nach Erklärung der Mobilmachung*, pp. 11–12.

32. Ibid., p. 5. The previous wars that Troeltsch cited were the mid-sixteenth-century religious wars of the Reformation, the Thirty Years' War, the wars of Louis XIV, the wars of Frederick the Great, the Napoleonic wars, and the wars of the *Reichsgründung*. Ibid., pp. 4–5. Troeltsch used the same volcano imagery after the war in "Die Aussichten der Weltrevolution und die Zersetzung der Sozialdemokratie," *Kunstwart*, 32 (July 1919):211.

33. *Unser Volksheer* (Heidelberg: Carl Winters Universitätsbuchhandlung, 1914), p. 7.

34. Herbert J. Muller, *Freedom in the Modern World* (New York: Harper & Row, 1966), p. 228.

35. *Unser Volksheer*, pp. 18–19.

36. Ibid., p. 5. Cf. the later "Das Ende des Militarismus," *Kunstwart*, 32 (Dez. 1918):175, where Troeltsch recorded his complaint that because of the prolonged course of the war the *Volksheer* concept had broken down to the point that "in spite of its appearance as a people's army, in actuality the army was identified with the officer corps."

37. *Unser Volksheer*, p. 14.

38. Ibid., p. 19.

39. *Das Wesen des Deutschen*, p. 3.

40. In this anti-English bias Troeltsch was not untypical of widespread German wartime sentiment, which reached an early peak in the *"Hasslied"*—the Hymn of Hate against England—made available in translation for the English-speaking world early in the war in the *New York Times* of 15 October 1914. To Troeltsch's credit, he did emphasize the need to get to know England better, criticizing German stereotypes of England as contained, for example, in Bernhardi. See, for example, *Der Kulturkrieg* (Berlin: C. Heymanns, 1915), pp. 32–33.

41. *Das Wesen des Deutschen*, pp. 3–5.

42. Ibid., p. 5.

43. On this important maneuver, see, for example, Robert B. Asprey, *The First Battle of the Marne* (Philadelphia: Lippincott, 1962).

44. Ernst Kris and Nathan Leites, "Trends in Twentieth Century Propaganda," in Bernard Berelson and Morris Janowitz, eds., *Reader in Public Opinion and Communication*, 2nd ed. (New York: Free Press, 1966), p. 268.

45. "Der Geist der deutschen Kultur," in Otto Hintze et al., eds., *Deutschland und der Weltkrieg* (Berlin and Leipzig: Teubner, 1915), p. 55.

46. *Der Kulturkrieg*, pp. 6, 20, 16. Copy like this illustrates the empirical generalizations that propaganda from World War I vis-à-vis that from World War II generally tended to lack sobriety, to be more emotionally charged and moralistic, and to disregard the facts more often. Kris and Leites, "Trends in Twentieth Century Propaganda," p. 269.

47. *Der Kulturkrieg*, p. 11.

48. Ibid., p. 14.

49. "Der Geist der deutschen Kultur," p. 56.

50. Gerhard Ritter, *The German Problem: Basic Questions of German Political Life, Past and Present*, trans. Sigurd Burckhardt (Columbus, Ohio: Ohio State University Press, 1965), p. 189.

51. *Das Wesen des Deutschen*, p. 6.

52. "Der Geist der deutschen Kultur," p. 56.

53. *Der Kulturkrieg*, p. 26.

54. "Der Geist der deutschen Kultur," p. 56.

55. *Der Kulturkrieg*, p. 27. For a fuller disavowal of any German imperialist aspirations, see further "Imperialismus," passim: and cf. the works of Fritz Fischer.

56. *Humanismus und Nationalismus in unserem Bildungswesen* (Berlin: Weidmannsche Buchhandlung, 1917), p. 42.

57. *Deutscher Glaube und deutsche Sitte*, p. 11.

58. *Das Wesen des Deutschen*, p. 19.

160   *Notes*

59. Ibid. On the relation of German national values to more universal classical and humanistic values, see further *Humanismus und Nationalismus*, passim.

60. In an article dated 5 September 1914—barely a month after war had been declared—Troeltsch still nostalgically held out the prospect and hope of a broader, less nationalistic, cultural allegiance, as seen in "Der Krieg und die Internationalität der geistigen Kultur," *Internationale Monatsschrift für Wissenschaft, Kunst und Technik*, 9 (1 Okt. 1914):51–58.

61. *Humanismus und Nationalismus*, p. 11.

62. See especially "Der Geist der deutschen Kultur," passim; "Konservativ und Liberal," *Die Christliche Welt*, 30 (1916):663–64; and "Ueber einige Eigentümlichkeiten der angelsächsischen Zivilisation," *Die neue Rundschau*, 28 (Feb. 1917):230 and passim.

63. *Humanismus und Nationalismus*, p. 38.

64. Cf. the parallel though less developed structure of an earlier address, *Das Wesen des Deutschen*, especially pp. 20 ff.

65. "Der Geist der deutschen Kultur," p. 90.

66. Partially because of this largesse of spirit, it was possible for Troeltsch only several years after war's end to contract a speaking tour in England, the product of which was the never delivered but posthumously published series of addresses, *Christian Thought*.

67. "Der Geist der deutschen Kultur," p. 59, n. 7.

68. Ibid. Troeltsch thought the Russian way of life—at least before the 1917 Revolution—more akin to German *Kultur* than to Anglo-French civilization. Ibid., pp. 63–64. Further on this important distinction see Johann Knobloch, Hugo Moser, Wolfgang Schmidt-Hidding, Mario Wandruszka, Leo Weisgerber, Margarete Woltner, eds., *Europäische Schlüsselwörter*, vol. 3: *Kultur und Zivilisation* (Munich: M. Hueber, 1967), especially pp. 288 ff.

69. "Der Geist der deutschen Kultur," p. 76.

70. Ibid., p. 79.

71. Ibid., p. 80.

72. Ibid.

73. Ibid., p. 81.

74. Ibid., p. 83.

75. Ibid., p. 84.

76. Ibid., pp. 84–85.

77. *Der Kulturkrieg*, p. 33; and "Die deutsche Idee von der Freiheit," *Die neue Rundschau*, 27 (Jan. 1916):55. See also ibid., p. 61.

78. "Der Ansturm der westlichen Demokratie," in *Die deutsche Freiheit: Fünf Vorträge von Harnack, Meinecke, Sering, Troeltsch, Hintze* (Gotha: F. A. Perthes, 1917), p. 86.

79. "Die Ideen von 1914," pp. 618–20. National comparisons occur in Troeltsch, for example, for English-French-German, in "Der Geist der deutschen Kultur," pp. 87–88; for English-French-American-German, in "Die deutsche Idee von der Freiheit," pp. 61–65; and cf. for English-French-American-Russian liberal-democratic ideas, "Der Ansturm der westlichen Demokratie," pp. 97–109. In these capsule sketches of non-German nation-states, Troeltsch may have veered towards resuscitating antiquated stereotypes (as Georg Iggers suggests in *The German Conception of History*), but these exaggerations undoubtedly encouraged by the context of the *Kulturkrieg* do not diminish the principle he was intent on pursuing, namely, the benefits of comparative history in understanding current events.

80. Cf. Leonard Krieger, *The German Idea of Freedom: History of a Political Tradition* (Boston: Beacon, 1957). In pursuit of this theme, that different historical experiences significantly determine a people's idea of freedom, Troeltsch went so far as to state—in a late 1915 speech in the capital of the Austro-Hungarian Empire, Germany's chief ally in the war—that even within the central European block of German powers different variations of freedom were visible. "Die deutsche Idee von der Freiheit," p. 53.

81. "Die Ideen von 1914," p. 618.

82. "Die deutsche Idee von der Freiheit," p. 68.

83. "Der Geist der deutschen Kultur," p. 89.

84. "Die deutsche Idee von der Freiheit," p. 59.

85. "Die Ideen von 1914," p. 618; and "Die deutsche Idee von der Freiheit," p. 74.

86. "Die deutsche Idee von der Freiheit," p. 70.

87. "Der Geist der deutschen Kultur," p. 89.

88. Further on these "ideas of 1914" see, of course, "Die Ideen von 1914," passim; as well as "Konservativ und Liberal," pp. 662–63, where Troeltsch contrasted "der Geist von 1914" with Western European values.

89. "Der Geist der deutschen Kultur," p. 90.

90. *Unser Volksheer*, p. 16. See also "Ueber einige Eigentümlichkeiten," p. 247 and passim, where Troeltsch countered the image of the "two Germanies" with remarks about the "two Englands."

91. *Der Kulturkrieg*, p. 29. Cf. "Das Wesen des Weltkrieges," in Max Schwarte, ed., *Der Weltkrieg in seiner Einwirkung auf das deutsche Volk* (Leipzig: Quelle & Meyer, 1918), pp. 19–20, 22; and "Die Ideen von 1914," p. 606. On Prussia "cast both as the hero and the villain of German history," see further E. J. Feuchtwanger, *Prussia: Myth and Reality: The Role of Prussia in German History* (Chicago: H. Regnery, 1970).

92. "Die deutsche Idee von der Freiheit," p. 75.

93. *Der Kulturkrieg*, pp. 20 ff.

94. "Der Ansturm der westlichen Demokratie," p. 81. As one climbs the grand staircase to the main reading room in Harvard University's Widener Library, one passes a huge patriotic mural that was informed by the mentality of this period, depicting American doughboys; the inscription is, "They Crossed the Seas Crusaders Keen to Help / The Nations Battling in a Righteous Cause."

95. "Das Wesen des Weltkrieges," p. 23; and "Die Ideen von 1914," p. 624. Despite these expressed hopes, Troeltsch also felt a foreboding of dire consequences. See, for example, "Das Wesen des Weltkrieges," pp. 18–19; and cf. the earlier *Der Kulturkrieg*, p. 34.

96. "Das Ende des Militarismus," p. 172.

97. Ibid.

98. Sebastian Haffner, *Failure of a Revolution: Germany, 1918–19*, trans. Georg Rapp (London: Deutsch, 1973), p. 178.

99. "Das Ende des Militarismus," p. 174. Cf. Gerhard Thomée, *Der Wiederaufstieg des deutschen Heeres, 1918–1938* (Berlin: Verlag "Die Wehrmacht," 1939).

100. "Das Ende des Militarismus," p. 174.

101. See, for example, ibid., p. 178.

102. "Die Schuldfrage," *Kunstwart*, 32 (Juli 1919):6.

103. "Das Ende des Militarismus," p. 176.

104. Ibid.

105. "Was man vor einem Jahre in Berlin von der Revolution persönlich erleben konnte," *Kunstwart*, 33 (Dez. 1919):272. Although written in November 1918, this *Spektator* letter was not actually published until more than a year later.

106. "Für unsre Selbsterkenntnis," ibid., 32 (Jan. 1919):26.

107. "Allmähliche Klärung," ibid., 32 (März 1919):121; and "Die Aussichten der Weltrevolution," p. 210.

108. "Zentralisation und Dezentralisation," ibid., 33 (Nov. 1919):116.

109. "Wahnsinn oder Entwicklung? (Schluss)," ibid., 32 (März 1919):113.

110. "Rück- und Umblick 2," ibid., 32 (Feb. 1919):98.

111. Sefton Delmer, *Weimar Germany: Democracy on Trial* (London: Macmillan, 1972), p. 54.

112. "Sozialismus," *Kunstwart*, 33 (Feb. 1920):98. See also "Die Aufnahme der Friedensbedingungen," ibid., 32 (Juli 1919):191, where Troeltsch also commented that if the terms of the Versailles Treaty were fulfilled "das wäre die Helotisierung Deutschlands."

113. "Nach Pfingsten," ibid., 32 (Juli 1919):30. For a sampling of world opinion in this same vein see, for example, the multilingual anthology, Alfred von Wegerer, ed., *Das Ausland urteilt! Amerikaner, Engländer, Franzosen, Italiener, Japaner, Russen, Neutrale gegen das Versailler Urteil* (Berlin: G. Stilke, 1929).

114. Quoted in Troeltsch, "Nach Pfingsten," p. 31.

115. Ibid.

116. See the lengthy article on this question contributed to *Der Kunstwart* virtually on the eve of signing the treaty, "Die Schuldfrage," passim.

117. Ibid., p. 6.

118. "Nach Pfingsten," p. 30.

119. "Wieder in Berlin," *Kunstwart*, 33 (Dez. 1919):223.
120. "Nach der Entscheidung," ibid., 32 (Juli 1919):72. See also "Die Schuldfrage," p. 2.
121. "Nach der Entscheidung," p. 73.
122. Ibid., p. 75.
123. "Nach Pfingsten," p. 28.
124. "Links und Rechts," *Kunstwart*, 32 (März 1919):168.
125. "Neue Finsternisse," ibid., 32 (Apr. 1919):26. See also "Die intimen Seiten der deutschen Lage," ibid., 35 (Apr. 1922):25–31.
126. "Nach Pfingsten," p. 28.
127. "Der Beginn der eigentlichen Schwierigkeiten," ibid., 34 (Juni 1921):160.
128. "Die Welle von rechts," ibid., 33 (Jan. 1920):79.
129. "Was man vor einem Jahre," p. 271.
130. "Die Aussichten der Weltrevolution," p. 210.
131. Ibid., p. 209. See also "Nach Pfingsten," p. 29.
132. "Rück- und Umblick," *Kunstwart*, 32 (Feb. 1919):73; and "Demokratie," ibid., 32 (Aug. 1919):95.
133. "Rück- und Umblick 2," p. 99.
134. Other reversals were, for example, his transformation from a Ritschlian to an anti-Ritschlian; his serious Berlin quarrels with the neo-Kantianism he had endorsed in the decade before the war; and his late judgments about the inadequacies of the sociological method in which he had pioneered. These are all treated in previous chapters.
135. "Der Geist der deutschen Kultur," p. 70.
136. Ibid., p. 84. Similar comments are found elsewhere, for example, in *Der Kulturkrieg*, "Konservativ und Liberal," "Privatmoral und Staatsmoral," "Der Ansturm der westlichen Demokratie," and "Die deutsche Idee von der Freiheit."
137. "Demokratie," p. 99.
138. Ibid. See also "Das Ende des Militarismus," p. 178; and cf. "Sozialismus," p. 97.
139. "Demokratie," p. 96. Cf. "Der neue Geist," *Kunstwart*, 33 (Okt. 1919):28.
140. See, for example, "Aristokratie," *Kunstwart*, 33 (Okt. 1919):51.
141. Ibid., pp. 50–51.
142. "Demokratie," pp. 93 ff.; as well as "Wahnsinn oder Entwicklung?," pp. 83–84; *Unser Volksheer*, p. 13; and "Aristokratie," p. 49.
143. "Sozialismus," p. 97. See also "Aristokratie," p. 50.
144. "Demokratie," p. 101. Such an accommodationist attitude justifies calling Troeltsch a "modernist" in the sense of Fritz Ringer, *The Decline of the German Mandarins*, passim.
145. "Demokratie," p. 99.
146. Ibid., p. 100.
147. Ibid., pp. 100–101. See also "Bethmann-Hollweg," *Kunstwart*, 34 (Feb. 1921): 291–92.
148. "Die Republik," *Kunstwart*, 36 (Nov. 1922):108–10; and "Demokratie," p. 102.
149. "Demokratie," p. 101.
150. "Das Ende des Militarismus," p. 178.
151. See "Aristokratie," passim; "Das Ende des Militarismus," pp. 174–75; and "Wahnssin oder Entwicklung?," pp. 109 ff.
152. "Sozialismus," pp. 98, 100–101.
153. Ibid., p. 101.
154. "Demokratie," passim.
155. For an early overview see, for example, "Rück- und Umblick," pp. 72–73; "Rück- und Umblick 2," pp. 92–99; and then "Allmähliche Klärung," pp. 121–23; as well as "Die Aufgaben der Reichsregierung," *Kunstwart*, 33 (Feb. 1920):179–83.
156. "Allmächliche Klärung," p. 123; and "Die Aufgaben der Reichsregierung," p. 180.
157. "Die Ideen von 1914," p. 615; "Die Aufgaben der Reichsregierung," pp. 180–81. Troeltsch wanted to "smashed to pieces the entire paper-splendor which today counterfeits an appearance of well-being." "Allmähliche Klärung," p. 123.
158. "Die Ideen von 1914," p. 616. A discussion of the economic consequences of the war is found in "Wahnsinn oder Entwicklung?," pp. 109–13; and for the economic aspects of problems

of centralization, see "Zentralisation und Dezentralisation," pp. 115–20; and "Kritik am System: Die Kammer der Arbeit," *Kunstwart*, 33 (Juni 1920):261–66.

159. "Die Aufgaben der Reichsregierung," p. 181.

160. "Produktivität," *Kunstwart*, 32 (Sept. 1919):252. See also "Die Republik," p. 93.

161. "Produktivität," p. 253.

162. Ibid., p. 252. On the related contemporary attitudes of nihilism and anarchism, see "Der neue Geist," pp. 30–31.

163. "Productivität," p. 254.

164. "Die Aufgaben der Regierung: Kulturfragen," *Kunstwart*, (Juni 1920):315. This article is anticipated in "Die Aufgaben der Reichsregierung," p. 182, where Troeltsch isolates "the socalled cultural question" as one of six great tasks facing the government.

165. "Die Aufgaben der Regierung: Kulturfragen," p. 314.

166. Ibid., pp. 315–19.

167. "Die Aufgaben der Reichsregierung," p. 182.

168. "Allmähliche Klärung," p. 123.

169. "Die Aussichten der Weltrevolution," p. 209; "Äussere und innere Politik," *Kunstwart*, 33 (Mai 1920):169; and "Neue Krisen von Aussen," ibid., 34 (März 1921):349.

170. "Neue Eingriffe von Aussen," ibid., 33 (März 1920):220. See also "Die Aufgaben der Reichsregierung," p. 183.

171. See, for example, "Kritik am System," *Kunstwart*, 33 (Apr. 1920):31; as well as "Die Aufgaben der Reichsregierung," p. 182.

172. "Die Aussichten der Weltrevolution," p. 211. See also "Links und Rechts," pp. 167–70.

173. "Links und Rechts," p. 167.

174. See, for example, the opening pages of "Aristokratie," pp. 49 ff.

175. See, for example, "Neue Eingriffe von Aussen," pp. 223–24.

176. "Kritik am System: Das Parteiwesen," *Kunstwart*, 33 (Juni 1920):212–13.

177. Ritter, *Sword and Scepter*, vol. 4: *The Reign of German Militarism and the Disaster of 1918* (Coral Gables, Florida: University of Miami Press, 1973), p. 17.

178. "Kritik am System: Das Parteiwesen," p. 213.

179. "Die Aufgaben der Reichsregierung," p. 179. See also "Ideologien und reale Verhältnisse," *Kunstwart*, 34 (Aug. 1921):287–93.

180. "Aristokratie," p. 51.

181. Ibid., and "Kritik am System," pp. 32–34.

182. For example, the few sentences tucked away in "Kritik am System," p. 34.

183. Troeltsch astutely detected that the real object of these repeated attacks was not Erzberger himself but the democratic, parliamentary system Erzberger represented, with a magnificent parallel existing in the recent Dreyfus affair whereby the person of Dreyfus had been used as a covering symbol for competing systems of values and institutions. Ibid.

184. "Der Enthüllungssturm," *Kunstwart*, 32 (Sept. 1919):212–13.

185. "Der Ansturm gegen die Demokratie," ibid., 32 (Mai 1919):148.

186. "Wider in Berlin," pp. 222–23.

187. "Neue Finsternisse," p. 27.

188. "Neue Krisen und Möglichkeiten," *Kunstwart*, 32 (Aug. 1919):123–24; and "Neue Finsternisse," p. 26. See also on the Bolshevik threat to Germany and Europe, "Die preussiche Nationalversammlung," ibid., 32 (Apr. 1919):82–83, and "Die Aussichten der Weltrevolution," pp. 209–10; and on the danger of socialism leading to "terror by the minority," "Demokratie," pp. 94–95.

189. "Links und Rechts," p. 168. Troeltsch tended to be highly critical of intellectuals meddling in politics; for example, in rebuffing the scapegoating of his own Democratic party by many intelligent Germans—including some of his own colleagues—as the classic story of "nothing learned and nothing forgotten," Troeltsch remarked that "indeed, in Germany scholarly importance often has little to do with political savvy." "Links und Rechts," p. 170.

190. Compare, for example, the remarks scattered in the following four *Kunstwart* articles dated January, May, October, and December, 1919: "Rück- und Umblick," "Die Aufnahme der Friedensbedingungen," "Wieder in Berlin," and "Die Welle von rechts."

191. "Links und Rechts," pp. 169–70.
192. Ibid., p. 170. See also, "Neue Krisen und Möglichkeiten," p. 123.
193. "Die Welle von rechts," pp. 80–81.
194. "Links und Rechts," p. 169.
195. "Die Welle von rechts," p. 82. See also "Die innere Entwicklung der deutschen Revolution," *Kunstwart*, 34 (Dez. 1920):164.
196. "Die Enthüllungssturm," p. 212.
197. "Vorherrschaft des Judentums?," *Kunstwart*, 33 (Jan. 1920):13.
198. Ibid., pp. 12–13, 15.
199. Ibid., p. 14.
200. Ibid.
201. Ibid., p. 16.
202. "Der Putsch der Prätorianer und Junker," *Kunstwart*, 33 (Apr. 1920):82.
203. "Das Ende des Militarismus," p. 178.
204. "Der Putsch der Prätorianer und Junker," p. 83.
205. Ibid., p. 85.
206. "Klassenkampf und Bürgerkrieg," *Kunstwart*, 33 (Mai 1920):126–30; "Aüssere und innere Politik," pp. 169–73; and "Kritik am System: Das Parteiwesen," pp. 210–11.
207. "Kritik am System: Die Kammer der Arbeit," pp. 261–62; and "Kritik am System: Das Parteiwesen," p. 210.
208. "Die Aufgaben der Regierung: Kulturfragen," pp. 313–14.
209. For a convenient statistical breakdown not only of this election but of Reichstag elections 1871–1912 and 1919–1933, see Koppel S. Pinson, *Modern Germany: Its History and Civilization* (New York: Macmillan, 1954), Appendices A and B, pp. 572–75; and for the twenty-one Reich cabinets of the Weimar Republic, Pinson's Appendix C, p. 576. Troeltsch did make passing comments on the succession of cabinets, whose general governmental incompetence in dealing with pressing problems considerably impressed him. See, for example, "Nach der Annahme des Ultimatums," *Kunstwart*, 34 (Juli 1921): 236.
210. "Die innere Entwicklung der deutschen Revolution," p. 163. See also "Die Reichstagswahlen: Eintritt der Revolution in ein neues Stadium," *Kunstwart*, 33 (Aug. 1920):374; "Der Bolschewismus," ibid., 34 (Okt. 1920):36; and "Der Versuch zur Wiedereröffnung des Krieges und die preussischen Wahlen," ibid., 34 (Apr. 1921):37.
211. "Die Reichstagswahlen," p. 375; "Der Bolschewismus," pp. 38–39; and "Die Reparation und Amerika," *Kunstwart*, 34 (Mai 1921):101.
212. "Die Reichstagswahlen," pp. 373–74.
213. "Die innere Entwicklung der deutschen Revolution," p. 166.
214. "Kritik am System: Das Parteiwesen," p. 215.
215. "Die Republik," p. 108.
216. Ibid., p. 107; "Neue Krisen von Aussen her," pp. 353–54; "Die Amerikanisierung Deutschlands," *Kunstwart*, 35 (Jan. 1922): 234; and "Die Reichstagswahlen," p. 376.
217. "Die Reichstagswahlen," p. 376.
218. "Der Versuch zur Wiedereröffnung des Krieges," p. 37; and "Der Beginn der eigentlichen Schwierigkeiten," *Kunstwart*, 34 (Juni 1921):161. See also "Die Amerikanisierung Deutschlands," p. 234; and "Die deutsche Uneinigkeit," *Kunstwart*, 35 (Feb. 1922):288.
219. "Die Verfassungskrise," p. 28. The year before Mussolini's "March on Rome" Troeltsch had already noted the emergence of fascism in Italy. "Nach der Annahme des Ultimatums," pp. 235–37.
220. "Gefährlichste Zeiten," *Kunstwart*, 35 (Aug. 1922):294–96. See also, on Rathenau, "Wieder bei der Reparationskommision," ibid., 35 (July 1922):240; and on the rebellious youth movement which helped form the assassins, "Die geistige Revolution," p. 231.
221. "See- und Landmächte," *Kunstwart*, 35 (März 1922):347; "Die intimen Seiten der deutschen Lage," pp. 25–31; and "Die Republik," p. 110.
222. "Die innere Entwicklung der deutschen Revolution," p. 165.
223. Ibid., p. 166. On signs in foreign politics corresponding with the new phase in the domestic November Revolution, see, for example, "Die Reichstagswahlen," p. 379; and "Der Bolschewismus," p. 37.
224. See, for example, "Die Amerikanisierung Deutschlands," p. 231; "Die Republik," p.

107; "Nach der Annahme des Ultimatums," p. 235; "Wieder bei der Reparationskommision," p. 237; and "Die neue Weltlage," *Kunstwart*, 35 (Juni 1922):158–64, 167.

225. "Das Weltsystem der Entente," *Kunstwart*, 34 (Nov. 1920): 102.

226. Ibid., p. 105; "Die geistige Revolution," p. 227; "Die Reparation und Amerika," p. 100.

227. "Das Weltsystem der Entente," p. 103; and "Die Amerikanisierung Deutschlands," pp. 230–31. The real victor of the war, in Troeltsch's opinion, had been American capitalism.

228. "Ideologien und reale Verhältnisse," pp. 288–89. See also "Der Bolschewismus," pp. 36–44; "Das Weltsystem der Entente," p. 102; and "Die neue Weltlage," pp. 163–64.

229. "Der Beginn der eigentlichen Schwierigkeiten," pp. 160–61; and "Neue Krisen von Aussen her," pp. 350–51; but cf. for the growing tension and diplomatic struggles between England and France, "Die neue Katastrophe und die Stellung des Bürgertums zur Republik," *Kunstwart*, 35 (Dez. 1921):156; "Die deutsche Uneinigkeit," p. 287; and "See- und Landmächte," p. 346.

230. "Der Versuch zur Wiedereröffnung des Krieges," p. 35; "Die deutsche Uneinigkeit," p. 287; and "Die intime Zeiten der deutschen Lage," p. 31.

231. "Neue Krisen von Aussen her," p. 351.

232. "Der Beginn der eigentlichen Schwierigkeiten," p. 163.

233. "Ideologien und reale Verhältnisse," p. 287; and "Die intime Zeiten der deutschen Lage," p. 26; as well as "Der Beginn der eigentlichen Schwierigkeiten," p. 163; "Eine Reise in Holland," *Kunstwart*, 35 (Mai 1922):95; "Die Reparation und Amerika," p. 102.

234. "Die neue Katastrophe," p. 159.

235. "Der Beginn der eigentlichen Schwierigkeiten," pp. 160–62.

236. Ibid., p. 163. See also "Die intime Zeiten der deutschen Lage," p. 31.

237. "Ideologien und reale Verhältnisse," p. 288. See also "Nach der Annahme des Ultimatums," pp. 236–37.

238. See, for example, "Die Republik," p. 107.

Chapter 6

1. Geoffrey Barraclough, *An Introduction to Contemporary History* (Baltimore, Maryland: Penguin Books, 1973), pp. 9, 45–46.

2. Fritz Ringer, *Decline of the German Mandarins*, p. 4.

3. "The Common Spirit" (1923), *Christian Thought*, p. 143.

4. Benjamin A. Reist, *Toward a Theology of Involvement*, p. 201. For further critiques of the Bodenstein-Reist appraisal see, for example, B. A. Gerrish, "Ernst Troeltsch and the possibility of a historical theology," in John Powell Clayton, *Ernst Troeltsch*, pp. 111–12; A. O. Dyson, "Ernst Troeltsch and the possibility of a systematic theology," ibid., p. 98; Hans-Georg Drescher, "Ernst Troeltsch's intellectual development," ibid., pp. 30–31; and Robert Morgan, "Troeltsch and Christian Theology," p. 212. In the 1970s, James Luther Adams repeatedly made the same point in published articles as well as in private correspondence.

5. C. E. Craig, "Ernst Troeltsch," *Methodist Review*, p. 963.

6. Georg Wünsch, "Ernst Troeltsch zum Gedächtnis," p. 107. Troeltsch's death came as a result of a sudden illness, partially due to privations in post-war Germany. Cf. Wilhelm Schenk, "Ernst Troeltsch's Conception of History," p. 29; H. R. Mackintosh, "Troeltsch's Last Book," *The Expository Times*, 35 (1923–24):137; anon., "Notes," ibid., p. 198; Adolf von Harnack, "Rede am Sarge Ernst Troeltschs," p. 102; John Herman Randall, Jr., *The Making of the Modern Mind*, rev. ed. (Boston: Houghton Mifflin, 1940), p. 566.

7. Drescher, "Ernst Troeltsch's intellectual development," pp. 11.

8. *Gesammelte Schriften* (hereafter, *G.S.*), III:vii.

9. Karl Bornhausen, "Ernst Troeltsch und das Problem der wissenschaftlichen Theologie," p. 198.

10. Hugh Quigley, "Ernst Troeltsch," p. 291.

11. H. Stuart Hughes, *Consciousness and Society*, p. 246. It goes without saying that Hughes did not so offhandedly dismiss all of Troeltsch's ideas. See ibid., especially pp. 229–42, 374.

12. T. K. Oesterreich, ed., *Grundriss der Geschichte der Philosophie. Die Deutsche Philosophie des XIX. Jahrhunderts und der Gegenwart* (Basel: B. Schwabe, 1951), p. 602.

166 Notes

13. Sleigh, *Sufficiency of Christianity*, p. 27.
14. Cf. R. M. Wenley, "Friedrich von Hügel," *Anglican Theological Review*, 5 (Oct. 1922):89.
15. Albrecht Dietrich, quoted by Hügel in his Introduction to Troeltsch's *Christian Thought* (1957), p. 16.
16. On the general tendency of all the neo-Kantians to avoid system-making, see Alban G. Widgery, "Classical German Idealism, The Philosophy of Schopenhauer and Neo-Kantianism," in V. Ferm, ed., *A History of Philosophical Systems* (New York: Philosophical Library, 1950), p. 303.
17. "Meine Bücher" (1922), *G.S.* IV:3.
18. Harnack, "Rede am Sarge," p. 103.
19. Wünsch, "Ernst Troeltsch," p. 105.
20. Harnack, "Rede am Sarge," p. 103.
21. Sleigh, *Sufficiency of Christianity*, p. 22. Wilhelm Pauck records similar recollections in *Harnack and Troeltsch*, pp. 45–50.
22. Wünsch, "Ernst Troeltsch," p. 105.
23. *G.S.* III:6; emphasis mine.
24. *The Social Teaching of the Christian Churches* (1960), 1:20; emphasis mine.
25. H. Richard Niebuhr, Introduction, ibid., p. 7.
26. Harnack, "Rede am Sarge," p. 102.
27. Hugh Ross Mackintosh, *Types of Modern Theology*, p. 216.
28. The metaphor of an "incomplete torso" has been used by Walther Köhler, *Ernst Troeltsch*, p. 332; Otto Hintze, "Troeltsch und die Probleme des Historismus," p. 324; and Walter Bodenstein, *Neige des Historismus*, p. 143.
29. Reist, *Toward a Theology of Involvement*, p. 14. Cf. Troeltsch's own demurrer in a letter of Aug. 1921 to Friedrich von Hügel, quoted in Hügel, "Ernst Troeltsch" (letter to the editor), *The Times Literary Supplement* (London), March 29, 1923, p. 216; as well as Friedrich Meinecke's comment in "Ernst Troeltsch und des Problem des Historismus," pp. 367–68.
30. Mackintosh, *Types of Modern Theology*, p. 188.
31. Troeltsch, letter (Feb. 1912) to Friedrich von Hügel, quoted in Hügel, ibid.; emphasis mine.
32. "Politics, Patriotism, Religion" (1923), *Christian Thought*, pp. 177–78; emphasis mine. The wife of Max Weber wrote of Troeltsch, "He is no fighter, but rather disposed to conciliation, compromise, and accommodation to human weaknesses." Marianne Weber, *Max Weber: Ein Lebensbild* (Heidelberg: L. Schneider, 1950), p. 262.
33. "Politics, Patriotism, Religion," p. 177.
34. Ibid., p. 168.
35. Sleigh, *Sufficiency of Christianity*, p. 33. See also Johannes Wendland, "Philosophie und Christentum bei Troeltsch," *Zeitschrift für Theologie und Kirche*, 24 (1914):131; and Hügel, Introduction to *Christian Thought*, p. 31.
36. Bodenstein, *Neige des Historismus*, p. 17.
37. Hervey Ganse Little, "Ernst Troeltsch and the Scope of Historicism," p. 343.
38. *Protestantism and Progress* (1958), p. 198. Cf. "Das neunzehnte Jahrhundert" (1913), *G.S.* IV:645.
39. See, for example, Eugene N. Anderson, "Meinecke's *Ideengeschichte* and the Crisis in Historical Thinking," in *Medieval and Historiographical Essays in Honor of James Westfall Thompson*, ed. James Lea Cate and Eugene N. Anderson (Chicago: University of Chicago Press, 1938); Georg Iggers, "The Dissolution of German Historism"; and Iggers, *The German Conception of History*, especially the last several chapters.
40. Simon, *Germany: A Brief History* (New York: Random House, 1966), p. 307.
41. Bodenstein, *Neige des Historismus*, p. 143.

Selected Bibliography

Following is a list of some useful secondary sources on Troeltsch. All the available writings are not included, nor, with only a few exceptions, are general background works cited here. Selected major works of Troeltsch are also listed, but for other primary source references the reader is referred to footnote documentation throughout the book. The most extensive (though still incomplete) bibliography of Troeltsch's writings published thus far is contained in the fourth volume of his collected works: "Bibliographie der von Troeltsch im Druck erschienen Schriften," *Aufsätze zur Geistesgeschichte und Religionssoziologie, Gesammelte Schriften*, Bd. IV, ed. Hans Baron (Tübingen: J. C. B. Mohr, 1925), pp. 863–72. (*Gesammelte Schriften* is abbreviated in notes as *G.S.*)

Listings of Troeltsch's works in English translation appear as an appendix to Robert Morgan and Michael Pye, trans. and eds., *Ernst Troeltsch: Writings on Theology and Religion* (Atlanta: John Knox Press, 1977), pp. 253–55; and in the bibliography compiled by Jacob Klapwijk in John Powell Clayton, ed., *Ernst Troeltsch and the Future of Theology* (London: Cambridge University Press, 1976), pp. 197–200. In keeping with the renewed interest in Troeltsch studies, further projects are being planned, including the published translation of *Der Historismus und seine Probleme* (*G.S.* III) and *Glaubenslehre*, as well as the compilation of an entirely new volume in his collected works (to become *G.S.* V).

Adams, James Luther. "Ernst Troeltsch as Analyst of Religion." *Journal for the Scientific Study of Religion* 1 (1961):102–6.

———. Introduction to *The Absoluteness of Christianity and the History of Religions*, by Ernst Troeltsch. Trans. David Reid. Richmond, Virginia: John Knox Press, 1971, pp. 7–20.

———. "Troeltsch, Ernst." *Encyclopaedia Britannica*, 1973 ed.

———. "Why the Troeltsch Revival?" *The Unitarian Universalist Christian* 29 (1974):4–15.

Antoni, Carlo. *From History to Sociology: The Transition in German Historical Thinking*. Trans. Hayden V. White. Detroit: Wayne State University Press, 1959.

———. "Problemi e methodi della moderna storiografia: la 'sociologia' e la 'filosofia della storia' di Ernst Troeltsch." *Studi Germanici* 2 (1937):385–416.

———. "Problemi e methodi della moderna storiografia: 'la teologia storica' di Ernst Troeltsch." *Studi Germanici* 2 (1937):255–77.

Apfelbacher, Karl-Ernst. *Frömmigkeit und Wissenschaft: Ernst Troeltsch und sein theologisches Programm*. Munich/Paderborn/Vienna: Schöningh, 1978.

Bainton, Roland H. "Ernst Troeltsch—Thirty Years Later." *Theology Today* 8 (1951):70–96.

Beer, Rainer. *Selbstkritik der Geschichtsphilosophie bei Ernst Troeltsch*. Munich: UNI-Druck, 1958.

Benckert, Heinrich. "Der Begriff der Entscheidung bei Ernst Troeltsch: Ein Beitrag zum Verstandnis seines Denkens." *Zeitschrift für Theologie und Kirche*, N. F. 12 (1931):422–42.

———. *Ernst Troeltsch und das ethische Problem*. Göttingen: Vandenhoeck & Ruprecht, 1932.

Bodenstein, Walter. *Neige des Historismus: Ernst Troeltschs Entwicklungsgang*. Gütersloh: Gerd Mohn, 1959.

Bornhausen, Karl. "Ernst Troeltsch und das Problem der wissenschaftlichen Theologie." *Zeitschrift für Theologie und Kirche*, N. F. 4 (1923):196–223.

Bosse, Hans. *Marx, Weber, Troeltsch: Religionssoziologie und marxistische Ideologiekritik*. Munich: Kaiser, 1970.

Brachmann, Wilhelm. *Ernst Troeltschs historische Weltanschauung*. Halle: Max Niemeyer, 1940.

Bras, Gabriel le, and Séguy, Jean. "Christianismes sociaux et sociologie du Christianisme chez Ernst Troeltsch." *Archives de Sociologie des Religion* 11 (1961):3–14.

Brünning, Walther. "Naturalismus—Historismus—Apriorismus (Das Werk Ernst Troeltsch)." *Studia Philosophica* 15 (1955):35–52.

Christie, Francis A. "Spiritual Values in the Work of Ernst Troeltsch." In *Methods in Social Science*, pp. 415–23. Ed. Stuart A. Rice. Chicago: University of Chicago Press, 1931.

Clayton, John Powell, ed. *Ernst Troeltsch and the Future of Theology*. London: Cambridge University Press, 1976.

Craig, Clarence E. "Ernst Troeltsch." *Methodist Review* 106 (1923):959–63.

Currie, Cecil. "Ernst Troeltsch's Philosophy of History." Ph.D. dissertation, Harvard University, 1946.

D'Arcy, M. C. "Ernst Troeltsch" (review of *Social Teachings*). *Dublin Review* 193 (1933): 13–30.

Dietrich, Albert. "Troeltsch, Ernst Peter Wilhelm." *Deutsches Biographisches Jahrbuch, 1923*. Berlin and Leipzig: Deutsche Verlags-Anstalt, 1930.

Drescher, Hans-Georg. "Das Problem der Geschichte bei Ernst Troeltsch." *Zeitschrift für Theologie und Kirche*, N. F. 57 (1960):186–230.

————. "Glaube und Vernunft bei Ernst Troeltsch: Eine kritische Deutung seiner religionsphilosophischen Grundlegung." Ph.D. dissertation, Marburg University, 1957.

Dyson, Anthony Oakley. "History in the Philosophy and Theology of Ernst Troeltsch." Ph.D. dissertation, Oxford University, 1968.

————. *The Immortality of the Past*. London: SCM Press, 1974.

Englemann, H. *Spontaneität und Geschichte: Zum Historismusproblem bei Ernst Troeltsch*. Frankfort a. M.: Dipa-Verlag, 1972.

Escribano Alberca, Ignacio. *Die Gewinnung theologischer Normen aus der Geschichte der Religion bei E. Troeltsch: Eine methodologische Studie*. Munich: Max Hueber, 1961.

Fellner, Karl. *Das überweltliche Gut und die innerweltliche Güter: Eine Auseinandersetzung mit Ernst Troeltschs Theorie über das Verhältnis von Religion und Kultur*. Leipzig: J. C. Hinrichs, 1927.

Fort, W. F. "Troeltsch's Theory of History." *The Personalist* 28 (1947):59–71.

Frei, Hans W. "The Relation of Faith and History in the Thought of Ernst Troeltsch." In *Faith and Ethics: The Theology of H. Richard Niebuhr*, pp. 53–64. Ed. Paul Ramsey. New York: Harper & Brothers, 1957.

Freisberg, D. *Das Problem der historischen Objektivität in der Geschichtsphilosophie von Ernst Troeltsch*. Emsdetten: Lechte, 1940.

Fülling, Erich. *Geschichte als Offenbarung: Studien zur Frage Historismus und Glaube von Herder bis Troeltsch*. Berlin: Töpelmann, 1956.

Gabriel, Hans-Jürgen. *Christlichkeit der Gesellschaft?: eine kritische Darstellung der Kulturphilosophie von Ernst Troeltsch*. Berlin: Union Verlag, 1975.

Gerrish, B. A. "Jesus, Myth, and History: Troeltsch's Stand in the 'Christ-Myth' Debate." *Journal of Religion* 55 (1975):13–35.

Getzeny, Heinrich. "Ernst Troeltsch als Theologe und Soziologe." *Höchland* 25 (1928):582–97.

Gustafson, Paul M. "UO-US-PS-PO: A Restatement of Troeltsch's Church-Sect Typology." *Journal for the Scientific Study of Religion* 6 (1967):64–68.

Harnack, Adolf von. "Rede am Sarge Ernst Troeltschs." *Die Christliche Welt* 37 (1923):101–5.

Hashagen, Justus. "Troeltsch und Ranke." *Philosophischer Anzeiger* 4 (1930):1–12.

Henderson, Kenneth T. "Ethics and the Control of History: A Study of Troeltsch." *Church Quarterly Review* 32 (1924):116–44.

————. "Troeltsch's Philosophy of History." *Australasian Journal of Psychology and Philosophy* 3 (1925):254–64.

Herberger, Kurt. *Historismus und Kairos: Die Ueberwindung des Historismus bei Ernst Troeltsch und Paul Tillich*. Marburg: H. Bauer, 1935.

Herman, E. "Death of a Great German Thinker." *Homiletic Review* 85 (1923):283–88.

Herring, H. "Max Weber und Ernst Troeltsch als Geschichtsdenker." *Kant-Studien* 59 (1968): 410–34.

Heussi, Karl. *Die Krisis des Historismus*. Tübingen: J. C. B. Mohr, 1932.

Hintze, Otto. "Troeltsch und die Probleme des Historismus." In *Soziologie und Geschichte, Gesammelte Abhandlungen*, 2:323–73. Göttingen: Vandenhoeck & Ruprecht, 1964.

Honigsheim, Paul. "Troeltsch, Ernst." *Handwörterbuch der Sozialwissenschaften*. 1959 ed.

Hügel, Friedrich von. "On the Specific Genius and Capacities of Christianity, Studied in Connection with the Works of Professor Ernst Troeltsch." *Constructive Quarterly* 22 (1914):68–98, 673–701.

——. *The German Soul*. London: J. M. Dent, 1916.

Hughes, H. Stuart. *Consciousness and Society: The Reorientation of European Thought, 1890–1930*. New York: Knopf, 1961.

Iggers, Georg G. "The Dissolution of German Historism." In *Ideas in History*. Ed. Richard Herr and Harold T. Parker. Durham, North Carolina: Duke University Press, 1965.

——. *The German Conception of History: The National Tradition of Historical Thought from Herder to the Present*. Middletown, Connecticut: Wesleyan University Press, 1968.

Ittel, Gerhard Wolfgang. "Die Hauptgedanken der 'religionsgeschichtlichen Schule.'" *Zeitschrift für Religions- und Geistesgeschichte* 10 (1958):61–78.

Johnson, Benton. "On Church and Sect." *American Sociological Review* 28 (1963):539–49.

Johnson, Roger A. "Troeltsch on Christianity and Relativism." *Journal for the Scientific Study of Religion* 1 (1962):220–23.

Kasch, Wilhelm F. *Die Sozialphilosophie von Ernst Troeltsch*. Tübingen: J. C. B. Mohr, 1963.

Kesseler, Kurt. "Ernst Troeltsch als Geschichtsphilosoph." *Monatschrift für höhere Schulen* 23 (1924):87–91.

——. "Ernst Troeltsch als Theologe." *Zeitschrift für den evangelischen Religionsunterricht* 34 (1923):13–17.

Klapwijk, Jacob. *Tussen Historisme en Relativisme: een Studie over de Dynamiek van het Historisme en de Wijsgerige Ontwikkelingsgang van Ernst Troeltsch*. Assen: Van Gorcum, 1970.

Köhler, Walther. *Ernst Troeltsch*. Tübingen: J. C. B. Mohr, 1941.

——. "Ernst Troeltsch." *Zeitschrift für deutsche Kulturphilosophie* 9 (1943):1–21.

Kollman, Eric C. "Eine Diagnose der Weimarer Republik: Ernst Troeltschs politische Anschauungen." *Historische Zeitschrift* 182 (1956):291–319.

Lee, Dwight E., and Beck, Robert N. "The Meaning of 'Historicism.'" *American Historical Review* 59 (1954):568–77.

Leidreiter, Erich. *Troeltsch und die Absolutheit des Christentums*. Mohrungen: Rautenberg, 1927.

Lessing, Eckhard. *Die Geschichtschilosophie Ernst Troeltschs*. Hamburg: Reich, 1965.

Lewis, Leicester C. "Troeltsch vs. Ritschl: A Study in Epochs." *Anglican Theological Review* 1 (1918):42–57.

Liebert, A. "Ernst Troeltsch letztes Werk: Der Historismus und seine Probleme." *Kant-Studien* 29 (1924):359–64.

Liebrich, Hans. *Die historische Wahrheit bei Ernst Troeltsch*. Giessen: R. Glagow, 1937.

Littell, Franklin H. "Church and Sect." *Ecumenical Review* 6 (1954):262–76.

Little, David. "Religion and Social Analysis in the Thought of Ernst Troeltsch." *Journal for the Scientific Study of Religion* 1 (1961):114–17.

Little, Hervey Ganse. "Ernst Troeltsch and the Scope of Historicism." *Journal of Religion* 46 (1966):343–64.

——. "History, Decision, and Responsibility: Examination of a Problem Central to the Thought of Ernst Troeltsch and Rudolf Bultmann." Ph.D. dissertation, Harvard University, 1965.

Lyman, Eugene W. "Ernst Troeltsch's Philosophy of History." *Philosophical Review* 41 (1932):443–65.

Mackintosh, Hugh Ross. *Types of Modern Theology: Schleiermacher to Barth*. London: Nisbet, 1937.

Mandelbaum, Maurice. *The Problem of Historical Knowledge: An Answer to Relativism*. New York: Harper & Row, 1967.

Mannheim, Karl. *Essays on the Sociology of Knowledge*. London: Routledge & Kegan Paul, 1964.

——. "Troeltsch, Ernst." *Encyclopaedia of the Social Sciences*, 1935 ed.

Masur, Gerhard. *Prophets of Yesterday: Studies in European Culture, 1890–1914*. New York: Harper & Row, 1966.

Meinecke, Friedrich. "Ernst Troeltsch und das Problem des Historismus." *Die Deutsche Nation* 5 (1923):183–92.

170 Bibliography

———. "Nachruf auf Ernst Troeltsch." *Historische Zeitschrift* 128 (1923):185–87.
Mertineit, Johannes. *Das Wertproblem in der Philosophie der Gegenwart unter besonderer Berücksichtigung von Ernst Troeltsch.* Berlin: Reuther & Reichard, 1934.
Miller, Donald E. "Conscience and History." Ph.D. dissertation, Harvard University, 1962.
———. "Troeltsch's Critique of Karl Marx." *Journal for the Scientific Study of Religion* 1 (1961):117–21.
Morgan, Robert. "Introduction: Ernst Troeltsch on Theology and Religion." In *Ernst Troeltsch: Writings on Theology and Religion*, pp. 1–51. Trans. and ed. Robert Morgan and Michael Pye. Atlanta: John Knox Press, 1977.
———. "Troeltsch and Christian Theology." In *Ernst Troeltsch: Writings on Theology and Religion*, pp. 208–33. Trans. and ed. Robert Morgan and Michael Pye. Atlanta: John Knox Press, 1977.
Müller, Gotthold. "Die Selbstauflösung der Dogmatik bei Ernst Troeltsch." *Theologische Zeitschrift* 22 (1966):334–46.
Müller-Lauter, Wolfgang. "Konsequenzen des Historismus in der Philosophie der Gegenwart." *Zeitschrift für Theologie und Kirche* 59 (1962):226–55.
Neumann, Carl. "Zum Tode von Ernst Troeltsch." *Deutsche Vierteljahrsschrift für Literaturwissenschaft und Geistesgeschichte* 1 (1923):161–71.
Niebuhr, H. Richard. "Ernst Troeltsch's Philosophy of Religion." Ph.D. dissertation, Yale University, 1924.
———. "Troeltsch, Ernst." *An Encyclopaedia of Religion*, 1959 ed.
Obayashi, Hiroshi. "Pannenberg and Troeltsch: History and Religion." *Journal of the American Academy of Religion* 38 (1970):401–19.
O'Dea, Thomas F. "Troeltsch, Ernst." *International Encyclopedia of the Social Sciences*, 1968 ed.
Ogletree, Thomas Warren. *Christian Faith and History: A Critical Comparison of Ernst Troeltsch and Karl Barth.* New York/Nashville: Abingdon Press, 1965.
Pannenberg, Wolfhart. *Basic Questions in Theology*, 3 vols. London: SCM Press, 1970–1973.
———. *Wissenschaftstheorie und Theologie.* Frankfort a. M.: Suhrkamp, 1973.
Pauck, Wilhelm. *Harnack and Troeltsch: Two Historical Theologians.* New York: Oxford University Press, 1969.
Pye, Michael. "Troeltsch and the Science of Religion." In *Ernst Troeltsch: Writings on Theology and Religion*, pp. 234–52. Trans. and ed. Robert Morgan and Michael Pye. Atlanta: John Knox Press, 1977.
———, and Morgan, Robert, eds. *The Cardinal Meaning: Essays in Comparative Hermeneutics: Buddhism and Christianity.* The Hague: Mouton, 1973.
Quarberg, David. "Historical Reason, Faith and the Study of Religion." *Journal for the Scientific Study of Religion* 1 (1961):122–24.
Quigley, Hugh. "Ernst Troeltsch." *The Quest* 14 (1923):289–94.
Rand, Calvin G. "Two Meanings of Historicism in the Writings of Dilthey, Troeltsch, and Meinecke." *Journal of the History of Ideas* 25 (1965):503–18.
Rapp, Arrigo. *Il Problema della Germania negli Scritti Politici di E. Troeltsch (1914–1922).* Rome: Giuffrè, 1978.
Reist, Benjamin A. *Toward a Theology of Involvement: The Thought of Ernst Troeltsch.* Philadelphia: Westminster, 1966.
Ringer, Fritz K. *The Decline of the German Mandarins: The German Academic Community, 1890–1933.* Cambridge, Massachusetts: Harvard University Press, 1969.
Rinteln, Fritz-Joachim von. "Der Versuch einer Ueberwindung des Historismus bei Ernst Troeltsch." *Deutsche Vierteljahrsschrift für Literaturwissenschaft und Geistesgeschichte* 8 (1930):324–72.
Ritzert, G. *Die Religionsphilosophie Ernst Troeltschs.* Langensalza: H. Beyer & Söhne, 1924.
Robertson, Roland. *The Sociological Interpretation of Religion.* New York: Schocken, 1970.
Röhricht, Rainer. "Zwischen Historismus und Existenzdenken: Die Geschichtsphilosophie Ernst Troeltschs." Ph.D. dissertation, Tübingen University, 1954.
Rossi, Pietro. *Lo storicismo tedesco contemporaneo.* Turin: Einaudi, 1956.
Rubanowice, Robert J. "An Intellectual in Politics: The Political Thought of Ernst Troeltsch." *Journal of Social Sciences and Humanities* 3 (1974):5–29.

————. "Ernst Troeltsch: Fifty Years After." *Cithara: Essays in the Judaeo-Christian Tradition* 13 (1973):16–28.

————. "Ernst Troeltsch's History of the Philosophy of History." *Journal of the History of Philosophy* 14 (1976):79–95.

————. "The Original Heidelberg Historicizer." *The Heythrop Journal: A Quarterly Review of Philosophy and Theology* 13 (1972):436–41.

Rupp, George. *Culture-Protestantism: German Liberal Theology at the Turn of the Twentieth Century.* Missoula, Montana: Scholars Press, 1977.

Salis, Jean R. de. "La théorie de l'histoire selon Ernst Troeltsch." *Revue de Synthèse historique* 43, n.s. 17 (1927):5–13.

Schaff, Julius Jakob. *Geschichte und Begriff: Eine kritische Studie zur Geschichtsmethodologie von Ernst Troeltsch und Max Weber.* Tübingen: J. C. B. Mohr, 1946.

Scheler, Max. "Ernst Troeltsch als Soziologe." *Kölner Vierteljahrshefte für Sozialwissenschaften* 30 (1923):7–21.

Schenk, Wilhelm. "Ernst Troeltsch's Conception of History." *Dublin Review* 214 (1944):25–34.

Schlippe, Gunnar von. *Die Absolutheit des Christentums bei Ernst Troeltsch auf dem Hintergrund der Denkfelder des 19. Jahrhunderts.* Neustadt a. d. Aisch: Degener, 1966.

Schmidt, Gustav. *Deutscher Historismus und der Uebergang zur parlamentarischen Demokratie: Untersuchungen zu den politischen Gedanken von Meinecke-Troeltsch-Max Weber.* Lübeck and Hamburg: Matthiesen, 1964.

Schmidt, Martin. "Zuge eines theologischen Geschichtsbegriffs bei Ernst Troeltsch." In *Reformatio und Confessio.* Ed. Friedrich W. Kantzenbach and Gerhard Müller. Berlin: Lutherisches Verlagshaus, 1965.

Schrey, Heinz-Horst. "Ernst Troeltsch und sein Werk." *Theologische Rundschau* N. F. 11 (1940):130–62.

Schwarz, G. M. "Deutschland und Westeuropa bei Ernst Troeltsch." *Historische Zeitschrift* 191 (1960):510–47.

Séguy, Jean. *Ernst Troeltsch et sa sociologie du Christianisme.* Paris: Cahiers du Cercle Ernest Renan, 1961.

Shippey, Frederick A. "Sociological Forms of Religious Expression in Western Christianity." *Religion in Life* 27 (1958):172–84.

Sleigh, Robert S. *The Sufficiency of Christianity: An Enquiry Concerning the Nature and the Modern Possibilities of the Christian Religion, With Special Reference to the Religious Philosophy of Dr. Ernst Troeltsch.* London: J. Clarke, 1923.

Spaleck, Gerhard. *Religionssoziologische Grundbegriffe bei Troeltsch.* Bleicherode am Harz: C. Nieft, 1937.

Spiess, Emil. *Die Religionstheorie von Ernst Troeltsch.* Paderborn: F. Schönigh, 1927.

Stackhouse, Max L. "Troeltsch's Categories of Historical Analysis." *Journal for the Scientific Study of Religion* 1 (1962):223–25.

Swatos, William H., Jr. "Weber or Troeltsch?: Methodology, Syndrome, and the Development of Church-Sect Theory." *Journal for the Scientific Study of Religion* 15 (1976):129–44.

Tasker, J. G. "Troeltsch on the Nineteenth Century." *Expository Times* 35 (1924):274–76.

Tönnies, Ferdinand. "Troeltsch und die Philosophie der Geschichte." *Schmollers Jahrbuch* 49 (1925):147–91.

Tracy, David. *Blessed Rage for Order: The New Pluralism in Theology.* New York: Seabury, 1975.

Troeltsch, Ernst. *Die Absolutheit des Christentums und die Religionsgeschichte: Vortrag gehalten auf der Versammlung der Freunde der Christlichen Welt zu Mühlacker am 3. Oktober 1901,* erweitert und mit einem Vorwort versehen, 3. Aufl. Tübingen: J. C. B. Mohr, 1929. Republished Munich and Hamburg: Siebenstern Taschenbuch Verlag, 1970. *The Absoluteness of Christianity and the History of Religions.* Trans. David Reid. Richmond, Virginia: John Knox Press, 1971.

————. *Aufsätze zur Geistesgeschichte und Religionssoziologie, Gesammelte Schriften* IV. Ed. Hans Baron. Tübingen: J. C. B. Mohr, 1925. Republished Aalen: Scientia Verlag, 1966.

————. *Die Bedeutung des Protestantismus für die Entstehung der modernen Welt.* Munich: Oldenbourg, 1906; 2nd ed., 1911; 3rd ed., 1924. Republished Aalen: Otto Zeller Verlag, 1963. *Protestantism and Progress: A Historical Study of the Relation of Protestantism to the*

Modern World. Trans. W. Montgomery. New York: G. P. Putnam, 1912; Boston: Beacon, 1958.

———. *Deutscher Geist und Westeuropa: Gesammelte Kulturphilosophische Aufsätze und Reden.* Ed. Hans Baron. Tübingen: J. C. B. Mohr, 1925. Republished Aalen: Scientia Verlag, 1966.

———. "The Dogmatics of the 'Religionsgeschichtliche Schule.'" *American Journal of Theology* 17 (1913):1–21. Expanded version published as "Die Dogmatik der 'religionsgeschichtliche Schule,'" *Gesammelte Schriften* II:500–24.

———. *Der Historismus und seine Problem. Erstes Buch: Das logische Problem der Geschichtsphilosophie, Gesammelte Schriften* III. Tübingen: J. C. B. Mohr, 1922. Republished Aalen: Scientia Verlag, 1961.

———. *Der Historismus und seine Ueberwindung: Fünf Vorträge.* Berlin: R. Heise, 1924. Republished Aalen: Scientia Verlag, 1966. Translated as *Christian Thought: Its History and Application.* London: University of London Press, 1923; New York: Meridian Books, 1957.

———. "Die Krisis des Historismus." *Die Neue Rundschau* 33 (1922):572–90.

———. *Die Soziallehren der christlichen Kirchen und Gruppen, Gesammelte Schriften* I. Tübingen: J. C. B. Mohr, 1912. Republished Aalen: Scientia Verlag, 1961, 1965. *The Social Teaching of the Christian Churches,* 2 vols. Trans. Olive Wyon. New York: Macmillan, 1931; Harper & Row, 1960.

———. *Spektator-Briefe: Aufsätze über die deutsche Revolution und die Weltpolitik 1918/22.* Ed. Hans Baron. Tübingen: J. C. B. Mohr, 1924.

———. *Vernunft und Offenbarung bei Johann Gerhard und Melanchthon: Untersuchung zur Geschichte der altprotestantischen Theologie.* Göttingen: Vandenhoeck & Ruprecht, 1891.

———. *Zur religiösen Lage, Religionsphilosophie und Ethik, Gesammelte Schriften* II. Tübingen: J. C. B. Mohr, 1913. Republished Aalen: Scientia Verlag, 1961.

Van Pelt, John R. "Ritschl and After." *Methodist Review* 106 (1923):36–58.

Vermeil, Edmond. *La pensée religieuse de Troeltsch.* Strasbourg and Paris: Librarie Istra, 1922.

Waismann, A. *Ernst Troeltsch o el drama del historicismo.* Córdoba, Argentina: University of Córdoba, 1955.

Wichelhaus, Manfred. *Kirchengeschichtsschreibung und Soziologie im neunzehnten Jahrhundert und bei Ernst Troeltsch.* Heidelberg: C. Winter, 1965.

Wienecke, Friedrich. *Die Entwicklung des philosophischen Gottesbegriffs bei Ernst Troeltsch.* Soldin: H. Madrasch, 1929.

Williamson, Clark M. "The Dilemma of Historical Relativity and Historical Revelation: An Analysis of the Theology of Ernst Troeltsch." Ph.D. dissertation, University of Chicago, 1969.

Wölber, H. O. *Dogma und Ethos: Christentum und Humanismus von Ritschl bis Troeltsch.* Gütersloh: C. Bertelsmann, 1950.

Wünsch, Georg. "Ernst Troeltsch zum Gedächtnis." *Die Christliche Welt* 37 (1923):105–8.

Yinger, J. Milton. "The Sociology of Religion of Ernst Troeltsch." In *An Introduction to the History of Sociology,* pp. 309–15. Ed. H. E. Barnes. Chicago: University of Chicago Press, 1948.

Index

Absoluteness of Christianity, 29–30, 33–35, 36–37
Adams, James Luther, ix–xix, xxi, xxiii, 29
Accident, category of, 85–86
Anthropology, 96, 97
Antoni, Carlo, 29
Apfelbacher, Karl-Ernst, xxii
Apriorizing philosophers of form, 75, 76
Archimedes, 90
Aristocracy, 110, 113, 120
Armistice, 113, 114, 119, 129
Arnold, Matthew, 5–6, 25
Aron, Raymond, 102
Art, xiii, 2, 7, 72, 108, 109
"August, days of," 102–104, 107
Augustine, Saint, 65, 66, 101
Axiology, 90–99. See also Cultural values; Formal values

Bainton, Roland H., 43–44
Barraclough, Geoffrey, 131
Barrett, William, 10, 18
Bendix, Reinhard, 46
Bergson, Henri, 70, 76–77
Bismarck, Otto von, 108, 113, 117, 122, 131
Bodenstein, Walter, xxii, 137
Bornhausen, K., 132
Bossuet, Bishop, 66
Boulding, Kenneth E., 3
Bradbury, Malcolm, 8–9
Brunner, Emil, 37
Bryce, James, 120
Burckhardt, Jakob, 5, 8, 66, 82

Carlyle, Thomas, 5
Carr, E. H., 60
Cartesianism, 52–53, 67, 68
Cassirer, Ernst, 76
Causality, 5, 79, 83
Chance, category of, 85–86
Christ, myth of, 27, 36

Christian Thought, 17
Christianity: absoluteness of, 29–37, 39, 41, 56; churchless, 26–29; in crisis, 17, 18–25; missionary, 35–36
Churches: decline of, 18, 20, 25–29; as sociological type, 46–47
Churchless Christianity. See Christianity
Church-state relations, 25, 26, 108, 109, 122
Clayton, John Powell, xviii
Communism, 125, 129. See also Marxism; Socialism
Compromise, Troeltsch's tendency to, 54, 69, 101, 128, 133, 134, 135, 136
Comte, Auguste, 70, 74
Contemporary cultural synthesis, xvii, xix, 71, 72, 73, 75, 92–95, 98, 137
Creative, category of the, 84–85
Crisis, age of, x, xvi, xvii, 1–2, 4–11, 18–20, 29, 60–61, 89, 90, 93, 99, 135, 138
Critical philosophy of history, 68, 78
Croce, Benedetto, 70, 76
Cultural synthesis, xvii, xix, 71, 72, 73, 75, 92–95, 98, 137
Cultural values, xvii, 90–92, 94, 97, 101, 107, 108, 110
Cunliffe-Jones, Hubert, 37

Decline of the West (Spengler), 93
Deism, 24, 40
Delbrück, Hans, 108
Democracy, 106, 109, 112, 117–18, 119–21, 123, 128, 130
Descartes, René, 52–53, 67, 68
Development, category of, xi, xv, xvii, 50–51, 76, 77, 86–88, 96
Diehl, Hermann, 100
Dietrich, Albrecht, 133
"Diktat," 113
Dilthey, Wilhelm, 11, 12, 14, 48, 54, 70, 75, 88
Dostoevsky, Fyodor, 4, 5, 8, 75

Smiles, Samuel, 5
Smith, Page, 4
Socialism, 120, 124, 125, 126. *See also*
    Marxism; Communism
*Social Teachings of the Christian
    Churches*, ix, 11, 19, 43–49, 56,
    135
Sociology of religion, 29, 31, 40–49
Sorel, Georges, 6
Sorokin, Pitirim A., 5
Spartacists, 125
Speculative philosophy of history, 68,
    71, 78
Spencer, Herbert, 73, 93
Spengler, Oswald, 8, 75, 93, 96
Spektator-Briefe, 100. *See also
    Kunstwart*
Spirits, general and particular, category
    of, 83
Stackhouse, Max L., xxiii
Stromberg, Roland N., 1
System of the Sciences (Tillich), xii,
    xviii, xix

Tillich, Paul, xii, xviii, xix, 51   150
Totalitarianism, 8, 125
Troeltsch, Ernst: as compromiser, 54,
    69, 101, 128, 133, 134, 135, 136; as
    historicist, x–xi, 15, 20, 39–40, 45,
    49–55, 56, 60–61, 62, 64, 78, 95,
    110; marriage of, 13; personal life of,
    11–16, 99–101, 130; as philosopher
    of history, 15; political writings of,
    xxii, 15–16, 98, 99–130; and pre-
    occupation with crises, 9–10, 16, 29,
    38, 60–61, 62, 89–90, 98, 124,
    130, 131, 137; and religious studies,
    12–15, 17; and religious tempera-
    ment, 11, 13, 101–102, 103; as rep-
    resentative of his age, x, 1, 10–11,
    29, 37, 38, 115–16, 131, 137–38;
    reputation of, 1, 9, 10, 11, 14, 16,
    17, 18, 29, 30–31, 37–38, 39, 40,
    43–44, 46–47, 48, 49, 63, 78, 100,
    101, 119, 132–38; revival of, ix–x,
    xviii–xix, xxi–xxii; schooling of,
    11–12; as sociologist of religion, ix,
    14, 29, 31, 40–49; writing style of,

132–37; teaching career, 14–15,
    134–35; as wartime propagandist,
    15–16, 98, 99–114. *See also Abso-
    luteness of Christianity; Christian
    Thought; Historismus und seine Pro-
    bleme; Historismus und seine Ueber-
    windung; Kunstwart; Protestantism
    and Progress; Reason and Revela-
    tion; Social Teachings of the Chris-
    tian Churches; Spektator-Briefe*
Two Sources of Morality and Religion
    (Bergson), 77

Unconsciousness, category of the, 83–
    84, 85
Uniqueness, category of, 82
Universal history, 90, 95–98

Values. *See* Axiology; Cultural values;
    Formal values
Van Pelt, John R., 30
Vernunftrepublikaner, Troeltsch as, 119
Versailles Treaty, 114, 115, 129
Verstehen, 88
Vico, Giambattista, xv, 68
Volksbund für Freiheit und Vaterland,
    100
Vollgraft, Karl, 5
Voltaire, 69

Wagar, Warren, 29
Wallas, Graham, 7
War Guilt Question, 115, 130
Weber, Max, ix, xvii, 3, 44–49, 76, 100
Wells, H. G., 74, 93, 96
Whitehead, A. N., xiii
Williamson, Clark M., 131
Wilson, President Woodrow, 112, 114
Windelband, Wilhelm, 48, 76, 81, 86
Wolfe, Thomas, 7
World War I, 8, 15, 55, 98, 99, 100,
    101–15, 130
Wünsch, Georg, 132, 134

Yeats, William Butler, 4, 5
Yinger, J. Milton, 47

Zahrnt, Heinz, 37